SOME MAKERS OF
ENGLISH LAW

CAMBRIDGE
UNIVERSITY PRESS
LONDON: BENTLEY HOUSE
NEW YORK, TORONTO, BOMBAY
CALCUTTA, MADRAS: MACMILLAN
TOKYO: MARUZEN COMPANY LTD

SOME MAKERS OF
ENGLISH LAW

THE TAGORE LECTURES
1937–38

by

SIR WILLIAM HOLDSWORTH,
K.C., D.C.L., Hon. LL.D., F.B.A.

*Vinerian Professor in English Law and Fellow of
All Souls College in the University of Oxford
Bencher of Lincoln's Inn*

CAMBRIDGE
AT THE UNIVERSITY PRESS
1938

PREFACE

THESE lectures were given by me as Tagore Professor in Calcutta University in December 1937 and January 1938. My two objects are, first to give some account of the most important of the men whose work entitles them to be reckoned amongst the Makers of English Law, and, secondly, so to connect their biographies with the general history of the law that the book will be a short biographical history of English law. I hope that it will be a useful companion to books on the history of legal institutions and on the history of the sources and literature of the law. Most of the information is to be found at greater length in my *History of English Law*, and in articles of mine in the *Law Quarterly Review* and the *Cambridge Law Journal*; but I think that its statement in a new form, which is shorter and simpler, will be useful to the student.

I must thank my son, Mr R. W. G. Holdsworth, Stowell Fellow of University College, Oxford, for criticism and for his help in correcting the proof sheets.

W. H.

ALL SOULS COLLEGE

August 1938

CONTENTS

LIST OF CASES

LIST OF STATUTES

SOME MAKERS OF ENGLISH LAW

✣

INTRODUCTION

POLLOCK AND MAITLAND, in the last sentences of their great history of English law, emphasize both the length of time during which the work done by the lawyers of the twelfth and thirteenth centuries—the age of Glanvil and Bracton—was destined to endure, and the extent of the earth's surface over which it was destined to hold sway. "Nor can we part with this age", they say,[1] "without thinking once more of the permanence of its work. Those few men who were gathered at Westminster round Pateshull and Raleigh and Bracton were penning writs that would run in the name of kingless commonwealths on the other shore of the Atlantic Ocean; they were making right and wrong for us and for our children." In fact this estimate of the geographical extent of their work is an understatement; for they were penning writs which would run also in the name of the King-Emperor on the shores of the Indian Ocean. The eastern and western expansions of England have spread English law and the English language over the world. Just as from the twelfth to the sixteenth centuries the concepts and principles and rules of Roman law spread over Western Europe and influenced in different degrees the legal system of all its countries; so in India, the concepts and principles and rules of English law have spread over the provinces and states of India.

---

[1] *History of English Law* (1st ed.), ii, 670.

This permeation of English law was, at the outset, effected in a manner very similar to that in which the permeation of Roman law was effected in medieval Europe. Just as in medieval Europe it was effected by statesmen and judges who had learned the principles of Roman law from those great Italian law schools where the revival of the study of Roman law began, and from which it spread to other European countries; so in India it was effected by English administrators and judges who knew little of any system of law but their own. Just as these medieval statesmen and judges found it necessary to supplement the native bodies of customary law to meet the needs and solve the problems of an advancing civilization, so, for the same reason, these English administrators and judges found it necessary to supplement the Indian bodies of law. Necessarily both had recourse to the rules of the more advanced system which met their needs. When these medieval statesmen and judges were faced with new problems it was inevitable that they should apply the rules of that system of Roman law, which they had been taught to regard as the embodiment of human wisdom, as the legacy of an ancient civilization which was superior to their own. When the English administrators and judges were instructed to decide cases for which no clear rule was provided in Acts of Parliament or Regulations or Indian customary law, in accordance with "justice, equity, and good conscience",[1] they applied the rules of the one system they knew, which they also had been taught to regard as the embodiment of human reason. And so, as Sir Henry Maine has said,[2]

The higher courts, while they openly borrowed the English rules from the recognized English authorities, constantly used language which implied that they believed themselves to be taking them from some abstract body of legal principle which lay behind

[1] See Ilbert, *Government of India,* 359–360.
[2] *Village Communities,* 298–299.

all law; and the inferior judges, when they were applying some half-remembered legal rule learnt in boyhood, or culling a proposition of law from a half-understood English text book, no doubt honestly thought in many cases that they were following the rule prescribed for them, to decide "by equity and good conscience" wherever no native law or usage was discoverable.

Thus, just as in the states of medieval Europe Roman concepts and principles and rules permeated all those departments of law where native customs were scanty, because those concepts and principles and rules were regarded as the highest embodiment of reason and justice, so in India a similar set of ideas led to the permeation of the concepts and principles and rules of English law. And so, "under the name of justice, equity, and good conscience, the general law of British India, save so far as the authority of native laws was preserved, came to be so much of English law as was considered applicable, or rather was not considered inapplicable to the conditions of Indian Society".[1] And the process was essentially the same as the process by which Roman law was received in medieval Europe; for English law in India, like Roman law in medieval Europe, "enjoyed a persuasive authority as being an embodiment of written reason, and impressed its own character on a formally independent jurisprudence".[2]

The manner in which this permeation of English law took place was altered, but its extent was in no way diminished, when in the nineteenth century the law was codified. Macaulay's Penal Code, which both Stephen[3] and Bryce[4] regard as his most remarkable achievement, was the first of these codes. It was the model upon which the distinguished English lawyers[5] who prepared the

[1] Pollock, *The Expansion of the Common Law*, 133.   [2] *Ibid.* 134.
[3] Stephen, *History of Criminal Law*, iii, 299.
[4] *Studies in History and Jurisprudence*, i, 127.
[5] For the personnel of these commissions see Whiteley Stokes, *The Anglo-Indian Codes*, i, xii, xiii.

earliest of these codes worked. They used English law as the basis of their codes, but modified it to meet the Indian needs. And so, as Sir Frederick Pollock has said,[1]

in British India the general principles of English law, by a process which we may summarily describe as judicial application confirmed and extended by legislation, have in the course of the nineteenth century...covered the whole field of criminal law, civil wrongs, contract, evidence, procedure in the higher if not in the lower courts, and a good deal of the law of property.... It is not too much to say that a modified English law is thus becoming the general law of British India....It is something to say that the Common Law has proved equal to its task. The Indian Penal Code, which is English criminal law simplified and set in order, has worked for more than a generation, among people of every degree of civilization, with but little occasion for amendment. In matters of business and commerce English law has not only established itself but has been ratified by deliberate legislation, subject to the reform of some few anomalies which we might well have reformed at home, and were deemed unsuitable for Indian conditions. More than this, principles of equitable jurisprudence which we seldom have occasion to remember in modern English practice have been successfully revived in Indian jurisdictions within our own time for the discomfiture of oppressive and fraudulent money lenders.

It is clear that, to understand the spirit of the rules of English law which have been thus used in these codes and adapted to meet Indian needs, it is as necessary to know something of the authorities upon which these English rules are based, as it was necessary to know the authorities relied upon by the judges who borrowed the rules of English law in the earlier period before the codes. But since, like the Roman law, English law has had a long and a continuous history, these authorities come from all periods of that history. In the second edition of Sir Dinshah Mulla's book on the Transfer of

[1] Pollock, *The Expansion of the Common Law*, 16–17.

Property Act 1882, it has been found necessary to include in the commentary on some of the sections of that Act a discussion of cases which come from the sixteenth to the twentieth centuries; in Mr Ramaswamy Iyer's book on the Law of Torts old statutes and cases are as much in evidence as in any English text-book on this topic; and we see the same phenomenon in other Indian law books,[1] some of which have originated in these Tagore Lectures.[2]

But if it is necessary to rely upon authorities which come from all periods in the long history of English law, it is also necessary to know something of the men who made these authorities, and something of the intellectual, political, social, and economic environment in which they lived and worked. Without some knowledge of this kind it is impossible to understand fully the statutes which have been worked into the fabric of English law, the cases by which from age to age the law has been gradually adapted to meet new needs, and the authoritative text-books in which the results of the cases and the statutes have been summed up. I propose in these lectures to say something of all of these matters—of the lawyers to whose authority constant appeal is made in the courts, of their work which is recorded in cases and text-books, of the various influences—technical or political—in which they did their work of adapting the rules of English law to new conditions and new needs. I hope that this

---

[1] Dr S. C. Brahmachari, in the Preface to his book on *The Law of Carriage by Rail and Water*, says of the Indian Railways Act 1890 that "there is no piece of legislation on the Indian Statute book which more closely follows English Statute Law. There is scarcely a section or clause which has not received an inspiration from the English, Irish, or Scottish decisions, and to understand the Indian Law on the subject, we must refer to them ungrudgingly."

[2] E.g. D. F. Mulla, *The Law of Insolvency*; P. K. Sen, *The Law of Monopolies in British India*; cp. Harnam Singh's book on *The Law of Specific Relief in India*.

discussion will render these authorities more intelligible, and so will help the lawyers who have occasion to use them to understand their meaning more fully, and therefore to appreciate more accurately the conditions in which, and, in the case of some of the older authorities, the reservations with which, they must be received.

My first three lectures will deal with the medieval law —with Glanvil and Bracton, the fathers and founders of the common law, with Edward I, in whose reign we begin to see some of the larger outstanding characteristics of that law, and with Littleton and Fortescue, in whose books many of the characteristics of this medieval law are summarized. The next three lectures will deal with the development of the law in the sixteenth and first half of the seventeenth centuries—with the broad effects of the period of the Renaissance and the Reformation on English law, with the foundation of the English system of equity by St Germain, Sir Thomas More, Ellesmere, and Bacon, with Sir Edward Coke and the commanding position which he takes in English legal history. The seventh lecture will deal with the two great lawyers of the latter half of the seventeenth century—Hale and Nottingham. The next three lectures will deal with Holt and Mansfield—the two great common lawyers who completed the modern common law, with Hardwicke and Eldon—the two great Chancellors who completed the English system of equity, and with Leoline Jenkins, Stowell, and the Civilians. My eleventh lecture will deal with Blackstone—the first holder of my chair at Oxford, and with his great critic Bentham and Bentham's disciple Austin. My twelfth lecture will give some account of the rise of that historical school of English lawyers which has deprived the school of Bentham and Austin of the predominant control over legal theory which it once held, and of the three great representatives of this school—

Maine, Maitland, and Pollock. In conclusion I shall say something of the need to study those legal principles which all these Makers of English Law have in different ways and in different periods helped to establish; and of the manner in which, by the light of these principles, the enactments of the Legislature have been worked into and made part of the fabric of a system of law which has learned to give due weight to the maintenance both of the stability of the state and of the liberty of the subject.

Lecture I

GLANVIL AND BRACTON

"LEGAL MEMORY"—the time before which the memory of the law does not reach—goes back to the coronation of Richard I, September 3, 1189. It is an arbitrary date which was fixed by analogy to the period of limitation set for the writ of right by a statute of 1275.[1] But though it is a date arbitrarily fixed by statute, there is a substantial reason why the period of legal memory should be fixed in the last years of the twelfth century; for it was round about that period that the common law began to take shape, and it was at some period shortly after 1187 that the earliest text-book on the common law—the book which goes by the name of Glanvil—was written.[2] That book marks the true beginning of the common law; for, as Reeves said in his *History of English Law*,[3] it is, as compared with the Anglo-Saxon laws, "like the code of another nation".

There were three main reasons why the common law began to take shape in the latter half of the twelfth century. In the first place, it was a period of legal renaissance all over Europe; in the second place, in the second half of this century England got in Henry II an exceptionally able King in close touch with this legal renaissance; in the third place, centralized institutions of government, the acts of which were permanently recorded, were established.

In the first place, it was a period of legal renaissance all over Europe.[4] The Norman Conquest had brought

[1] Pollock and Maitland, *H.E.L.* (1st ed.), ii, 82.
[2] Glanvil, viii, 3; Holdsworth, *H.E.L.* ii, 189.
[3] Vol. i, 256.
[4] Holdsworth, *H.E.L.* ii, 135–137, 139–142, 145–149.

England into closer touch with continental politics and
continental thought than she had been under the Anglo-
Saxon Kings; and continental thought was dominated
by the revival of the study of Roman law, which was
bringing the nations of Europe into contact with a very
much more advanced set of legal and political ideas. The
original texts of Justinian's Code and the Digest were
being studied in the Italian cities. Lanfranc, William
the Conqueror's archbishop, was a distinguished member of a law school at Pavia; and at Bologna the lectures
of Irnerius on the Digest called the attention of Europe
to its original text in which the true spirit of Roman law
was preserved. From Bologna also came Gratian, who
by his *Decretum Gratiani*, which Maitland calls "a great
law book",[1] harmonized the discordant canons of the
church, and founded the medieval canon law. This new
learning made its way to England immediately after the
Conquest; for the Normans were perhaps the most
cosmopolitan race in Europe. Three archbishops—
Lanfranc, Anselm, and Theobald—were distinguished
Roman and canon lawyers; and Theobald brought in his
train Vacarius, who founded such flourishing schools of
Roman law at Canterbury and Oxford in the middle of
the twelfth century, that in 1180 it could be said the
liberal arts were silenced, and that Titius and Seius had
usurped the place of Aristotle and Plato.[2] It is obvious
that the foundation of a school in which the more advanced concepts and principles and rules of Roman law
were taught must quickly affect the comparatively primitive customs of which the law of England then consisted.
Both India[3] and Japan[4] in our own days illustrate the
influence, partly conscious partly unconscious, which a

---

[1] Pollock and Maitland, *H.E.L.* (1st ed.), i, 92.
[2] *Collectanea* (Oxford Hist. Soc.), ii, 172—a paper by T. E. Holland.
[3] Maine, *Village Communities*, 74–76.
[4] *L.Q.R.* xxiii, 44–45.

finished body of law has upon the vague and shifting customary rules of a primitive society. The rapidity with which this influence made itself felt was due to the second of the reasons why England got a common law at this period.

In the second place, in the second half of the twelfth century England got in Henry II an exceptionally able King in close touch with this legal renaissance.[1] Henry II was not only King of England. He was also a great continental potentate. He ruled over more of France than the King of France; and his dominions were so organized that his power was felt throughout their extent. That he was able thus to organize them was due to the fact that his court was filled with the ablest and most cultured men of the day. He was, as Stubbs has said,[2] "by his very descent a champion of literary culture. Not to speak of his grandfather Henry Beauclerc, whose clerkship was probably of a very elementary sort, he was the lineal descendant of Fulk the Good who had told King Lothar that rex illiteratus was asinus coronatus." Peter of Blois speaks of the court as a centre of literary culture;[3] and the man of letters and the man of action were often the same person. The best history of the reign was written by Richard bishop of London, Treasurer of England, who wrote also the *Dialogus de Scaccario*; and Glanvil, who gave his name to the earliest text-book on the common law, was justice in eyre, ambassador, and justiciar. Such men could not be unaffected by the new legal studies and new legal literature which were arising in Europe. They were all influenced by the school of the Glossators,[4] which was publishing Roman law to the nations of Europe and adapting it to their needs. Acquaintance with practical life saved their writings

[1] Holdsworth, *H.E.L.* ii, 174–175.
[2] *Lectures on Medieval and Modern History*, 136.   [3] *Ibid.* 164.
[4] For this school see Holdsworth, *H.E.L.* iv, 220–221.

from the vice of unreality, and their study of the principles of Roman law saved them from the mechanical formalism of the official or the mere practitioner. Therefore they were able to lay so firmly the foundations of the common law that it rules to-day not only in England, but also in the many lands beyond the seas in which Englishmen have settled. That its foundations were so firmly laid is due in no small extent to the third of the reasons which enabled the common law to take shape in this period.

In the third place, centralized institutions of government, the acts of which were permanently recorded, were established.[1] The King's court—the Curia Regis—conducted or supervised the whole machinery of government, exercising executive, legislative, and judicial functions, and making its power felt throughout the whole country. The character of its work is illustrated by the account which Richard bishop of London, the Treasurer, has left us, in his *Dialogus de Scaccario*,[2] of the organization and working of the Exchequer over which he presided, and by Glanvil's book on the working of the judicial side of the King's court. Both books testify to the great strides which had been made in the establishment of a centralized system of law and government in Henry II's reign. And the work, and therefore the influence, of this centralized system were permanent, because its acts were officially recorded. Many of the most important of our national records—Exchequer Rolls, Charter Patent and Close Rolls, and Plea Rolls—begin in this period. So firmly had this new system of centralized law and government been established on the basis of fixed rules of practice, which its series of records had made it possible to create, that it stood the strain of an absent King, a bad King, and an infant King. The fact that such a system was established is an all-sufficient

[1] Holdsworth, *H.E.L.* i, 32–54; ii, 165–166, 180–186.
[2] *Ibid.* ii, 186–188.

explanation of the fact that England obtained a common law. And here we may notice what may well prove to be an interesting historical parallel. On December 6, 1937, the Chief Justice of India, in his speech at the inaugural meeting of the Indian Federal Court, pointed out that the unifying effect upon English law of the establishment by Henry II of a central court for the whole of England may be repeated for Indian law by the establishment of the Federal Court, which is the first central court for the whole of India.

Because the two departments of the administration which had begun to be specialized in Henry II's reign were finance and law, special treatises were written about them. Just as Richard bishop of London, the Treasurer, wrote a special treatise about finance, so a few years later a special treatise was written about law, which bears the name of Glanvil, the justiciar. It is this book, and Glanvil's work as justiciar on which the book is based, which entitle him to his place as the earliest of the Makers of English Law.

Glanvil[1] was one of those many-sided statesmen, soldiers and lawyers who staffed Henry II's court. He was one of the leaders of the English army which defeated the Scots at Alnwick in 1174; and he served the King as justice in eyre, as ambassador, and as justiciar. As the King's principal adviser he suggested and helped to carry out some of Henry's legal reforms. He ceased to hold the office of justiciar on the accession of Richard I. He accompanied the King on his crusade and died at Acre in 1190. There is no doubt that he was one of the foremost of that band of statesmen and lawyers who founded the common law. Whether he actually wrote the book which bears his name is not certain. It seems probable that it was written by his nephew and secretary Hubert Walter, who afterwards became archbishop of

[1] Holdsworth, *H.E.L.* ii, 188–189.

Canterbury, chancellor, and justiciar, but it is certain that it was written with Glanvil's consent, and perhaps under his supervision. It long remained a standard text-book. Bracton made extensive use of it, and in the early part of the thirteenth century an edition of it was introduced into Scotland under the name of *Regiam Majestatem*.[1] A new and very adequate edition of the book, based on the study of twenty-seven MSS, was published by Professor Woodbine in 1932.

It is not a lengthy treatise. Its subject-matter is treated of in fourteen short Books. That subject-matter, Glanvil tells us in his Prologue, is the law laid down by the King's court—the common law. He cannot, he says, deal with the confused multitude of local customs of which a large part of English law was still composed. As yet the common law is only one of the many systems of law which bear rule in England—though even at this early period it is recognized as the most permanent, the most universal, and the strongest of all these systems.[2] We can see from Glanvil's book that the earliest branches of the common law are the law of procedure, criminal law, and the land law. In the law of procedure we see one very permanent feature of the common law—its dependence upon writs—the common law already knows a number of writs which corresponds to the various causes of action of which the King's court takes cognizance. But as yet there is no fixed number of causes of action, for the King is very free to issue new writs as he pleases; and since his court is not fettered by precedents it can administer equity as well as law. In the criminal law the new criminal procedure, which is based on presentment by a grand jury and trial by the petit jury,

---

[1] Holdsworth, *H.E.L.* ii, 189–192.
[2] "Legis eciam Anglice trina est particio; et ad eandem distanciam supersunt regis placita curiae, que usus et consuetudines suas una semper immobilitate servat ubique", *Leges Henrici Primi*, ix, 9.

exists side by side with the older procedure, which is based on the appeal, that is the accusation, of the private accuser. In the land law we can see that the principle that all land is held either mediately or immediately from the Crown is established—the land law is thoroughly feudalized; and for this reason a certain amount of uniformity in the land law is being established. But though we see some of the great types of tenure—knight service, frankalmoin, serjeanty, and socage—they are not as yet clearly defined. Still less do we get any final definition of the kinds of interest which tenants can have in the land. English law has not yet arrived at its doctrine of estates in the land.[1]

In the law as stated in Glanvil's book we can see two main elements. The first and most important element is the rules made by the court itself and recorded on its plea rolls. These rules, which will grow more detailed and more precise as more cases are decided, are the substratum of the law. The second element is the influence of Roman law, civil and canon.[2] This is by no means a negligible element—indeed the idea of writing such a book as this may have been derived from short tracts on civil and canon law procedure which appeared in this century in England and Normandy. The preface and introductory chapters are taken from Justinian's *Institutes*. The Roman law as to slavery is used to illustrate the position of the villein. The Roman *dos* is contrasted with the English dower. Roman contracts are referred to by their Roman names. One of Henry II's most successful reforms—the assize of novel disseisin—is derived, through the canonist *actio spolii*, from the Roman interdict *unde vi*. The rule that a tenant for term of years has no seisin and no real action, so that his interest is not real property, is derived from an attempt to follow rules of Roman law which denied possession to certain kinds of

[1] Holdsworth, *H.E.L.* ii, 192–202.   [2] *Ibid.* ii, 202–206.

occupiers of land and to certain holders of other kinds of property. But the greatest debt which English law owed at this period to Roman law was of another and more indirect kind. The book shows that Roman law has supplied a method of reasoning upon matters legal, and a power to create a technical language and technical forms, which will enable precise yet general rules to be evolved from a mass of vague customs and particular cases. This debt to Roman law is much emphasized, as we shall now see, in the following period of the rapid growth of the common law which is summed up in Bracton's great book.

The first seventy years of the thirteenth century are a disturbed period. The constitutional crisis which led to the granting of Magna Carta showed that the nation, led by the barons, was determined to have some share in the government of the country, and to correct abuses in the administration of the law. It is a testimony to the success of Henry II's reforms that his new machinery of centralized government, through which a common law was being created, is recognized and regulated; and that the clauses of the Charter which attempt to regain independent feudal jurisdiction are very few in number.[1] One of the results of that constitutional crisis was to show that the period in which the law was developed solely by the power of the Crown was over; and to show that the period which will end in the establishment of a body which will limit the power of the Crown and share in the making of laws was begun. The problem of how to organize this body, and the problem of how and in what way it could limit the power of the Crown, were difficult, and they were made more difficult by the character of Henry III. It is not surprising that the attempts to settle them led to the civil war which broke out in the latter part of his reign. But neither in Magna Carta nor in the struggles between

[1] Holdsworth, *H.E.L.* i, 58–63; ii, 212–213.

Henry III and his barons was there any attempt to get rid of the machinery of central government which Henry II had established. In spite of much disorder this machinery still functioned. The courts sat at Westminster, the judges went their circuits. Therefore the development of a common law made steady progress.

In the preceding period the eminent judge had also been an eminent statesman. Glanvil, as we have seen, was far from being a mere lawyer. But the new centralized machinery of government, and the growing differentiation of the judicial and administrative sides of the King's court, had led to the rise of a number of professional judges. These judges began their career as royal clerks, made their way to the bench, and gained their reputation as lawyers. They were generally ecclesiastics and knew something of the Roman civil and the canon law. It is because the development of the law was guided by these learned clerks that it made such rapid progress during this period.[1] Two of the most famous of them were Martin of Pateshull and William of Raleigh.[2] Pateshull was archdeacon of Norfolk and dean of St Paul's, and he had such a capacity for hard work that a brother judge asked to be excused from going on circuit with him because he wore out his colleagues by his incessant activity. William of Raleigh, who became bishop of Winchester, was one of the ablest lawyers of the day, and was said to have been the inventor of important writs. Both of them were recognized by Bracton as his masters in the law. It is principally from their plea rolls that he extracted the cases which he used as the foundation of his book.

Henry of Bratton, generally known as Bracton, was probably born at Bratton Fleming in Devonshire. He was an ecclesiastic, and when he died in 1268 he was chancellor of Exeter Cathedral. He was justice in eyre

[1] Holdsworth, *H.E.L.* ii, 226–228.   [2] *Ibid.* ii, 230–231.

in 1245 and 1246, and from 1248 till his death he was a judge of assize. From 1248 till 1257 he was a judge of the King's Bench, and one of the King's Council; and it was during these years of royal favour that he was allowed to keep the plea rolls which he used as the foundation of his treatise. Probably he sympathized with the baronial party. But his abilities were recognized by both sides. In 1267 he was one of a commission appointed to adjudicate upon the claims of the disinherited supporters of Simon de Montfort. He died in the following year.[1]

His works make this period in the history of English law pre-eminently the period of Bracton. His principal work is a treatise upon English law which had no competitor either in literary style or in completeness of treatment till Blackstone composed his commentaries five centuries later. As the foundation of that work he compiled a *Note Book*, in which he collected 2000 cases from the plea rolls of the first twenty-four years of Henry III's reign. In 1884 Vinogradoff suggested that this collection of cases was a *Note Book* made and used by Bracton in the compilation of his treatise. Maitland, who printed and edited this *Note Book*, proved that this conjecture was correct. These two works come at the end of a period of rapid growth, which they sum up and pass on to future generations of lawyers. But for them all memory of this period might easily have been lost, and, consequently, the future history of English law might have been very different.

The treatise on the laws of England is unfinished—it leaves off in the middle of the discussion of the writ of right; and it is clear that, though Bracton added to and revised his book from time to time, he never finally revised it, for it contains contradictory passages which would have been eliminated on a final revision. Internal evidence would seem to show that the book was written in or

[1] Holdsworth, *H.E.L.* ii, 232–234; Bracton's *Note Book*, i, 13–25.

about 1240, and that though he added a few later cases he did not seriously work at it after 1256.[1] The number of MSS extant proves its popularity, but we have not got Bracton's own autograph. The best account of these MSS and the relations between them is to be found in Professor Woodbine's unfinished edition of the treatise. The older printed editions—Tottell's edition of 1569 and the Rolls Series edition—are very defective.

The manner in which Bracton intended to arrange his treatise is a matter of conjecture—the book was unfinished, and perhaps Bracton had not made up his own mind on this matter. There is an introductory part, much influenced by Roman law, in which the Roman division into the law of persons, things, and actions is adopted. But this is a very small part of the treatise. Bracton knew very well that the whole of English law could not be grouped under these heads. And so the main body of the treatise is divided into tracts which deal with the most important actions—civil or criminal—which came before the King's courts. There are tracts on the pleas of the Crown, on the possessory assizes, on the action of dower, on the writs of entry, and on the writ of right.

The treatise shows us that English law has already acquired two of its permanent characteristics. As in Glanvil's book, it is clear that it depends on the writs and the forms of action. But Bracton's book makes it clear that it depends also on decided cases.[2] Wherever possible Bracton vouches a case, and he criticizes decisions of which he does not approve. As yet there are no reports, and so the cases are taken from the rolls. But in his citation and reliance on cases Bracton is in advance of his age. The law books of Edward I's reign do not

---

[1] Woodbine's ed. of Bracton, i, 302; Holdsworth, *H.E.L.* ii, 236–237.

[2] At f. 1 b he says, "si tamen similia evenerint, per simile judicentur, cum bona sit occasio a similibus procedere ad similia".

exhibit this characteristic in anything like the same degree. But there is another characteristic of Bracton's book which was not destined to be permanent—its reliance on Roman law. It is this characteristic which makes the treatise so interesting historically; for it shows us that it comes at the parting of the ways. It gives us a picture of English law as developed by judges who were not merely lawyers, and not merely English common lawyers, and just before the period when it was to be developed by lawyers who knew little or no law except English common law.

Bracton's treatise shows that English law had developed very rapidly during the half century that had elapsed since the writing of Glanvil's book.[1] Let us look at some of its characteristic features at this stage of its development. First, the number of writs and forms of action had increased. In the justice done through the machinery of these actions there was still a large measure of equity; and that meant that English law was a flexible system, capable of expansion to meet new needs. Secondly, the crisis which had led to the granting of Magna Carta had brought constitutional questions to the front. Bracton holds strongly that the law is supreme, and should govern all—King and subject alike. But what if the King did not obey the law—no abstract question in Henry III's reign? Bracton, in a passage not found in all the MSS but found in Fleta, who wrote in Edward I's reign, says that the counts and barons are the King's masters, who must restrain him if he breaks the law. Thirdly, the fact that a true criminal law is developing is shown by the decay of the old appeal of crime, and the growth of the procedure by way of indictment at the King's suit. The King's court takes cognizance of all the more serious crimes; and Bracton's treatment of homicide, which was influenced by a canon lawyer, Bernard

[1] For a detailed account see Holdsworth, *H.E.L.* ii, 244–267.

of Pavia, shows that the law is beginning to attach some importance to the existence of a *mens rea*. Fourthly, the land law shows considerable progress. The types of tenure are settled; and the various interests which a freeholder may have in the land are also being settled by the working of the real actions. But as yet the law has not acquired the notion of an estate in the land; and some important questions are still unsettled—notably the question whether it is possible to leave land by will, and the question whether the interest of a man to whose use another holds land will be recognized. Lastly, as yet the law of personal property is scanty, and the common law has not got a theory of contract. Disputes upon questions of contract and tort were still dealt with mainly by the local courts in the country and the towns, and the law which they applied was as yet rudimentary.

It was to fill these obvious gaps in the nascent common law that Bracton borrowed from Roman law.[1] The extent of his debt to Roman law has been most variously estimated. Maine thought that the whole of the form and a third of the contents were borrowed from Roman law.[2] Reeves, on the other hand, thought that, though terms and maxims were borrowed from Roman law, the actual doctrines borrowed would not fill three pages.[3] Maitland thought that though the influence of Roman law was marked in certain parts of the first 107 folios, though in parts of the book, relating to possession, criminal law, and marriage, Roman doctrines were borrowed, and though Roman ideas enabled him to plan and write such a treatise, the major part of it is genuine English law based on the procedure of the royal courts and the cases decided by it.[4] I think that it is now generally agreed that Bracton's debt to Roman law is larger than Maitland

[1] For a detailed account see Holdsworth, *H.E.L.* ii, 267–286.
[2] *Ancient Law*, 82.   [3] *History of English Law*, i, 531.
[4] Bracton and Azo (S.S.), Introd.; Bracton's *Note Book*, i, 9–10.

thought. His background of legal theory, his views as to law in general, as to the rights and duties which the law should protect, as to the procedure which should be employed to enforce those rights, were influenced by Roman law. Like many contemporary lawyers in other countries in Western Europe, he was inspired by the Roman civil law, which was being interpreted by the school of the Glossators, and by the canon law. He got his civil law from Azo, the leading lawyer of the school of Bologna; and we have seen that he was influenced in his treatment of criminal law by the canonist Bernard of Pavia. In fact the influence of Roman law on Bracton is similar to the influence of Roman law on the French law of this period in the *pays de coutumes*. Those who wrote summaries of these customs used Roman law to supply a theory of contract, and to fill up the gaps in the customary law. They used it as a "ratio scripta"—not because it had any imperative force as a "jus scriptum".[1] If in England the King's court had continued to be staffed by men like Bracton who were learned in the civil and canon law, Roman law would have continued to have this same authority in England, and would have played a large part in moulding the customs of the King's courts, and therefore the English common law. But we shall see in the next lecture that Roman law never had this extensive influence, because the judges in the King's courts ceased to be men who were learned in the civil and canon law.

Nevertheless the fact that Bracton's book contains this Roman element has helped to give the book its historical importance—for the following reason: because Bracton was learned in Roman law he was led to discuss many problems about which the nascent common law had as yet no authority. Thus he deals with such topics as accessio, specificatio, and confusio; and "where", says

[1] Esmein, *Histoire du Droit Française*, 791–792, 796–840.

Maitland,[1] "in all our countless volumes of reports shall we find any decisions about some questions that Azo has suggested to Bracton?" So too he deals with questions relating to contract, fraud, and negligence about which the common law had as yet no rules. It was because his treatise gave English law one authority upon many matters which were outside the routine of practising lawyers of the thirteenth, fourteenth, and fifteenth centuries, that its influence has been so lasting.

During the century after Bracton's death his influence was great. But in the course of the fourteenth and in the fifteenth centuries it somewhat declined. English lawyers were tending to become merely practitioners, learned only in their own system of law. They had ceased for the most part to care for broad principles, and they had ceased to be interested in the discussion of legal theory. The common law seemed to be losing its grasp of principle, and to be coming to be "an evasive commentary upon writs and statutes".[2] To such lawyers the large outlook and vigorous common sense of Bracton seemed strange, and they were quite incapable of understanding his Roman law; and so some of them denied that Bracton's book was authoritative.[3] A very small knowledge of the history of English law is sufficient to show the absurdity of such dicta. In the sixteenth century Bracton's *Note Book* was known to Fitzherbert. He cites cases taken from it in his Grand Abridgment. Through Fitzherbert the cases which he took from the *Note Book* were known to Coke. Coke also borrows largely from the treatise; and the issue of the contest for supremacy between the common law courts and the new courts and councils of the Tudor period, in which he was the protagonist, would have been more doubtful if he had

[1] Bracton and Azo (S.S.), xx.
[2] Pollock and Maitland, *H.E.L.* (1st ed.), i, 204.
[3] Holdsworth, *H.E.L.* ii, 288.

not been able to use Bracton's treatise to liberalize the
common law.[1] When the common law finally triumphed
and assumed the jurisdiction formerly exercised by the
Admiralty and the Star Chamber, Bracton's treatise
continued to be used by the judges. Holt C.J. used it in
the case of *Coggs* v. *Bernard*[2] to settle the law as to bail-
ments, and Bracton's borrowings from the Roman law
as to servitudes were used by later lawyers to settle the
law as to easements.[3] Hale put the authority of Bracton's
treatise on a level with that of the records of the courts,[4]
and Blackstone followed Hale in recognizing it as
authoritative.[5]

For these reasons, then, we must regard Bracton as
one of the most important of the Makers of English Law.
His works are the one authority which we have for this
period of the rapid growth of the common law, when it
was being developed by men who were learned in the
civil and canon law. If the memory of this period had
been lost, it may well be doubted whether the medieval
common law, as developed by the lawyers of the fourteenth and fifteenth centuries, would have been found
sufficient to guide the development of a modern state.
If the common law had been found insufficient and had
lost its supremacy, if in consequence there had been, as
there was on the continent, a reception of Roman law,
the issue of the constitutional controversies of the seventeenth century would have been much more doubtful;
for it was upon Bracton's statement as to the supremacy
of the law over all—King and subject alike—as well as
upon medieval precedents of the fourteenth and fifteenth
centuries supplied by the common lawyers, that the
Parliamentary statesmen relied in their contest with the
Stuart Kings. Since Bracton's works, by thus helping to

[1] Holdsworth, *H.E.L.* ii, 288.   [2] (1704) 2 Ld. Raym. 909.
[3] Holdsworth, *H.E.L.* vii, 323.
[4] *History of the Common Law*, 189.   [5] *Commentaries*, i, 72.

maintain the supremacy of the common law, helped to secure the victory of Parliament and the defeat of absolute monarchy, we may claim for Bracton and his works an influence not only on the development of English law, but also on the political and constitutional development of the English state, and of all those other states in the eastern and western worlds which have inherited England's ideas of constitutional government.

Lecture II

EDWARD I

HALE, writing in the second half of the seventeenth century, thus describes the reign of
Edward I:[1]

Upon the whole matter, it appears that the very scheme,
mould, and model of the common law, especially in relation to
the administration of common justice between party and party,
as it was highly rectified and set in a much better light and order
by this king than his predecessors left it to him; so in a very great
measure it has continued the same in all succeeding ages, to this
day.

This is a true description; for the substantial settlement
of the constitution of Parliament, the settlement of the
constitution and jurisdiction of the common law courts,
the settlement of the relations of the common law courts
to other courts and departments of state, and the
numerous statutes which travel over the whole field of the
law, all helped to determine some of the large outstanding
characteristics of English law which are visible to-day.

These large effects of the reign of Edward I are due
partly to the character of the age and partly to the
character of the King. The latter half of the thirteenth
century was an age of constructive legislation. Frederic II
in Sicily, Louis IX in France, Edward's father-in-law
Alfonso X in Castile were all great lawgivers.[2] Among
these great men Edward I is by no means the least. His
travels in Italy and the East, and his association with the
French crusaders, gave him an opportunity of becoming
acquainted with such monuments of the legislative
activity of the age as the Assizes of Jerusalem and the

---

[1] *History of the Common Law*, 194.
[2] Stubbs, *Const. Hist.* ii, 116; Nichols, *Britton*, i, xvii.

Institutes of St Louis, and with some of the famous
French jurists. But though he possessed some knowledge of foreign systems of law and foreign jurists, he
was one of the most English of our English statesmen.
He made no violent changes. But, like the great Kings
of the house of Tudor, he could almost silently impress
a new policy upon the country, suited to its altered circumstances, by judicious modifications of existing institutions and laws. He had, as Stubbs has said,[1] an
instinctive genius for "the definition of duties and
spheres of duty, and the minute adaptation of means to
ends". Sir Frederick Pollock, writing in 1904, has
bidden us remember that "if writs run in the name of
King Edward VII from the North Sea to the Pacific, it
is largely because King Edward I was a faithful servant
of his people and of the law".[2]

The outstanding event of the reign is the substantial
settlement of the constitution of Parliament. That event
went far to settle that constitutional problem, created by
the granting of Magna Carta, which had led to the civil
wars of Henry III's reign; and it had repercussions
which affected permanently both legal institutions and
the form and contents of English law. We see the beginnings of a House of Lords consisting of the greater
barons, and by its side a House of Commons in which
representatives from the counties and the boroughs take
their places. We see signs that this Parliament of two
Houses will become the legislative and taxing body in
the state. In 1294 Edward I told the clergy, when they
asked him to repeal the Statute of Mortmain in return for
a grant of money, that statutes passed by Parliament
could not be repealed without its consent;[3] and the constitutional crisis of 1297, which led to the Confirmation

[1] *Const. Hist.* ii, 116.
[2] *The Expansion of the Common Law*, 137.
[3] Stubbs, *Const. Hist.* ii, 137.

of the Charters, shows that Parliament was claiming to control taxation. No doubt the constitution of Parliament was not yet settled in its final form; and the extent of its powers was as yet far from being finally ascertained. But its form and some of its powers are foreshadowed; and so we get the beginnings of a separation between the legislative and the executive organs of the state on lines to which the events of the succeeding centuries will give an ever-growing emphasis and precision.

We see also foreshadowed another separation between the organs of government. The constitution and jurisdiction of the three courts of common law—King's Bench, Common Pleas, and Exchequer—were becoming settled. Though as yet the King's Bench was closely connected with the King's Council, and continued to be closely connected with it till nearly the end of the fourteenth century,[1] there are signs of a coming separation which will divide the Council from the common law courts, and will thus foreshadow the division between the executive and the judicial departments of the state. It is not till the statute of the Long Parliament, which abolished the Star Chamber and deprived the Council of all jurisdiction in England, that this separation became complete; and even then the Council retained and still retains its jurisdiction to hear appeals from India, the Dominions, the Colonies and other possessions of the Crown outside the United Kingdom.

It is because we see foreshadowed this separation of the legislative, executive, and judicial organs of the state that in Edward I's reign we see the beginning of some of the large outstanding characteristics of English law.

The immediate effect of the rise of Parliament, which went far to settle the constitutional controversies of Henry III's reign, and began to separate the legislative

[1] Holdsworth, *H.E.L.* i, 209–211.

from the executive organs of the state, was the enactment of a number of statutes, some of which have retained their importance till our own day. In fact it is no exaggeration to say that it was these statutes which played the principal part in settling the sphere of the medieval common law, on which our modern common law is founded. We must wait till the nineteenth century for another period in which direct legislation has had so great an influence on legal development. The following is a very short summary which will illustrate the variety of topics covered by Edward I's legislation.

The Statutes of Westminster I and II (1275 and 1285) travelled over the whole field of law—procedure, real property, criminal law, constitutional law—amending and constructing.[1] The first of these statutes was "to a large extent based upon the results of the inquests held upon the articles of the Eyre of 1274".[2] It contains fifty-one chapters. They dealt (*inter alia*) with such matters as maintenance, champerty, peine forte et dure, scandalum magnatum, wardship, distress, limitation of actions, and essoins. The second of these statutes contains fifty chapters. It created the estate tail,[3] and contained provisions dealing with distraint,[4] dower, advowsons, mortmain, approvement of common, the writ of account, the criminal appeals, remedies available to executors, the scope of the assize of novel disseisin, nisi prius, bills of exceptions,[5] process of execution for debt, and, perhaps most important of all, the issue of writs in consimili casu.[6] In a sense the most modern of Edward's statutes was the Statute of Wales (1284).[7] It was a codification of the rules of English law made for

---

[1] Statutes (R.C.), i, 26, 71; Reeves, *History of English Law*, ii, 22–51, 74–121.

[2] H. E. Cam, *Vinogradoff*, Oxford Studies, vi, 36.   [3] c. 1.

[4] c. 2.   [5] c. 31; Holdsworth, *H.E.L.* i, 223–224.

[6] c. 24; Holdsworth, *H.E.L.* i, 398 n. 3.

[7] Statutes (R.C.), i, 55.

the purpose of introducing that law into Wales. It reminds us of our Indian codes and other codifying Acts of the nineteenth century. Perhaps, indeed, it is more than a coincidence that it is only the reign of Edward I and the nineteenth century—our two most important periods of legislation upon matters legal—which have seen statutes of this nature. The Statute of Gloucester (1278) gave the landlord a remedy against termors who let their land lie waste, and protected termors whose landlords attempted to oust them by fictitious recoveries; it dealt with the case of killing in self-defence and by mischance; and it fixed the competence of the local courts.[1] The Statute de Viris Religiosis (1279) introduced the law prohibiting gifts of land in mortmain.[2] The Statute de Mercatoribus (1283) and another statute of 1285 made special provision for the recovery of debts owed to merchants.[3] The Statute of Winchester (1285) improved and consolidated the police system of the country.[4] The Statute of Quia Emptores (1290) gave the tenant in fee simple of land held by free tenure (other than a tenant in chief of the Crown) the power of free alienation, and defined the effect of such alienation.[5] The ultimate result of this statute has been the practical elimination of mesne tenure.

These statutes deal mainly with private law. Other statutes possess considerable constitutional importance. During the disturbed times of Henry III's reign the large landowners had usurped jurisdiction over their tenants and others. In 1274 Edward I sent out commissioners to enquire into these usurpations. The results of their enquiries are embodied in the Hundred Rolls.

---

[1] Statutes (R.C.), i, 45; Holdsworth, *H.E.L.* i, 72, 73; iii, 121, 214, 312.   [2] Statutes (R.C.), i, 51.
[3] *Ibid.* i, 53, 98; Holdsworth, *H.E.L.* iii, 131.
[4] Statutes (R.C.), i, 96.
[5] Statutes (R.C.), i, 106.

On these Rolls Edward I founded his quo warranto
enquiries. He sent out commissioners furnished with
copies of the Hundred Rolls to enquire quo warranto—
by what warrant—these landowners were exercising
their franchises. The King's pleaders adopted the theory
which had been stated by Bracton that all jurisdiction
belongs to the Crown; and that no landowner is entitled
to exercise jurisdiction unless he can show a royal
charter. Mere length of user, they contended, aggravated the offence, for "nullum tempus occurrit regi".
These proceedings roused so much resentment amongst
the barons and other large landowners that Edward I was
obliged to compromise his claims. In 1290 the two
Statutes of Gloucester[1] enacted that possession from the
beginning of Richard I's reign should give a good title.
But the theory of the King and his lawyers, that no
franchise could exist except by virtue of a royal grant,
became the law for the future. In 1297 there occurred
the constitutional crisis which led to the Confirmation of
the Charters;[2] and with these documents should be mentioned the Articuli super Cartas of 1300, which included
another confirmation of the Charters,[3] an enactment on
the subject of conspiracy,[4] and other legislative changes.
The Statute of Carlisle (1306–7),[5] directed against the
practice of sending money out of the kingdom, began the
series of statutes directed against the anti-national practices of ecclesiastics which culminated in the Statute of
Praemunire of Richard II's reign.[6] There are many less
comprehensive statutes—statutes concerning the office
of coroner,[7] the statute called Rageman,[8] statutes for the

---

[1] 18 Edw. I, Sts. 2 and 3.   [2] 25 Edw. I, c. 1.
[3] 28 Edw. I, c. 1.   [4] c. 10.
[5] 35 Edw. I.   [6] 16 Rich. II, c. 5.
[7] 4 Edw. I, St. 2.
[8] For this statute see H. E. Cam, *Vinogradoff*, Oxford Studies, vi, 41–
56. The term "Rageman" was a popular name for the Hundred Rolls,
derived from the ragged appearance of the original returns. By a

City of London,[1] statutes concerning malefactors in parks and prison breach,[2] and statutes concerning the levying of fines and false money.[3] And, since the form in which a statute is made is not yet fixed, we find included amongst the statutes documents which are statutory neither in form nor in substance, such as administrative rules relating to the conduct of business in the Exchequer,[4] the writ Circumspecte Agatis dealing with the spheres of lay and ecclesiastical jurisdiction,[5] a record of a case in Parliament dealing with waste,[6] a writ relating to joint tenants, and an ordnance relating to the royal forests.[7]

This great legislative activity illustrates the effect of the separation between the legislative and executive organs of the state which was created by the rise of Parliament. I pass now to the effects of the other separation between the organs of government—the beginning of the separation of the Council from the common law courts. This separation was the cause of many developments which affected, first, the personnel of the judiciary; secondly, the legal profession; thirdly, legal literature; fourthly, the character of the medieval common law; and, lastly, the character of the control exercised by the central government over persons and courts entrusted with the local government.

shifting of meaning (parallel to that which occurred in the case of the term "assizes", see Holdsworth, *H.E.L.* i, 275–276), it was applied first to the pleas instituted on these returns, and then to the statute which assigned justices to hear these pleas.

[1] 13 Edw. I.
[2] 21 Edw. I, St. 1; 23 Edw. I.
[3] 27 Edw. I, St. 1, c. 1; St. 3.
[4] Statutes (R.C.), i, 69.
[5] *Ibid.* i, 101.
[6] *Ibid.* i, 109.   [7] *Ibid.* i, 145, 147.

(1) *The personnel of the judiciary.*

Towards the end of Henry III's reign there had been signs of a change in the personnel of the bench. The judges were not always learned clerks of the type of Bracton. There are instances of judges who were laymen;[1] and one of them—Laurence de Broke—was perhaps an early instance of a man who was raised to the bench by reason of his eminence as a practitioner, for we know that he was taking the assizes in 1267 and 1268.[2] It is probable that Bracton saw the beginning of this change. These lay judges were often men of no very high principles—tales are told by Matthew of Paris to the discredit of Thomas de Muleton and Henry of Bath who were two of these lay judges;[3] and it is probable that they were not so learned as the clerical judges of the older type. At any rate Bracton tells us that one of the reasons why he wrote his book was the fact that unlearned and dishonest men had become judges and were perverting the law;[4] and in writing his treatise he chose deliberately to rely upon earlier rather than upon later decisions.

The political unrest which marked the close of Henry III's reign had further contributed to the deterioration of the bench, and indeed to all branches of the civil service of the state. The chroniclers and the political songs of the period are full of complaints of the corruption of these civil servants, lay and clerical alike.[5] Two causes had produced this result—first the want of a strong ruler,

---

[1] Thomas de Muleton, Robert de Thurkilby, and Henry of Bath, Pollock and Maitland, *H.E.L.* (1st ed.), i, 184.
[2] Foss, *Lives of the Judges*, ii, 267; but it is not certain that he was ever a judge of the King's Bench or Common Pleas.
[3] *Chron. Maj.* iv, 49; v, 213.   [4] At f. 1 b.
[5] *Political Songs* (Camden Soc.), 225–230; *Liber Mem. de Bernewelle*, 171; for similar abuses in the local government see H. E. Cam, *Vinogradoff*, Oxford Studies, vi, chap. iii.

and secondly the fact that these civil servants were underpaid and irregularly paid.[1] The absence of Edward I between 1286 and 1289 brought matters to a crisis. He was met on his return by such loud complaints that he appointed a commission of enquiry, at the head of which was his Chancellor, Robert Burnell. The results of the enquiries of this commission were disgraceful to all branches of the civil service, and more especially to the bench. They constitute, to use Maitland's words, "our one great judicial scandal".[2] Of the judges of the King's Bench two out of three were removed; of the judges of the Common Pleas four out of five. The only two judges of these courts who were found to be guiltless were John de Metingham and Elias de Beckingham. Five of the itinerant justices and many minor officials were found guilty of various crimes. Thomas of Weyland, the chief justice of the Common Pleas, who was accused of being accessory to murder, took sanctuary and abjured the kingdom; and Ralph de Hengham, the chief justice of the King's Bench, was found guilty of a gross perversion of justice and heavily fined. But he was one of the most learned lawyers of the day, a clerical justice of the type of Bracton, and the author of some valuable law tracts. That he was not amongst the most guilty can be seen from the fact that he was made chief justice of the Common Pleas in 1301.

This episode helped in no slight degree to forward the success of Edward I's reforms. Though there were other scandals in later years in the judicial and administrative branches of the civil service, it was never again necessary to resort to such sweeping measures to secure the purity of the administration of justice. That this was so was due partly to the formation of an organized legal profession.

[1] Holdsworth, *H.E.L.* ii, 294.
[2] *Mirror of Justices* (S.S.), xxiv–xxv; on the whole subject see *State Trials of the Reign of Edward I* (Royal Hist. Soc.).

To this second important development of Edward I's reign we must now turn.

(2) *The formation of an organized legal profession.*

In Edward I's reign a legal profession was being formed which consisted of two classes of persons—pleaders who became known as serjeants-at-law in later centuries, and attorneys. The distinction between the two is well marked and has ancient roots. Lord Brougham in 1839 explained the distinction as follows:[1] "If you appear by attorney he represents you, but when you have the assistance of an advocate you are present, and he supports your cause by his learning, ingenuity, and zeal." The idea that one man can stand in the place of another and represent him as his attorney does not come naturally to primitive systems of law; and so the appointment of an attorney was originally only allowed on special grounds, and it was effected with considerable formality. On the other hand, it was well recognized from an early period that one man can assist another in court, and so the appointment of a pleader is not a formal proceeding.

In the thirteenth century there was a well-known class of pleaders, employed both by the King and by private persons. The fact that they were specially exempted from Edward I's legislation as to maintenance[2] shows that they were a definite class; and in our earliest Year Books we see, says Maitland, that "the great litigation of the realm ...is conducted by a small group of men. Lowther, Spigornel, Howard, Hertpol, King, Huntingdon, Heyham—one of them will be engaged in almost every case."[3] But it is clear from the complaints made to the justices in eyre in 1292 and 1293 of the conduct both of

---

[1] *The Serjeants' Case*, Manning, *Serviens ad Legem.*
[2] 28 Edw. I, St. 3, c. 11; Plac. Abbrev. 295 b.
[3] Pollock and Maitland, *H.E.L.* (1st ed.), i, 195.

pleaders and attorneys, that some regulation of this
nascent legal profession was needed.[1] In 1292 the King
directed the judges to provide a certain number of
attorneys and apprentices to follow the court, who should
have the exclusive right of practising before it.[2] The
King considered that one hundred and forty should
suffice; but more were to be appointed if there was need.
Probably the King did not mean to interfere with the
established pleaders. He meant rather that there should
be in future some regulation of the "apprenticii"—the
learners who intended to follow the profession of the law.
It is quite possible that up to this time these apprenticii had got their training from the serjeants, or the
class of practitioners in the royal courts who answered to
the serjeants of later days.[3] It is probable that the immediate effect of this ordinance was the making of more
systematic arrangements for their legal education; and
it is not unlikely that the judges entrusted those who were
responsible for giving this education with the duty of
selecting those privileged to practise in the courts. There
is an incidental reference to the teaching of law in
London in 1293;[4] and shortly after this date we hear of
the discussions of the students. In 1305 Hengham C.J.
was puzzled by a knotty case which he suspected had
been manufactured by these students in order to ascertain
a doubtful point of law.[5] We shall see that in the following century the more eminent of these pleaders will
become the serjeants-at-law; that the apprenticii will be
organized in the Inns of Court and Chancery, where they
will get their legal education from the senior members of
the Inns; and that to these Inns the judges will entrust

[1] *Select Bills in Eyre* (S.S.), nos. 6, 88, 99; Introd. xlii–xlv.
[2] *Rot. Parl.* i, 84.
[3] *L.Q.R.* xxiv, 393–394.
[4] *Select Bills in Eyre* (S.S.), no. 79; Introd. xlv.
[5] Y.B. 33–35 Ed. I (R.S.), 64.

the duty of calling to the bar those who have made themselves sufficiently learned in the law.[1]

In the twelfth and early thirteenth centuries the power
to appoint an attorney was a privilege which must be
given by royal grant, and the appointment must be
formally made in court.[2] But a series of statutes beginning with the Statute of Merton (1235–6)[3] gave everyone the right to appoint an attorney. For that reason we
get the rise of a class of professional attorneys which was
regulated by the ordinance of 1292 which regulated the
pleaders. This ordinance was perhaps the origin of the
staffs of professional attorneys attached to the three
courts of common law. They were appointed by the
judges, by whom they were controlled. Thus we see the
beginnings of the process which will make the professional attorney an officer of the court, and will
accentuate his separation from the pleader.

The growth of this organized legal profession emphasized the tendency to appoint the judges from its
leading members. Thus out of nine serjeants-at-law of
Edward I's reign seven were raised to the bench;[4] and
in the following period the serjeants got the privilege,
which in form they retained till the Judicature Act,[5] that
only members of their order were qualified to become
judges. In Edward I's reign they had not got this
privilege. Hengham C.J. was a distinguished representative of the older school of clerical judges, and, like
Bracton, was chancellor of Exeter Cathedral. But his
writings bear little trace of his clerical profession. They
might have been written by a man who had made his
career at the bar. It is clear that the growth of this

---

[1] Below, pp. 48–50.   [2] Holdsworth, *H.E.L.* ii, 315–316.
[3] 20 Henry III, c. 10.   [4] Holdsworth, *H.E.L.* ii, 318.
[5] Only in form because as early as Elizabeth's reign any lawyer whom
the Crown wished to appoint as a judge was made a serjeant for that
purpose, *ibid.* v, 341; below, p. 48.

organized and privileged legal profession will have important effects upon the development of the law. One of its most salutary effects will be the growth of an organized professional feeling which will create standards of professional conduct, and so prevent those judicial scandals which marked the beginning of Edward I's reign. It also had other effects upon the literature of the common law and on its development which were not so salutary. Of these two effects I must now speak under the two following heads.

(3) *The change in the character of the legal literature of Edward I's reign.*

Britton and Fleta are the two important law books of Edward I's reign. Both owe much to Bracton. In fact they are, to a large extent, Bracton brought up to date, omitting the greater part of the Roman elements in Bracton's treatise. Britton was probably written about the year 1291–2. It is a practical book for lawyers practising in the royal courts, written in the law French of the day. Its form is unique. It purports to be a direct enactment and codification of the law by the King. The fact that it was given this form is very significant of the importance of the legislation of Edward I. The treatise known as Fleta was probably compiled in or about 1290 by an official in the royal household—perhaps he was guilty of some defalcations and had been committed to the Fleet prison where the book was written. It is written in Latin, and never had the popularity of Britton. Both Britton and Fleta were royal clerks—that is, they were something more than mere common lawyers. By borrowing from Bracton they can write a legal treatise. On the other hand the later legal writings of Edward I's reign, written by practising lawyers, are mere tracts on procedure and pleading.

There are several of these tracts.[1] Some were summaries or adaptations of Bracton's treatise. Thus the *Cadit Assisa* summarizes his account of the assize of mort d'ancestor; and Hengham's two tracts the *Parva* and the *Magna*, which deal with procedure in the real actions, owe much to Bracton. The aim of these two tracts is to give instruction in the rules of pleading and procedure to be followed at different stages in the real actions, with some account of the relation of the jurisdiction of the county court and the court baron to that of the King's courts in these cases. Other tracts deal with other aspects of the law of procedure and pleading. It is probable that two of them, the *Fet Assaver* and the *Judicium Essoniorum*, were also by Hengham. Two others, the *Cum Sit Necessarium* or *Modus Componendi Brevium* and the *Exceptiones ad Cassandum Brevia*, deal with the drafting of writs, and defences to writs—a subject which was perhaps the most important of all to the young practitioner. The tract known as *Brevia Placitata* is a collection of precedents of pleading—each precedent consists of a writ, a count, and a plea. The *Casus Placitorum* is a collection of the decisions of certain judges, all of whom lived before 1260. It is the most interesting of all these tracts because it foreshadows what was to be in the two succeeding centuries the main source of the common law—the Year Books.

Lastly, there is a mysterious book called the *Mirror of Justices* which is quite unlike any of the other books of Edward I's reign.[2] The book was first cited in court in 1550. Coke, as Maitland says,[3] "devoured its contents with uncritical voracity"; and through Coke's

---

[1] For these tracts see Holdsworth, *H.E.L.* ii, 322–326; Woodbine, *Four Thirteenth-Century Law Tracts*; Dunham's ed. of Hengham's *Summae*.

[2] Holdsworth, *H.E.L.* ii, 327–333; Maitland's Introd. to the Selden Society's edition.

[3] *Mirror of Justices* (S.S.), Introd. ix.

credulity it was long regarded as an important source
for the history of the Saxon period in our legal history.
Maitland in his Introduction to the Selden Society
edition has finally destroyed its claim to possess any
sort of authority. "If", he says,[1] "at the present day
a man wrote a law book, and said in it, Law forbids
that murderers should be hanged; estates tail cannot
be barred; bills of exchange are not negotiable instruments, he would be guilty of no extravagance for
which a parallel might not be found in the Mirror." It
is a legal romance—an attempt by a writer of the thirteenth century to construct an ideal system of law out of
the shifting legal panorama of his day, by going back to
biblical first principles, and letting his fancy play upon
the mixture of the archaic, the feudal, the Romanist,
the royalist, and the constitutional tendencies which
he saw reflected in the institutions and the law of his
time.

It is clear from the tracts which compose the regular
legal literature of the latter part of Edward I's reign that
the day for philosophical treatises upon the law has gone
by. The common law is becoming a special subject known
only to the practitioners of the royal courts; and the
principal need of the practitioner is for some simple
information as to the rules of court. The law itself lies
beyond. The rank and file of the profession, immersed in
the routine of practice, never attain to a conception of law
as a reasonable and logical science. What they want is
short rules about writs, up-to-date knowledge of the
rules of procedure, the most recent "cautelae" in the art
of tripping up an opponent. But these rules can be best
learned by attending to the decisions of the courts. And
so it is that the two last-mentioned of these tracts—the
Brevia Placitata and the *Casus Placitorum*—foreshadow
what (apart from the statutes) will be, in the following

[1] *Mirror of Justices* (S.S.), Introd. xxxvii.

period, the two chief sources of law—the Register of Writs and supplementary works on pleading, and the Year Books. In the Register and the supplementary works on pleading are contained the list of the remedies given by the law and information as to their use: in the Year Books the cases of practical importance and notes thereon.

As we shall now see this change in the character of the literature of the law foreshadows a change in the character of the law.

(4) *The characteristics of the medieval common law.*

The most important branch of the medieval common law was the land law. The law was feudal inasmuch as it was based upon tenure. But the jurisdictional and governmental elements in feudalism were being eliminated, so that it was becoming more distinctly the law of property. The list of free tenures is fixed in its final form; the law has evolved the conception of an estate in land; with the creation of the estate tail by the statute De Donis Conditionalibus[1] the list of estates is closed; the statute Quia Emptores[2] settled the question of freedom of alienation; the position of the tenant for term of years is becoming fixed; the rules as to seisin and possession are beginning to take shape. It was the elaboration of the complex rules of the land law, on the lines fixed by Edward I's legislation, which was the main part of the work of the common lawyers of the two succeeding centuries.

The other important branch of the common law was the criminal law. The offence of treason is not as yet defined; but the conception of felony, and the chief classes of felonies have made their appearance. The procedure by way of indictment is gradually ousting the old

[1] 13 Edw. I, c. 1.   [2] 18 Edw. I.

criminal appeals. In the rise of the action of trespass[1] we see a new form of action which will leave deep marks on the criminal law, and still deeper marks on the law of tort. It is the trespasses which are presented to the itinerant justices which will develop into the misdemeanours of later law. Around the action of trespass, and trespass on the case, a large part of the law of tort will grow up. But as yet the scope of the law of tort is narrow. Parliament solemnly declared in 1295 that the common law gave no action for defamation;[2] and the only fraud remedied by the action of deceit was some deceitful act committed or coming to the notice of the court in the course of the conduct of a case.[3] As yet the common law had no theory of contract. By means of the actions of debt and covenant certain agreements could be enforced. But the idea that the law should enforce agreements as such is not yet recognized.[4] In fact we can see from the scope of such actions as debt and detinue that the line between actions founded on property, on tort, and on contract is very indistinctly drawn. But I think that it would be true to say that the amorphous character of these and other personal actions, and of the law which centred round them, made further developments in the law easier. It is doubtful if English law could have developed an original theory of contract from developments in the actions on the case, if the scope of such actions as debt and detinue and the law which centred round them had been more precisely fixed.

---

[1] For the early history of the action see Maitland, *Harv. Law Rev.* iii, 177–197; Holdsworth, *H.E.L.* ii, 364–365; cp. *Yale Law Journal*, xxxiii, 806–808, 812–816, where Professor Woodbine points out that the most characteristic feature of the action—the fact that damages could be obtained—was derived through the assize of novel disseisin from Roman law.

[2] *Rot. Parl.* i, 133.

[3] Pollock and Maitland, *H.E.L.* ii, 533–534.

[4] Holdsworth, *H.E.L.* ii, 367.

The substantive rules of the common law were thus growing more certain and more fixed. But it was the adjective law—the law of procedure and pleading—which was showing most markedly this quality of growing fixity. Consequently the common law was beginning to acquire a rigidity which it had never had before. An unfortunate result of this rigidity was the elimination of those equitable characteristics which it had possessed in the days of Bracton. This elimination did not come all at once; and in the Bills in Eyre, which are complaints addressed to the justices in eyre, we see a procedure which in some respects foreshadows the Bills which were later addressed to the Chancellor.[1] But though the decay of the equity once administered by the courts of common law was slow it was sure. The hardening of the common law into a rigid and technical system, of which we see the beginnings in Edward I's reign, proceeded very rapidly in the fourteenth century for the two following reasons: In the first place, the increasing number of the ordinary forms and processes of the common law tended to concentrate the attention of the lawyers upon the working of this complicated machinery. In the second place, the courts of common law had ceased to be so closely identified with the person of the King that they could assume his prerogative to administer equity. In Edward III's reign the courts of common law definitely decided not to recognize the interest of the cestui que use.[2] For these reasons litigants who wanted equity were driven into the court of Chancery—a court which, because it had maintained its close connection with the King, was able to exercise his prerogative to administer equity. Thus we see foreshadowed in the legal developments of Edward I's reign the reasons why in England alone the administration of law and equity came to be

[1] *Select Bills in Eyre* (S.S.); Holdsworth, *H.E.L.* ii, 336–344.
[2] Holdsworth, *H.E.L.* ii, 593–595; iv, 416.

entrusted to separate courts, and why, therefore, law and equity came to be more separate than they are in any other system.

(5) *The character of the control exercised by the central government over persons and courts entrusted with the local government.*

Though the separation of the common law courts from the person of the King made for the decay of the equity which they had formerly administered, they still retained a jurisdiction which they had acquired before this separation became complete. This was a jurisdiction to supervise and control, by means of the prerogative writs of certiorari, mandamus, prohibition, and quo warranto, as well as by other means, the doings of all those subordinate courts and officials through whom the local government was conducted. This jurisdiction had both a legal and a constitutional importance.

It had a legal importance for the following three reasons: First, it defined spheres of jurisdiction. The quo warranto enquiries helped to settle the sphere of the jurisdiction of the franchise courts, and statutes, such as the Statute of Gloucester, settled the sphere of the jurisdiction of the communal courts of the counties and hundreds. Secondly, this jurisdiction helped to control the exercise of jurisdiction. This control was exercised both by the itinerant justices and by the courts of common law. In civil cases writs of error and false judgment brought the doings of these local courts to the notice of the common law courts. Both in civil and criminal cases their irregularities were punished both by the itinerant justices and the common law courts by amerciaments. Thirdly, this control helped to produce uniformity of rule. The rolls of manorial courts and borough records show that much law was still administered in the local courts. But those rolls also show that the example and control of the central courts were producing many uniformities; and the jurisdiction assumed by the courts of common law to hold the by-laws of those communities void, if in their opinion they were unreasonable, prevented any large divergencies from the common law. Sir F. Pollock has remarked upon the power of the common law to impose its own conceptions upon other systems of law. He has pointed out that it has shown this power in modern times on a large stage.[1] It was showing this same power upon a smaller stage in the reign of Edward I and the following centuries, with the result that the law of England became truly a common law.

This control exercised by the common law over subordinate courts and officials had also a constitutional importance. The communities of county, hundred, and township, of manor and borough, and in later centuries their successors the justices of the peace, through whom local government was carried on and local jurisdiction was exercised, could act freely, subject only to the judicial control of the common law courts. They were subordinated to the law without losing their individual character and their independent life. It followed, in the first place, that the supremacy of the law was emphasized; and, in the second place, that the "self-government" which is characteristic of the English system of local government was secured. The fact that the English local government was thus based on communities which could act freely subject only to the control of the law, and not upon persons or bodies which acted only as delegates of a sovereign state, is the essence of the English system of local self-government.[2] It is to this system of self-government that the success of Parliamentary government is largely due, for it educated those who worked it,

---

[1] *The Expansion of the Common Law*, 16–19.
[2] Gneist, *English Constitution*, ii, 112.

and thus fitted them for the work of government in a higher sphere. Thus the constitutional effect of this jurisdiction exercised by the common law courts has been very great; for it has helped forward the development of two fundamental characteristics of the English constitution—the rule of law and the system of self-government.

For all these reasons the reign of Edward I is a turning point in English legal history. At the end of the reign we see foreshadowed some of the most important features of English law public and private, and of the machinery by which it will be developed. How these characteristics of the law were elaborated, and how this machinery worked in the two following centuries, will be the subject of the next lecture.

Lecture III

LITTLETON AND FORTESCUE

THE completion of the medieval common law, upon the foundation of which the modern English public and private law is built, was the work of many lawyers of the fourteenth and fifteenth centuries, the majority of whom are anonymous. It was these lawyers who founded the Serjeants' Inns, the Inns of Court, and the Inns of Chancery, through which the legal profession got its organization, its discipline, and its education. They helped to form the Register of Writs which was the ground plan upon which these builders of the medieval common law worked—"the very skeleton", Maitland says,[1] "of the Corpus Juris". They wrote the Year Books in which from term to term and year to year the work of the courts in developing the law was recorded. Being pre-eminently practitioners, they were principally interested in the procedure of the courts in which they practised, and they knew no other law but the law, adjective and substantive, administered in those courts. Therefore they developed the common law on very technical lines, with the result that they often seem to be more interested in the working of the technical procedure which they had created than in the principles of substantive law. No doubt some of these lawyers, as judges or counsel, show some grasp of principle; and many showed very considerable powers of logical reasoning; for their training and outlook made for great precision in thought and language. But there is no doubt that their outlook was less broad and more technical than that of the lawyers of the age of Bracton; with the result that, till the latter part of the fifteenth century, there is no legal

[1] *Collected Papers*, ii, 110.

literature to speak of, except the purely utilitarian Year Books. The lawyers were kept too busy by their professional work in the courts to write books; and, for all but exceptional lawyers, immersion in professional work, then as now, prevents any desire to write systematic expositions of the law. But in the middle of the fifteenth century two such exceptional lawyers made their appearance—Littleton and Fortescue. Littleton wrote a classical book upon the land law, which was the most important branch of the private law of the Middle Ages. Fortescue wrote classical books upon the legal profession, upon the outstanding characteristics of English law public and private, and upon the causes of the evils which oppressed the state and the administration of the law at the end of the medieval period.

In this lecture I must begin by saying something of the main features of legal development during the fourteenth and fifteenth centuries, because, to understand the contribution made to English law by Littleton and Fortescue, we must bear in mind these features. In the second place, I shall say something of Littleton and the development of private law. Thirdly, I shall say something of Fortescue and his books on the legal profession and the development of public law. Lastly, I shall say something of the strong and weak points of the medieval common law.

(1) *The main features of legal development during the fourteenth and fifteenth centuries.*

There are three features in the legal development of this period which have had a very permanent effect upon the development and character of the common law, upon the position in the state which is held by the common law and the common lawyers, and upon the form taken by the constitutional law of the English state. The first of these features is the formation of an organized, disciplined, and learned profession. The second is the creation by this profession of technical bodies of legal doctrine formed around the writs and forms of action, and developed by the decisions of the cases which came before the courts. The third is the great part played by the members of this profession, and by the law which they were creating, in developing the machinery of government, and the principles and rules by which it was regulated.

(i) It was during these centuries that an organized, disciplined, and learned profession was formed.[1] The highest rank in that profession consisted of the serjeants-at-law and the judges. It was from the serjeants-at-law that the judges were chosen. Right down to the Judicature Act it was only a serjeant-at-law who was qualified to be a judge of the common law courts—though in fact from the sixteenth century onwards this rule had been coming to be a merely formal one. The lawyer whom the King wished to make a judge was made a serjeant-at-law for that purpose.[2] The serjeants and the judges were brothers of one order—the Order of the Coif. Lawyers who were made serjeants left their Inns of Court and joined one of the serjeants' Inns, where they and the judges lived together as members of the same society; for the serjeants, like the judges, held a recognized official position in the state. They were called on to act as itinerant justices, they attended Parliament, they acted as triers of petitions addressed to Parliament, they considered doubtful questions of law referred to them by the Council and Parliament, and from their ranks the King retained certain members, styled King's serjeants, who performed the functions of the modern attorney- and solicitor-general.

The members of the legal profession under the degree of serjeant—the barristers and students—were

---

[1] Holdsworth, *H.E.L.* ii, 484–512.　　　[2] Above, 36 n. 5.

organized in the Inns of Court and Chancery. The four Inns of Court—Lincoln's Inn, the Inner and Middle Temple, and Gray's Inn—and the Inns of Chancery dependent upon them, attained substantially their final form in this period. We see the existing three grades of membership—the benchers who are the governing body of the Inn, the barristers, and the students. Probably these Inns originated in bodies of lawyers living together and teaching their juniors—the apprentices of the law— who in return assisted these lawyers in their work. These bodies of lawyers probably attained the position which they held in the fifteenth century by the privileges given to them by the serjeants and the judges. The serjeants and the judges helped these lawyers to maintain order and to educate their apprentices, and they allowed those, and those alone, whom they called to the bar of the Inn to practise in the courts. Thus originated the call to the bar by the Inns which to-day gives the barrister the right to practise in the courts. In this way the Inns became universities for the study of the law. And they were very efficient universities. The benchers of the Inns appointed readers every year whose duty it was to lecture on some legal topic. Each reading was followed by an argument upon some point of law raised by the reader in his reading, in which the barristers and students took part. Every day in term time there were discussions of cases after dinner by the readers and benchers, and moots were held after supper in which the benchers acted as judges and the barristers and students as counsel; and in the vacations moots continued to be held, at which the barristers acted as judges. Thus the Inns gave a legal training which was very practical—it produced the men who wrote the Year Books, and made the common law a system of case law. At the same time it gave opportunity for the discussion of principles. It was also a collegiate system, which gave a moral and a social as well as an intellectual training; and so the Inns attracted many students who had no thought of becoming professional lawyers. It is not surprising that a legal profession thus organized and disciplined and educated should have left very deep marks upon the law which it administered and developed. This brings me to the second of the main features in the legal development of this period—the creation by this profession of technical bodies of legal doctrine.

(ii) Maitland, speaking of the legal education provided by the Inns of Court, says:[1] "It would, so I think, be difficult to conceive any scheme better suited to harden and toughen a traditional body of law than one which, while books were still uncommon, compelled every lawyer to take part in legal education, and every distinguished lawyer to read public lectures." Moreover this toughening process was accentuated by the procedural and therefore practical angle from which the study of the law was approached. The student began with the study of the original writs;[2] and throughout his professional career the learning of writs and forms of action was of the first importance to him. These writs were said in a Parliamentary petition of Edward III's reign to be "the chiefest part of the law which is the sovereign law of King and kingdom". And so the Register of Writs, which was growing and expanding throughout the fourteenth century, was one of the most important books for the medieval lawyer. It was in fact the basis of the medieval common law, a guide to its leading principles, and a commentary upon their application. The first step in an action was the choice of a writ; and the choice of a writ meant the choice of a remedy which could only be

---

[1] *English Law and the Renaissance*, 27–28.

[2] For the history of the Register of Writs and Forms of Action see Maitland, *Collected Papers*, ii, 110–173: Lectures on the Forms of Action; Holdsworth, *H.E.L.* ii, 512–525.

made effectual by following rigidly the procedure appropriate to it. It must be brought in the right court. Each
writ had its peculiar process for getting the defendant
before the court. Modes of pleading, of trial, and of
execution differed according to the writ chosen. In 1317
these characteristics of the medieval law of procedure
were summed up epigrammatically by Bereford C.J.
in the phrase—"Writ, count, and action—to each its
own kind of reasoning."[1] It is not surprising that
Littleton told his son that "it is one of the most honourable, laudable, and profitable things in our law to have the
science of well pleading in actions reals and personals".[2]

But if the rules of procedure and pleading which
gathered around these writs were to be published to the
profession, reports of the decisions of the courts must be
made. And so the Year Books[3]—reports made by lawyers for lawyers—arose. The old legend that they were
official publications is now entirely exploded. The earliest
of them, Maitland thinks, were made by young lawyers
whose object was to note down the latest points for the
use of themselves or their friends. The earliest printed
Year Book comes from 1292; and during the succeeding
two and a half centuries, from term to term and from year
to year, they give us first-hand accounts of the doings of
the courts, and therefore of the legal doctrines laid down
by the judges of these centuries, who, building on the
foundations laid by Glanvil and Bracton, constructed the
medieval common law. They are the precursors of those
libraries of reports which accumulate whenever the common law, or any legal system which has come under its
influence, is studied and applied. No other nation has
anything like them. They are as unique as the common

---

[1] Y.B. 10 Edw. II (S.S.), 86 (1935).   [2] Litt. § 534.
[3] For the Year Books see Bolland, *Three Lectures on the Year Books*;
Jacques Lambert, *Les Year Books de Langue Française*; Holdsworth,
H.E.L. ii, 525–556.

law itself. "Instruction for pleaders", says Maitland,[1] "rather than the authoritative fixation of points of substantive law", was the aim of the makers of the early Year Books. It never ceased to be an important aim of these reporters. But their reports developed as the years passed; they gave fuller and better accounts of the arguments of counsel and the judges on matters both of procedure and substance; and so they became the only first-hand authorities for the history of the development of the principles of the medieval common law.

It was in this technical procedural environment that the doctrines of the medieval common law were created. We see the beginnings of the rules of pleading, some of which lived on till the reforms of the nineteenth century. Partly by means of the enactments of the Legislature, and partly by means of the decisions of the courts, the criminal law was developed. We see some development in the law as to the ownership and possession of chattels through the working of the actions of trespass and detinue, and some development of the law of contract through the working of the actions of covenant and debt. In the actions of trespass and case developments were being made in the law both of tort and contract. In fact, in the fifteenth century, some of the modern rules of the law of tort and contract were beginning to emerge through these actions on the case. As to the origin of these actions on the case, which were destined to take the place of many of the older actions through which the medieval common law was developed, and by the means of which very many of the rules of the modern common law were created, there has been recently much learned controversy.[2] The older view was that they originated in chap. 24 of the Statute of Westminster II (1285). But it has been

---

[1] Y.B. 1, 2 Edw. II (S.S.), xiv.

[2] Plucknett, *Col. Law Rev.* xxxi, 778, and *L.Q.R.* lii, 220; Landon, *L.Q.R.* lii, 68.

thought by Professor Plucknett that they are not connected with this statute. The true view is, I think, this :[1]
A clause in the Provisions of Oxford (1258) had provided that the Chancellor should seal no writ except a
writ of course without the consent of the King and
Council. This enactment had prevented the free manu-
facture of new remedies for new wrongs, and it was to
give back to the Chancellor the power to devise such new
remedies that the clause of the Statute of Westminster II
was passed. Not very much use was at first made of it.
But the principle that the remedies provided by the law
should not be unduly narrow had been laid down; and
when, in the fifteenth century, changing conditions demanded new remedies, and the need to meet the competition of rival courts was felt, effect was given to it by
the growth of actions on the case.

All through this period the most highly developed
body of law was the land law. The many intricate relations
of many different kinds of tenants were governed by the
real actions. They were a complex apparatus of remedies
governed by highly technical rules, which gave abundant
opportunities for the skill of the pleader. Through their
working the complex rules of the medieval land law grew
up. This body of law covered far more ground than is
covered to-day by the land law. There are two main
reasons for this. In the first place, society was still
organized on feudal principles, that is, it still depended
largely on tenurial relations. For this reason it covered
many relations which would now fall under the rubric
Master and Servant. It was not till the fifteenth century
that the hired agricultural labourer replaced the villein
tenant. In the second place, the law of contract was still
rudimentary. Many transactions which would now fall
under the rubric *Contract* were regarded as branches of
the land law. Much, for instance, could be done by the

[1] *L.Q.R.* xlvii, 334.

creation of proprietary rights. "The man of the thir-teenth century", says Maitland,[1] "does not say, I agree that you may have so many trees out of my copse in every year; he says, I give and grant you so much wood. The main needs of the agricultural economy of the age can be met in this manner without the creation of any personal obligations." In Littleton's book many topics which we do not regard as belonging to the land law, such as tender, payment, and persons under disability, are dis-cussed in connection therewith. We shall see that it is for this reason that Littleton's book is so important. It summed up the most highly developed branch of the medieval common law, to which many other branches were related, and around which many of its principles were developed.

But the field of the common law was not limited to these branches of private law. The common law had from the first been made by the royal judges, and, consequently, had always been intimately allied with public law. Indeed it was generally recognized that King and state depended on the law. The law was, as a Year Book of Henry VI's reign says,[2] "the highest inheritance which the King has; for by the law he and all his subjects are ruled, and if there was no law, there would be no King and no inheritance". It is this aspect of the medieval common law which brings me to the third of its characteristic features—the part played by it in developing the machinery of govern-ment and the principles and rules by which it was regulated.

(iii) It was a commonplace of medieval political thought that law of some sort was supreme over all persons and causes—the law of God, the law of nature, or the law of the state. Even the King was bound by the law, and political writers argued in the fourteenth and

---

[1] Pollock and Maitland, *H.E.L.* ii, 145.
[2] Y.B. 19 Henry VI, Pasch. pl. 1.

fifteenth centuries, as they had argued in the thirteenth century, that this limitation was no diminution of the royal power, for it merely limited his power to do wrong.[1] Practical effect was given to this political theory by the growth of the legislative and taxing powers of Parliament; and I think that it was the lawyers who so developed the procedure of Parliament that it became a workable assembly, and the only one of the medieval representative assemblies which survived, and became an integral part of the machinery of government. They regarded Parliament as a court with many of the features of those courts in which they practised, but a court with peculiar functions of its own, and superior to all other courts. Its rules of procedure, its rules of debate, its committee system, its privileges, its records—all had affinities to the similar characteristics of courts of law.[2] Because the lawyers regarded Parliament as a superior court they never allowed it to be hampered by the archaic rules which fettered the activities of some of the continental representative assemblies.[3] Because they regarded it as the highest court known to the law they never took a narrow view of its powers and privileges; and they never questioned its legislative power.[4] They obeyed its enactments; and by the manner in which they interpreted them they worked them into the fabric of the medieval common law.

Thus the common law and the common lawyers played a great part in constructing the medieval constitution. Sometimes they were entangled in political questions. In Richard II's reign the judges were arrested and condemned to death for their opinions as to the extent of the royal prerogative. They played a more prudent part in Henry VI's reign, and declined to give an opinion as to the validity of the Duke of York's claim to the throne.

[1] Holdsworth, *H.E.L.* ii, 253–254, 435.   [2] *Ibid.* ii, 431–433.
[3] *Ibid.* ii, 433–434; iv, 168.   [4] *Ibid.* ii, 434, 442–443.

But then and at other times they did not shrink from vindicating the majesty of the law and their own independence. Markham C.J. was dismissed from his post of chief justice of the King's Bench in 1469 because he declined to strain the law in order to secure a conviction for treason.

Just as Littleton summed up in his book the most important branch of the private law of these centuries, so Fortescue summed up in his books the public law. All these books, as we shall see in the two following parts of this lecture, have had so large an influence upon future development of English law, that they entitle their writers to a high place amongst the Makers of English Law.

(2) *Littleton and the development of private law.*[1]

It is between the years 1440 and 1450 that we begin to hear of Littleton as a rising member of the legal profession. In 1447 he was recorder of Coventry—a post afterwards filled by his great commentator Coke. About the same time he was reader in his Inn, the Inner Temple —the earliest recorded reader of that Society. The subject of his reading—the statute De Donis Conditionalibus— shows that he was then especially interested in the subject which was to make his name famous. He became a serjeant-at-law in 1453, and King's serjeant in 1455. In 1466 he was made a judge of the court of Common Pleas —a post which he held till his death in 1481.

Five books stand out pre-eminently in the history of English law—Glanvil, Bracton, Littleton, Coke, and Blackstone. Littleton's *Tenures* was written in the professional law French of the day. It summed up the results of the professional development of the most important branch of the common law during the fourteenth and fifteenth centuries. It showed that the com-

[1] Holdsworth, *H.E.L.* ii, 571–588.

mon law was not merely a collection of rules of procedure
and pleading which could be compendiously strung
together in the short tracts which for the last century and
a half had been the only law books, besides the Year
Books, which the legal profession had produced. It
showed that it possessed principles and doctrines of its
own which were scientifically exact and yet eminently
practical, because they were founded upon the actual
problems of daily life. The book was founded upon the
Year Books, but it was no mere summary of decisions.
The author tries to get beyond the decisions to the
"arguments and reasons of the law", and thus to construct from the already vast number of decisions upon
the various parts of his subject a coherent body of legal
doctrine by which "a man more sooner shall come to the
certainty and knowledge of the law".[1] It is the pioneer
of a long series of text-books upon various branches of
the common law in its completed form. It has been and
it is a model both in its methods and in its style to
succeeding writers.

The book was designed to assist the author's son
Richard to a knowledge of the law, and it soon obtained
and long retained its position as a first book for the
student. When it was written is not quite clear—probably towards the close of the author's life. There are two
MSS of it which were almost certainly written while he
was alive, but we have not got the autograph. It seems
to have been at once accepted as a classic. Mr Wambaugh
tells us that it was printed by Lettou and Machlinia in
1481 or 1482, "being one of the earliest books printed
in London, and the earliest treatise on the English law
printed anywhere". There was a second edition in 1483,
and before 1628 (the year when Coke's edition and
commentary was published) it had run to more than
seventy editions.[2] Early in the sixteenth century it

[1] Epilogue.   [2] Wambaugh's ed. of Littleton's *Tenures*, lix–lxi.

was translated, and it obtained a commentator before Coke.

These few facts speak more strongly for the intrinsic merits of Littleton's book than pages of elaborate eulogy. Here I would call attention to the characteristic which gives it a unique value from the historical point of view. It describes the land law as it existed at the end of a period of continuous and purely logical development, and just before a period when its doctrines were to be profoundly modified. When Littleton wrote, the new doctrines as to Uses were beginning to modify the strict common law rules; and, whether or not to meet the competition of the new kinds of interests in the land which they rendered possible, the common law was beginning to think of admitting the validity of the contingent remainder. An effective method had at length been devised of barring an entail and so of undoing the effect of the statute De Donis. The action of trespass and its offshoots were soon to encroach upon the sphere of the real actions. Littleton both knew and understood the doctrines of Uses, as his will shows; but the undoubted references to them in his book are of the slightest. He denies the validity of a contingent remainder. There is no hint either that un-barrable entails are things of the past, or that the supremacy of the real actions will shortly be threatened. In fact, the historical interest of Littleton's book is closely parallel to that of Blackstone's *Commentaries*. It summed up and passed on to future generations the land law as developed by the common lawyers of the Middle Ages, before it was remodelled by the changes inspired by the growth of the new equitable principles administered in the Chancery, just as Blackstone's *Commentaries* summed up and passed on the common law, as developed mainly by the work of the legal profession, before it was re-modelled by the direct legislation inspired by the teaching of Bentham.

(3) *Fortescue and his books on the legal profession and the development of public law.*[1]

Fortescue belonged to a Devonshire family. He was a member of Lincoln's Inn and acted as its governor in 1425, 1426, and 1429. He became a serjeant in 1429 or 1430, and in 1442 he was made chief justice of the King's Bench. When the Wars of the Roses broke out, he, unlike his brethren on the bench, took a side and joined the Lancastrian party. The fortunes of war varied. But by 1464 the Yorkists had prevailed. The year before Fortescue had left England with the Queen and her son. For the next seven years they lived in exile in France. In 1470 the Earl of Warwick joined the Lancastrian party, secured the expulsion of Edward IV, and a brief Lancastrian restoration. But Edward returned, defeated Warwick at the Battle of Barnet, and finally defeated the Lancastrians at Tewkesbury. Prince Edward the Queen's son was killed, and she was taken prisoner. It was obvious that the Lancastrian cause was lost, and so Fortescue made his peace with the Yorkists. He was pardoned, and made a member of the King's Council, and, on his writing a retractation of his arguments against the Yorkist title to the throne, his estates were restored to him. The last notice that we have of him comes from 1476.

But for the Wars of the Roses, and but for the fact that Fortescue, unlike his brethren, took a side in those wars, we should probably only know him, as we know most of the other lawyers of this period, as giving certain decisions and arguing certain cases. His exile made him a political thinker. He used his leisure to reflect upon the condition of his country and its law, and to embody the results of those reflections in books which have had a permanent influence on the course of English constitu-

---

[1] Holdsworth, *H.E.L.* ii, 566–571.

tional and legal history. The permanence of their influence is due to the fact that they were written by a lawyer who had been at the centre of affairs in many spheres of activity. He correctly diagnosed the cause of the evils which were afflicting his country, and he suggested the remedies which were adopted in the following century.

The two most important of Fortescue's books are the *De Laudibus Legum Angliae* and the *Monarchia* or *The Governance of England*.

The *De Laudibus* was written for the benefit of Prince Edward while Fortescue was in exile in France. It is written in the form of a dialogue between Fortescue and the Prince, and its aim is to instruct the Prince in the laws of the country over which he was one day to rule. He explains to the Prince the difference between an absolute and limited monarchy—taking France and England as the types of these two forms of government. He then goes on to compare the English common law with the Roman civil law—greatly to the advantage of the former. As part of his description of English law he gives us our earliest account of the Inns of Court, legal education, and the ranks of the legal profession. In his account of the law itself he abstains from going into technical details. He explains only its elementary doctrines and salient features. It was because the book was written to instruct a person who was not a lawyer and never would be a lawyer that it contains information which, being well known to all contemporary lawyers, we get from no other person. The lucidity of its style, and the unique character of the information which it contains, explain why amongst lawyers it has always been the most popular of Fortescue's books.

The *Monarchia* or *The Governance of England* is one of the latest of Fortescue's works. Its date depends upon the question whether we think that the book was addressed to Henry VI or Edward IV. If it was addressed to the former it was probably written during the brief period of the Lancastrian restoration in 1470: if it was addressed to the latter it was written after Fortescue had made his peace with the Yorkist government. There is much in common between the *Monarchia* and the *De Laudibus*. Both contain a discussion of the differences between an absolute and a limited monarchy. Both contrast the state of France and England in order to show the goodness of English institutions. But whereas the object of the *De Laudibus* is to instruct in English law, the object of the *Monarchia* is to probe the causes of that want of governance which had led to the Wars of the Roses.

Fortescue's analysis of the causes of that want of governance is masterly—its truth is borne out by all the contemporary authorities for the history of this period. During Henry VI's minority the government had been in the hands of the leading nobility who composed the King's Council. These "overmighty subjects", as Fortescue called them, ran the country in their own interests, and used the machinery of government to aggrandize themselves, and to help them to prosecute their feuds with one another. They had, he tells us,[1] always business of their own to be treated of in the Council, as well as the business of the King.

Wherethrough when they come together, they were so occupied with their own matters, and with the matters of their kin, servants, and tenants, that they attended but little...to the King's matters. And also there were but few matters of the King's, but the same matters touched also the said counsellors, their cousins, their servants, tenants, or such other as they owed favour unto. And what lower man was there sitting in that Council, that durst say against the opinion of any of the great lords? And why might not these men make by means of

[1] *The Governance of England*, chap. xv.

corruption some of the servants and counsellors of some of the lords
to move the lords to partiality, and to make them also favourable
and partial as were the same servants or the parties that so moved
them? Then could no matter treated in the Council be kept
privy. For the lords often times told their own counsellors and
servants, that had sued to them for those matters, how they had
sped in them and who was against them.

Fortescue's practical experience, and his reading and
reflection upon political questions, made him both an
original political thinker and a statesman who could
suggest practical reforms. That it made him an original
political thinker has been shown by Mr Chrimes in his
recent book on *English Constitutional Ideas in the Fifteenth
Century*. Mr Chrimes has shown that it was Fortescue's
knowledge of the machinery of the English government
which led him to originate the theory of a *dominium
politicum et regale*—that is the theory of constitutional or
limited monarchy. No writer on political theory had
envisaged such a form of government; but Fortescue
"wanted a theory to cover the facts of the English polity
as he knew them.... He therefore made the combination."[1] That it made him a statesman who could suggest
practical reforms is shown by his recommendations
for the reform of the Council. He recommended a
Council of twelve spiritual and twelve temporal men "of
the wisest and best disposed that can be found in all
parts of this land". They were to take an oath like that
of the judges; they were to have a president to be chosen
by the King; and they were to meet at certain hours and
deliberate upon all matters of state and suggest legislative changes to Parliament. The Chancellor, Treasurer,
and Lord Privy Seal should be ex-officio members; the
judges should be summoned as occasion demanded;
and the Council should keep a book of rules for its
own procedure. Thus, without departing from the

[1] Chrimes, *English Constitutional Ideas in the Fifteenth Century*, 318.

constitutional position which he had taken up in both his books, he suggested reforms which were carried out by the Tudors. It is for this reason that the influence of Fortescue's books has been curiously double. They suggested the measures which led to the establishment of the strongest monarchy which England had had since the Norman and Angevin kings, and the arguments which in the seventeenth century were used by the opponents of arbitrary rule.

In fact in the fifteenth century the constitution and the constitutional law of England were very nebulous. Certain institutions of government existed and functioned—the King, Parliament, and the courts. All of them were recognized as essential parts of the government of the state, and, as such, all of them had a more or less defined legal position. But though the exigencies of litigation compelled the lawyers to theorize about their position when cases bearing on it came before the courts, there was very little general theory on these questions. English political thought, like English law, was very insular.[1] Even Fortescue's books are more concerned with the machinery and the conduct of government than with speculation.

If we look at this machinery we can see many medieval elements and some of those modern elements which will, in the following century, reduce the medieval ideas in which they originated to a position of relatively small importance. Thus in the position ascribed to the King we can see both a religious element and a feudal element; and there is also a national element—he is the chief magistrate in the nation. We see in germ the idea that the King has a double capacity—though there was a

---

[1] "The stream of stimulus and inspiration from the Continent, which has at all times irrigated the seeds of English intellectual movements, seems to have dried up till the end of the century, when the trickle begins to widen, to flow, and to enrich the harvest once again", Chrimes, *English Constitutional Ideas in the Fifteenth Century*, 301.

reluctance, to which much later Coke gave expression, to draw practical consequences from the distinction. There is a disposition to attribute to the King a prerogative which puts him above any mere feudal lord, and to say that these prerogatives are inseparable from his person. But there are limitations on these prerogatives—he cannot legislate or tax; and though the discussion of his prerogatives in the courts is introducing some precise rules in respect of certain matters, the process of defining them in this way is only in its initial stages. It is the same with Parliament. The older ideas which regarded it primarily as a court are still held; but they are being overshadowed by other ideas which regard it as a body representing the state—ideas which enabled Coke to say as Speaker in 1592–3 that though it was a court it was not only a court.[1] The exigency of the facts of Parliamentary history in this century was forcing Fortescue and many other lawyers to realize that though Parliament might be a court, it was also "a representative political assembly possessing attributes in excess of those accorded to any ordinary court of law".[2] It is recognized that it is only by Parliament that statutes can be enacted; but it is not as yet clearly recognized that there are no limitations on Parliament's legislative powers. The universally received political theories of the Middle Ages imposed the limit that it would enact nothing contrary to the law of God or nature; and this limitation died hard.[3] Whether or not there were other limitations was uncertain—the answer to it depended to some extent on the strength at any given moment of the Yorkist and Lancastrian factions. At one time it was said that the Duke of York's claim was barred by Acts of Parliament: at another that by the law of God his hereditary right must prevail. Then,

[1] D'Ewes, *Journal*, 515.
[2] Chrimes, *English Constitutional Ideas in the Fifteenth Century*, 140.
[3] Holdsworth, *H.E.L.* ii, 443–444.

too, though the assent of the Commons was necessary to legislation, the King and his Council had some power of amendment, some control over the drafting of statutes, and some control over the Acts which should be enrolled as statutes. On the other hand it is clear that the judges recognized the imperative force of statutes; and that they were evolving canons of interpretation by means of which they were fitting them into the structure, and, where possible, were harmonizing them with the principles of the common law.

From the state of the English constitution and constitutional law as described by Fortescue three general conclusions can I think be drawn. In the first place, the precedents on which the Parliamentary statesmen of the seventeenth century relied were by no means so conclusive in their favour as they and the Whig historians of the nineteenth century imagined. In the second place, the fact that it was possible to develop the constitution as it emerged from the fifteenth century in two different directions in the two following centuries was not the least of the reasons why it was possible for the lawyers to develop continuously the principles of English constitutional law, and to make them fit the needs of a constantly changing society. In the third place, the state of the English constitution and constitutional law sheds considerable light upon the strong and weak points of the medieval common law. Of this last conclusion I must now speak in somewhat greater detail.

(4) *The strong and weak points of the medieval common law.*

The medieval common law was a close-knit, logical, and practical system. The common lawyers were a learned well-taught body of men who made very tough law. This law was, within its technical limits, capable of a certain amount of expansion to meet new needs. In the fourteenth and fifteenth centuries new principles of criminal and civil liability were being developed. A new theory of contract was beginning to emerge. The interests of the lessee for years and the copyholder were gaining protection. The statutes passed by Parliament were being worked into the technical fabric of the law, and in some cases they introduced new ideas into the law—one illustration is the series of the Statutes of Labourers. The weakness of the common law was its technicality and consequent rigidity. It had been developed too exclusively by lawyers who were learned only in the intricacies of a very insular and a very technical system, who consequently thought more of the logical development of technical rules than of making the principles of substantive law conform to the needs of a developing society. The result was that the common law was coming to be incapable of developing the rules needed by such a society. One striking instance of this fact is its failure to protect the interest of the cestui que use. The result was that the cestui que use was obliged to go to the Chancery for protection; and the use, as Maitland has said, made the fortune of the court of Chancery. And so we must ascribe the division of English law into the two separate systems of law and equity to the development of the common law in these centuries by a very close, a very specialized, and a very insular profession.

The thirteenth century had reaped the benefits of a fixed and centralized system of law: the fourteenth and fifteenth centuries paid the penalty. The common law at the close of the medieval period was suffering from a development which was too narrowly and exclusively professional. The unrestrained efforts of a hierarchy of professional lawyers is apt to produce results similar to those attributed by Maine to a hierarchy of priests— "Usage which is reasonable generates usage which is unreasonable."[1] And these defects were aggravated by

[1] *Ancient Law*, 19–20.

the weakness of the government. The overmighty subjects knew well how to turn to their own use the technicalities of the law. They used the forms of law merely
to further their own interests and to aid them in the
prosecution of their feuds. In 1440 Mr Justice Paston
strongly advised a friend not to go to law with one who
had the support of the Duke of Norfolk. "For if thou do,
thou shalt have the worse, be thy cause never so true, for
he is in the pay of my lord of Norfolk, and much is of his
counsel; and also thou canst get no man of law in Norfolk
or Suffolk to be with thee against him; and therefore my
counsel is, that thou make an end whatsoever thou pay,
for he shall else undo thee and bring thee to nought."[1]
Men used the technicalities of the law and physical force
alternatively, as policy dictated, to further their quarrels.
Well might Jack Cade say in 1450 that "the law servyth
of nowght ellys in these days but for to do wrong, for
nothyng is sped almost but false maters by coulour of
law for mede, drede, and favor".[2]

The machinery of the law was still intact; and the
lawyers still professed to maintain the high ideals which
they had inherited from their great predecessors of the
twelfth and thirteenth centuries. Both the lawyers and
the Legislature tried to curb the growing lawlessness;
and the strictness with which the courts interpreted the
laws against maintenance[3] was an attempt to restrain one
of the principal means by which the overmighty subjects
consolidated their power. But the weakness of the state
frustrated all the endeavours of the lawyers and Parliament. The restoration of the strength of the state was,
as Fortescue saw, the chief need. But it was not the
only need. The limitations of the medieval common law
and its rigidity and technicality were making the law

---

[1] *Paston Letters*, i, 42.
[2] *Three Fifteenth Century Chronicles* (C.S.), 96.
[3] Holdsworth, *H.E.L.* i, 334–335.

incapable of devising new rules for the guidance of new social and economic conditions. It was already becoming obvious that, however much the common lawyers might dislike the jurisdiction exercised by the King's Council and the Chancery, its exercise was needed to introduce new life and new ideas into the law. This need was intensified in the new age of Renaissance and Reformation which, in the following century, was substituting modern for medieval ideas and institutions. Would England get a government strong enough to restore the strength of the state? Would that government be able to introduce new ideas and a new spirit into English law, which would enable it to guide the destinies of the state and the activities of individuals in this new age? What would be the effect of these necessary changes upon the tough and technical system of the medieval common law? Upon the answer to these questions the future of the law and constitution of England depended. With the answer which was given to them in the following century and a half I shall deal in the next three lectures.

Lecture IV

RENAISSANCE, REFORMATION, AND RECEPTION OF ROMAN LAW

ICEY in his lectures on *Law and Public Opinion in England*[1] has said that

There exists at any given time a body of beliefs, convictions, sentiments, accepted principles or firmly rooted prejudices, which, taken together, make up the public opinion of a particular era, or what may be called the reigning or predominant current of opinion. . . . It may be added that the whole body of beliefs existing in any given age may generally be traced to certain fundamental assumptions, which at the time, whether they be actually true or false, are believed by the mass of the world to be true with such confidence that they hardly appear to bear the character of assumptions.

It was this character of these "assumptions" which created the public opinion of the Middle Ages, and gave to medieval history its distinguishing characteristics. It was the Renaissance and Reformation of the sixteenth century which substituted other "assumptions", created a new public opinion, and thus started the modern history of Europe. The Reception of Roman law, which was experienced in many states in Europe in varying degrees of intensity, was the consequence of the political, economic, and social changes following upon the Renaissance and Reformation. These changes caused the rise of the modern territorial state, and the need for more mature systems of law to govern the relations of rulers and subjects of those states, and of the states themselves in their dealings with one another. England and English law were affected by these three allied movements; but, owing to the different course taken by English legal and

[1] At pp. 19–20.

constitutional history in the Middle Ages, in a way which differed from that in which other European countries were affected. If therefore we would understand the course of English legal history in the sixteenth and early seventeenth centuries we must know something of the effects of these three allied movements abroad. It is only in the light of this preliminary study that we can understand the salient and peculiar features of the course taken by English legal history during this period. In the first place, therefore, I shall describe very shortly the legal and constitutional effects of these three allied movements abroad, and then explain the very different effects which they had in England.

THE CONTINENTAL DEVELOPMENTS

The Renaissance and the Reformation.

I have summarized the effects of the Renaissance and the Reformation in my *History of English Law*,[1] and on this matter I shall repeat what I have there said.

The Renaissance of classical studies had begun in Italy in the last half of the fourteenth century. In the last years of that century, and in the fifteenth century, the study of the Greek classics was pursued side by side with the study of the Latin classics; and this revival of classical studies soon produced a complete break with medieval modes of thought. The older monuments of learning and art were no longer looked at through the spectacles of the scholastic philosophy and theology. They were studied in and for themselves. Human reason, unfettered by preconceived theories, theological or otherwise, tried to discover the meaning which they had to the men who made them; and this necessarily gave a wholly new meaning to the older studies—to grammar, to history, to literature—and led to the growth of new standards of

[1] *H.E.L.* iv, 11–13.

taste, both in literature and art. It was the real world of classical antiquity which was thus revealed—a wholly new world of thought to that age; and of that world man and man's intellect and aspirations and desires were the centre. These things were no longer to be regarded as pomps and vanities of this wicked world except in so far as they were used to further that logical system, which took the doctrines of the church as its premises, and viewed all human knowledge in the light of deductions from them. This world might be wicked and it might be transitory, but it was meant to be lived in. Man's senses and faculties were given him to use, not to mortify; and he was under no obligation to view all knowledge from one particular standpoint. He was the master of his fate; and it was his duty to act and think and reason freely and fearlessly, not only upon art and literature, but upon history sacred and profane, upon religious doctrine,[1] and eventually upon physical science. These views were disseminated throughout Europe by lectures, by schools, by academies, and by the printing press. Students flocked to Italy to study the new learning, as in former days they had flocked thither to study Roman law. The results may be seen and illustrated by the writings of men of such opposite characters as Machiavelli and Sir Thomas More. In *The Prince* the whole scheme and theory on which medieval thought rested is simply disregarded. He "consistently applied the inductive or experimental method to political science". "An appeal was to be made to history and reason; the publicist was to investigate, not to invent—to record, not to anticipate —the laws which appear to govern man's actions."[2] Similarly in the *Utopia* of Sir Thomas More the actual facts of society are looked at with a critical eye, and its faults are satirized by the comparison with his ideal

[1] Cp. Acton, *Lectures on Modern History*, 77–79.
[2] L. A. Burd, *Camb. Mod. Hist.* i, 212–213.

republic, which rests on bases very different to any which could have been deduced from the old premises of the scholastic philosophy.

As we can see from the *Utopia*, the discovery of the New World intensified the tendency to abandon the ancient ways. Ralph Hythlodaye, who relates his adventures in Utopia, "for the desire that he had to see and knowe the farre Countreyes of the worlde", had "joyned himselfe in company with Amerika Vespuce"; and it was on one of these voyages that he had found this ideal commonwealth. In fact, it was not merely the premises of the old philosophy which were being undermined. The physical world was being enlarged and changing its shape. New countries, new nations, new phenomena of all kinds were emerging. With these things the old learning, the old modes of thought and reasoning were powerless to deal. These things must be investigated; and the results of that investigation necessarily led to the abandonment of old theories, not only as to the physical constitution and position of the universe, but also as to men's relations to it and to one another.

Theological ideas and dogmas dominated the old learning in all its branches. Any fundamental change therefore in any branch of knowledge necessarily involved some reconsideration of men's religious beliefs. Could these beliefs be reconsidered and restated in such a way as to bring them into harmony with the new order? Some, notably Erasmus, thought that this was possible. And if there had been merely the intellectual difficulty arising from the necessity of readjusting an old theology to new points of view, the sixteenth century might have managed to effect such a readjustment as skilfully as the nineteenth century. But, in the sixteenth century, the intellectual difficulty was far greater, nor was it by any means the only difficulty. In the first place, theology was not merely a special branch of knowledge: its conceptions dominated all knowledge. In the second place, church and state were in a sense one society; and therefore any questioning of the dogmas of the church, and of its position in relation to the state, meant far more than the alteration of one particular society within the state. It meant rather the unsettling of the foundations of all society. In the third place, the church had enormous vested interests in the maintenance of the old order. Finally, the abuses rampant in the church had been thrown up into stronger relief by the changed political and intellectual conditions of Europe; and they had inspired a hatred of the church and of churchmen which made it certain that no peaceable readjustment of the old ideas to the new could be effected. Any attempt at change was sufficient to upset a system which had long been growing more and more unstable, and to begin a religious revolution. The acts which were the immediate and proximate causes of the movement—Luther's ninety-five theses and his bonfire of the papal bull and the books of the canon law, the divorce question in England—were merely sparks which produced their far-reaching effects because they touched a mass of explosive matter.

Thus began the religious Reformation of the sixteenth century. It stopped all thoughts of peaceable change in the religious world. It stopped for a time the gradual spread and peaceable development of the new learning, and in the end it changed the course and modified the results of the Renaissance upon the intellectual world.

The constitutional and legal effects of these two allied movements were the consolidation of the power of the state, and the formation of the modern territorial state. That state, having assumed much of the divinity which in the Middle Ages was more especially the attribute of the church, could assert its supremacy over all persons and causes. It was this new territorial state which put an end to the turbulence of the Middle Ages, and so made possible a more orderly and a more civilized life. No doubt in the first instance the Reformation seemed to impede the growth of the modern state. Religious differences supplied a cause for wars in which the old turbulent feudalism played its part. But in the long run the Reformation assisted the growth of the modern state. The horrors of the religious wars strengthened the desire and the need for efficient government which the modern territorial state alone could satisfy. And with the growth of the power of the state national feeling began to prevail over religious animosity. Thus the medieval political theory of a universal church and a universal state was disposed of, and, consequently, the victory of the new learning and new modes of thought was assured. The several independent states of modern Europe were an environment in which new opinions could be formed, new ideas arise, and new discoveries increase, because their independence and diversity taught men that it was possible to tolerate diverse opinions. But it was obvious that to settle the new relations of these states to their subjects and to one another, and to settle the more complex private relations of subject to subject, which were the result of the new social and economic developments rendered possible by the rise of the modern state, new and more elaborate systems of law were needed. It is for this reason that the Renaissance and the Reformation were accompanied in many states by a Reception of Roman law.

The Reception of Roman law.

Roman law had, as the result of the legal Renaissance of the twelfth and thirteenth centuries, influenced the law of many countries in Europe. We have seen that it had had a large influence on the development of the

English common law in the age of Glanvil and Bracton.[1]
The rules of Roman law, and the legal and political ideas
which came in their train, helped forward the development of legal and political thought; and the necessity of
continuously reconciling these ideas with the gradually
changing facts of medieval life produced an intellectual
ferment from which emerged the legal and political
factors of our modern world. This work of reconciling
the rules of the classical Roman law to the conditions of
medieval life was skilfully done by the Italian law schools
and more especially by the school of the Bartolists. They
created, on the basis of the civil and canon law, a set of
legal and political principles adapted to the Italy of the
fourteenth and fifteenth centuries; and those conditions
were sufficiently like the political and commercial conditions prevailing in Europe in the sixteenth century to
make these principles applicable to the new order. Thus
the law which was received was not the classical Roman
law. It was Roman law adapted to the needs of the day.
It was the text of the Roman law as glossed by the
glossators and Bartolists. "What the gloss does not
recognize," it was said, "the court does not recognize."
That is, the passages of the Corpus Juris which were not
glossed were not living law.[2]

The victory of a Roman law as thus modified and
supplemented by the work of the medieval civilians and
canonists is the outward sign, the legal expression, of the
sovereignty of the state. In fact its rules and ideas were
the necessary instruments of publicists, statesmen, and
lawyers who were seeking answers to the political, the
administrative, and the legal problems set by this new
age. Publicists in search of arguments wherewith to
attack, or support, or criticize a government, found a
well-stocked arsenal in the texts of the civil and canon

[1] Above, pp. 14–15, 20–22.
[2] Holdsworth, *H.E.L.* iv, 242–244.

law, and in the books of the medieval glossators and commentators. Statesmen set to govern a world in which the growth of a capitalistic organization, both of foreign trade and of domestic industry, was breaking up the medieval guilds, and the medieval agricultural arrangements based on the manor and the feudal tie between lord and tenant; a world in which the competition between the several states of modern Europe emphasized the need to organize all industry, agricultural or commercial, with a view to national power—found there principles which aided them to assert the supremacy of the state, to organize its machinery, and to regulate the working of that machinery. Lawyers seeking to give legal expression to these political, constitutional, and economic changes, found that they were obliged to talk and reason in terms derived from the only system of law which seemed to be as capable of meeting the needs of the modern state as of the medieval empire. Lawyers and statesmen who were seeking a new basis for international intercourse had recourse to theories of jus gentium, and a law of nature, which medieval civilians and canonists had elaborated from Roman law, from classical philosophy, and from Christian doctrine, to provide a new international law.[1]

Necessarily this Reception of Roman law had large effects not only on the law of the state, but also upon its machinery and structure, and upon the political theories held by its rulers. In the twelfth and thirteenth centuries the lawyers who had learned from Justinian's books had given the King a position higher than that of a mere feudal lord; and, as the theory of the Holy Roman Empire came to be more and more unreal, there was a tendency to put the King, *qua* his own dominions, into the place formerly occupied by the emperor.[2] The Kings

---

[1] Holdsworth, *H.E.L.* v, 25–60.
[2] *Ibid.* iv, 190–191.

both of France and England claimed to be emperors.[1] The Reception of Roman law in the sixteenth century made for the further magnification of the kingly office; and the consequences of this magnification were developed in detail. New machinery was devised to give effect to them; and, under the influence of the changed ideas as to the relationship of church and state which came with the Reformation, the King, as representative of the state, began to hedge himself about with that divinity, which in medieval times had been more especially the attribute of the church. The way was prepared for the theory of sovereignty and its application to the King which was enunciated by Bodin in 1576 in his book on *The Republic*—the most important book on political science, it has been said, which had been written since Aristotle.[2] The medieval courts, the medieval system of local government, the medieval representative assemblies, disappeared; and with them went the medieval idea that, because the King owed duties to his subjects to maintain justice, resistance to a King who neglected these duties was lawful. When these medieval restraints had vanished Titius was left without rights against an omnipotent state,[3] represented by an absolute King, accountable only to God, and subject to no duties enforceable by merely human law.[4] The King was himself the state.

---

[1] Esmein, *Histoire du Droit Français*, 384, n. 2; Gierke, *Political Theories of the Middle Age* (Maitland's tr.), xlv, n. 4; in the preamble to Henry VIII's Statute of Appeals, 24 Henry VIII, c. 12, it is said that "This realm of England is an empire."

[2] For an account of Bodin and his book see Holdsworth, *H.E.L.* iv, 193–195.

[3] Maitland says, "Titius and the State, these the Roman lawyers understood, and out of them and a little fiction, the legal universe could be constructed", Gierke, *Political Theories of the Middle Age* (Maitland's tr.), xxviii.

[4] Esmein, *Histoire du Droit Français*, 391–392; Lavisse et Rambaud, *Histoire Générale*, iv, 139.

In many of the states of Western Europe these results had followed from these three allied movements of Renaissance, Reformation, and the Reception of Roman law. We shall now see that their effects upon the English state and English law were very different.

THE ENGLISH DEVELOPMENTS

England and English law were influenced by these three allied movements; but, owing to the peculiarities of English constitutional and legal history in the Middle Ages, their effects on English law were different from their effects on continental law, with the result that, in the middle of the seventeenth century, both the constitution of the English state and English law were wholly different from the constitution and the law of continental states.

The Renaissance and the Reformation.

During Henry VII's reign the New Learning had been making its way in England. A few Englishmen had studied in Italy, and what they had learned in Italy they had begun to teach in England. Of the progress of this New Learning Erasmus wrote enthusiastically. Henry VIII was its friend; and Erasmus said that there were more men of learning to be found in his court than at any university.[1] Though in England, as elsewhere, the Reformation, and more especially the dissolution of the monasteries and the destruction of the monastic libraries, were a shock to learning and literature,[2] there

---

[1] Holdsworth, *H.E.L.* iv, 29–30, 41.

[2] *Ibid.* 42; but Mr Baskerville, *English Monks and the Dissolution of the Monasteries*, 280–281, points out that though "no care seems to have been taken to preserve books and manuscripts", many books were saved. They were taken or borrowed by individual monks or abbots. Thus "practically the whole of the library of the Yorkshire priory of Monk Bratton was bought by the prior and monks, and twenty years after nearly a hundred of its books are found in the possession of one or other of them".

is gain to set against loss. Henry VIII was no enemy to learning. He founded regius professorships at the universities, and refounded Wolsey's great college at Oxford. Cambridge in the reign of Edward VI was the home of the best kind of humanism; and from Cambridge came many of Elizabeth's most eminent statesmen. Elizabeth —the daughter of Anne Boleyn—was bound by her birth to stand by the Reformation. By choosing as her ministers such men as Burghley, Bacon, Cooke, and Smith, who had been educated under the influence of the Renaissance and in the principles of the reformed religion, she showed that she meant to build upon the foundations laid by her father and her brother. The brilliant success of her policy domestic and foreign fostered a national pride and self-confidence, which showed itself in that wonderful outburst of literary activity which makes the Elizabethan age the true period of the English Renaissance and the golden age of English literature. Her reign is the real dividing line between medieval and modern in law, in institutions, in thought, and in literature. In the works of Francis Bacon[1] we see the most decisive break with medieval ideas, and the most complete acceptance of modern modes of thought.

England had fully accepted the modern ideas and modern modes of thought which are summed up in the word "Renaissance". And she had done so the more completely because Henry VIII had identified her with the Reformation. But it was a Reformation very different from that which took place in any other country. In the Reformation Parliament (1529–36) Henry gradually worked out the constitution of a national church with himself as supreme head, and by deft Parliamentary management he partly persuaded, partly forced the Houses to give it legislative sanction. This national church was not to be a heretic church. It was to be the

[1] Below, p. 103.

historic Catholic church of England restored and reformed. There was to be only so much change as was
needed to adapt the medieval universal church to the
wants of the new territorial state. The power of the Pope
was exchanged for the supremacy of the King—the new
papacy the Spanish ambassador aptly called it;[1] and the
papal canon law, so far as it was inconsistent with the new
order, ceased to be applicable. Subject to these necessary
modifications there was to be little change in doctrine,
discipline, or organization.

It was to this religious settlement that Elizabeth
returned. It satisfied many moderate men; for it had in
it elements which appealed alike to men of Catholic and
men of Protestant tendencies, and thus enabled it to
include within itself many divergent sects. At the same
time the violence of the changes actually made was
skilfully disguised by the fiction of the restoration of
an old independence, which was first propounded by
Henry VIII in the preamble to his Statute of Appeals,[2]
and has since been accepted as good law by the lawyers
and as sound doctrine by the theologians.[3]

We shall now see that these peculiarities in the Reformation settlement effected by Henry VIII and
Elizabeth, and more especially the claim that this settlement made no break with the past, are paralleled by the
manner in which the modern English state and English
law were developed continuously from their medieval
origins.

The Reception of Roman law.

In European countries the extent to which Roman
law was received depended upon the state of the law of
each country. The more backward the legal system and
the less fitted to guide the state in the new conditions

---

[1] *Letters and Papers*, v, no. 114.   [2] 24 Henry VIII, c. 12.
[3] Holdsworth, *H.E.L.* i, 590–591, 596.

of the sixteenth century, the more wholesale was the Reception which it experienced, and the greater the break with its legal past. Countries like Germany and Scotland, where the law had been customary and bookless, were more deeply affected by the Reception than the Latin countries, the basis of the laws of which had, throughout the medieval period, been Roman.[1] From this point of view the position of England and English law was peculiar. Though the institutions, the ideas, and the law of England in the Middle Ages contained many medieval ideas, they were not purely medieval. Centralized institutions which made for the supremacy of the state, and a common law, had been created by the strong Kings of the twelfth and thirteenth centuries. In those centuries there had been a reception of the more civilized legal and political ideas, which had come with the twelfth-century revival of the study of Roman civil law, and the rise of the canon law; and those ideas had created an English state, and a law which, after the end of the thirteenth century, was developed on its own lines by a learned profession. It is true that the recrudescence of semi-feudal disorder, which marked the greater part of the fifteenth century, and culminated in the Wars of the Roses, prevented the proper working of the central government and reduced the common law to impotence. But, for all that, the institutions of government and the law were intact; and when order had been restored, and they were able to work again, they were sufficient for many of the needs of the modern state.

The result was that in the sixteenth century England differed from many continental countries in that there was no scrapping of medieval institutions, medieval ideas, and medieval laws. In the sphere of local government hundred and county courts, courts leet and other franchise jurisdictions in town and county, justices of the

[1] Holdsworth, *H.E.L.* iv, 246–250.

peace, the organization of the parish—all contributed to
the formation of a system which was remarkable for its
unsystematic character by reason of the historic diversity
of its various parts. Then, again, medieval juries of one
sort or another—juries of presentment and trial juries—
continued to play an important part both in administration and in judicature. The medieval Parliaments had
asserted their right to control taxation and legislation,
and, within limits, to offer advice to the Crown, and even
occasionally to criticize its policy. We shall see that
Parliaments, controlled by the Crown, continued to
legislate and tax, that they continued to have an important position in the state, and consequently that they
were able to consolidate their powers and their privileges.[1] The medieval idea of the rule of law continued
to permeate the whole system of government, local and
central. All the officials of the government were controlled by the law. Subject to the law they could act
freely in their several spheres, a freedom of action which
is unknown to officials who are merely the delegates of
a central board. Though, as we shall see,[2] this freedom
of action was being curtailed by the Council and Star
Chamber, much of it was still left; and in the seventeenth
century it contributed largely to the failure of the Stuart
Kings to establish a system of prerogative government.
Some of the most important parts of English law, the
land law, the law as to treason and felony, the law as to
contract and tort, were medieval in their origin, and
based upon medieval books and precedents.

The Tudors did not find it necessary either to create
a new machinery of government, or to supersede the
common law. All they needed to do was, first, to restore
by a stern and intelligent control the proper workings of
the existing institutions of government and of the common law; and, secondly, to supplement those institutions

[1] Below, p. 84.   [2] Below, pp. 83, 85, 87.

and the common law where they were inadequate to meet the needs of the new age. Let us look at the work done by the Tudors from these two points of view: the way in which they strengthened the working of existing institutions; and the way in which they created new and supplementary institutions.

(1) The work of restoring the proper working of medieval institutions and medieval law was performed with very great skill by the Tudor sovereigns. Acting through their Privy Council, which all through this period was the real government of the country, they carefully supervised all the departments of government, and they saw to it that both the administrative and judicial officers of the government carried out the duties imposed upon them by the common and statute law. The manner in which the Privy Council, and also the provincial Councils of Wales and the North, supervised the work of the justices of the peace, both in town and country, and the manner in which the Star Chamber and the provincial Councils dealt with their sins of omission and commission, made the justices efficient instruments of the local government of a modern state. In fact, this supervision and control made these justices such efficient instruments that Coke could say of their rule: "It is such a form of subordinate government for the tranquillity and quiet of the realm, as no part of the Christian world hath the like."[1] The manner in which the Council and the Star Chamber dealt with corrupt jurors, and with persons who corrupted or terrorized them, restored the proper working of the jury system. That system had broken down in the fifteenth century. In the case of the jury, as in the case of many other parts of the machinery of justice of the common law, the Council and the Star Chamber restored its proper working; and they made the jury the most efficient instrument for the trial of

[1] *Fourth Institute*, 170.

disputed questions of fact that any legal system has ever possessed. It is true that the Star Chamber sometimes punished jurors who found verdicts which were displeasing to the government. The punishment of the jury which acquitted Throckmorton in 1554 is a notorious case; and the cases of this kind, having attracted the notice of constitutional historians, have been given by them an undue prominence. But I cannot doubt that the service done by the Star Chamber in restoring the proper working of the jury system outweighs any injustice it may have done by its interferences in political cases. Similarly, the use which the Tudor sovereigns made of Parliament consolidated both its powers and its privileges, and made it an integral part of the government of the state. Its members were drawn from the same class as that from which the justices of the peace were drawn; and this fact both helped to educate the justices in the larger field of national government, and also helped to give Parliament a first-hand knowledge of the problems of local government, and of the sort of measures which were best fitted to solve them. As Bacon said, "Those that have voices in Parliament to make laws they for the most part are those which in the country are appointed to administer the same laws; and from these two institutions if a man would make a commonwealth by a level, he could not find better than these."[1] As a result of these developments, Sir Thomas Smith, Elizabeth's secretary of state, could say that, "The most high and absolute power of the realm of England consisteth in the Parliament",[2] meaning, of course, the King in Parliament. In these ways then the Tudor sovereigns restored the proper working of many medieval institutions and made them useful instruments of the modern state.

(2) The Tudors supplemented the existing institu-

---

[1] Spedding, *Letters and Life of Bacon*, vi, 304.
[2] *De Republica*, bk. 2, c. 1.

tions of the common law where they were deficient. We can trace their action in these respects in several different directions.

In the first place, we get a great development of new courts and councils, administering bodies of law outside the sphere of the common law. The Star Chamber and the provincial Councils developed the criminal law in many directions. For instance, we get important developments of the law of libel, the law of conspiracy, and the law as to attempts to commit crimes. Moreover, their control over persons and bodies entrusted with governmental functions was beginning to introduce something very like a system of administrative law. Thus they protected, and supported the authority of, the officials of local government. "Let all men hereby take heede", it was said in 1603 in the Star Chamber, "how they complayne in wordes againste any magistrate, for they are gods; & he must haue verye good matter that will goe aboute to conuynce them, for feare he ouerthrowe not himselfe."[1] Conversely, they rebuked these persons and bodies, and disciplined them, if they abused their authority. The records of the Privy Council are full of such cases. For instance, the City of London found that it could not go on electing non-residents to municipal office with the view to enforcing a fine for not serving.[2] They settled disputes between officials and between communities. Thus in 1592 the Council had before it the case of two justices of Northampton who had attacked one another at the sessions;[3] and in 1597 it was listening to charges of malversation against the town of Newcastle.[4] The development of the jurisdiction of the court of Chancery, of the court of Requests, and of the court of Admiralty, was adding new and supplementary bodies

[1] Hawarde, *Les Reportes del Cases in Camera Stellata*, 177.
[2] Dasent, *Acts of the Privy Council*, xvii, 4.
[3] *Ibid.* xxiii, 286, 333, 367.   [4] *Ibid.* xxviii, 317–319.

of law to the common law, which dealt with matters which were outside its sphere. It is in some parts of the law made by these new courts, and in their procedure, that we can see traces of the influence of Roman law. Some of the ideas introduced into criminal law and procedure through the Star Chamber, many of the new rules of commercial and maritime law introduced through the court of Admiralty, some of the rules of procedure introduced through the court of Chancery and the court of Requests, can be ascribed to a reception of some of the political and legal ideas of Roman law.

In the second place, it was due to the initiative of the King and the Privy Council that comprehensive statutes of far-reaching and permanent importance were passed, which made English law fit for the needs of this new age. I will cite one or two instances: The statutes of Uses and Wills fixed the main lines of the development of the modern land law. The Elizabethan statutes on the law of master and servant and on the poor law fixed the main lines of the development of both of these branches of law; and they have retained their importance right down to modern times. The Tudor legislation as to enclosures did much to settle the position of the agricultural industry, and helped to solve the problem of unemployment. The legislation directed to fostering native industry had the effect of establishing the beginning of the wool and other industries.

Thus the Tudors had created the modern English state, but they had created it on medieval lines. The modern English state was a development of the medieval state with many new additions and developments. It contained within itself many medieval institutions and medieval ideas. Justices of the peace, juries, and Parliament were medieval institutions; and the medieval notion that the law was supreme, and that officials of the government could act freely, subject to the law, was a medieval idea. At the same time the new ideas, which emphasized the power of the Crown as representing the state, which tended to put the Crown and its servants above and outside the ordinary law, were making themselves felt. In fact, the modern English state which was being created by the Tudors, like the modern English law, contained within itself many various ideas medieval and modern; and these ideas were not always logically consistent. Neither the English state nor the English law could be justified on any one theory. But under Elizabeth the machinery of government worked; and it worked well; for it gave the nation not only prosperity, but the glory of great national achievements in many fields. But it is clear that, if and when the nation becomes less contented with its government or its law, the divergent tendencies in politics and law, which can be discerned in the Elizabethan age, will give rise to a schism which it will be difficult to heal.

At the end of Elizabeth's reign Parliament and the common law courts on the one hand, and the Council and its off-shoots on the other, had begun to develop rival theories of the state. The theory of Parliament and the common law, which was based upon the supremacy of Parliament and the common law, was in many points directly contradictory to the theory of the Council. The latter theory, since it was based upon the supremacy of the prerogative, had many affinities with the continental doctrine, which vested the powers of the state in an absolute King. This divergence of theory can be traced in local as well as central government. The Council tended to regard the justices of the peace as its agents or servants, subject to its jurisdiction and protected by its authority. The common law courts, on the other hand, regarded them as deriving their authority from the common law and from the statute law, and within these limits entitled to act freely and independently. Similarly,

the relation of the new bodies of law—such as the law
of the Chancery, the law of the Star Chamber, and the
law of the Admiralty—administered in the new courts
and councils of this period, to the common law was
very nebulous. In particular, who was to decide the
conflicting claims of these rivals? Was it the King or
was it the common law?

The Elizabethan age had left all of these political and
legal questions very hazy. They were precipitated by the
clear-cut political theory of James I. Hence it may be
said that, successful as was the Tudor regime in many
ways, it left a legacy of dispute to any dynasty which was
less able, and less capable of understanding the complex
constitution which the Tudors had created. In the
political and constitutional sphere those who supported
the Crown and the new machinery of prerogative government which the Crown had created, and those who supported the Parliament and the common law, fought out
their differences first in Parliament and the courts, and
then on the field of battle; and the fortune of war gave
the victory to Parliament and the common law. In the
purely legal sphere we see a counterpart of the constitutional struggle in the contest for supremacy between the
common law courts and common law, and the rival courts
and bodies of law which had been created or were being
developed in the sixteenth and early seventeenth centuries. Maitland, in his famous Rede lecture on *English
Law and the Renaissance*, suggested that, in the sixteenth
century, these rival courts and bodies of law were
threatening the existence of the common law. I do not
think that this is true. We have seen that the Tudors
maintained and strengthened the medieval institutions
of the English state, and the medieval common law on
which they depended.[1] The common law courts were
busy, and the common lawyers were active in many

[1] Above, pp. 83–84, 86.

spheres throughout the sixteenth century. But I think that there is no doubt that in the sixteenth and early seventeenth centuries the supremacy of the common law was in danger. If the King had won the constitutional struggle, all these rival courts would have flourished and cut into the jurisdiction of the common law courts; and the final arbiter as to conflicts of jurisdiction would have been the King. In so far as these courts had absorbed Roman rules and Roman ideas there might have been a larger reception of these ideas into the English legal system. It is significant that Sir Henry Martin, the judge of the court of Admiralty, said that the Long Parliament, the assembly of which marked the end of prerogative government, was likely to prove "the funeral of his profession".[1] It was not until the victory of the Parliament was assured that the supremacy of the common law was secure.

The court of Chancery and its nascent system of equity was the only one of these rival courts and bodies of law which made good its claims as against the common law courts and the common law; and the result of the victory of the court of Chancery was to divide English law into the two separate systems of law and equity. Over the other rival courts the victory of the common law was complete. That it won this complete victory was due largely to the achievements of Edward Coke. But without the work of the Tudor sovereigns and their Council even Edward Coke could not have won this victory. They had restored the power of the state, they had enabled the machinery of the common law to function regularly, and they had helped to modernize its rules. Maitland says[2]:

Somehow or other England after a fashion all her own had stumbled into a scheme for the reconciliation of permanence

[1] *S.P. Dom.* (1640–41), 197, cccclxxiv, 67.
[2] *Collected Papers*, ii, 495–496.

with progress. The old medieval criminal law could be preserved because a court of Star Chamber would supply its deficiencies; the old private law could be preserved because the court of Chancery was composing an appendix to it; trial by jury could be preserved, developed, transfigured because other modes of trial were limiting it to an appropriate sphere. And so our old law maintained its continuity.... If we look abroad we shall find good reason for thinking that but for these institutions our old fashioned national law, unable out of its own resources to meet the requirements of a new age, would have utterly broken down, and the "ungodly jumble" would have made way for Roman jurisprudence and for despotism. Were we to say that equity saved the common law, and that the court of Star Chamber saved the constitution, even in this paradox there would be some truth.

In my next lecture I shall give some account of the founders of our modern system of equity, and in the following lecture I shall deal with the career of Sir Edward Coke, his conversion of the medieval into the modern common law, and his settlement of its position in the state.

Lecture V

ST GERMAIN, MORE, ELLESMERE, AND BACON

THESE four men are the founders of the modern English system of equity. They settled the place taken by equity in English law, the procedure by which it operated, and its relation to the common law and to the other bodies of law which make up the whole body of English law.

Continuity is the characteristic feature of the history of the common law. An absence of continuity is the characteristic feature of the early history of equity. No doubt the root idea of equity, the idea that law should be administered fairly and that hard cases should so far as possible be avoided, is common to many systems of law at all stages of their development;[1] and this root idea came very naturally to the medieval mind, which regarded the establishment of justice, through or even in spite of the law, as the ideal to be aimed at by all rulers and princes. In England the medieval history of the application of this ideal to the law passed through two distinct stages. There is the stage in which it was applied in and through the common law courts, and there is the stage in which it was applied in and through the Council and the Chancellor.

The first stage ended in the course of the first half of the fourteenth century. In the latter half of the fourteenth and in the fifteenth centuries the common law tended to become a fixed and a rigid system. It tended to be less closely connected with the King, and therefore less connected with, and sometimes even opposed to, the exercise

[1] Cp. Pollock, "The Transformation of Equity", *Essays in Legal History* (1913), 287–289.

of that royal discretion which was at the base of the equitable modification of the law. Equity therefore came to be exercised by the Chancellor and Council who were in close touch with the King, because through them the King exercised his executive and his extraordinary judicial power.

This second stage in the history of equity differs in three important respects from the preceding stage. In the first place, its growth was caused, and its development was largely conditioned, by the rigidity which had become a marked characteristic of the common law, when it ceased to develop those equitable principles and ideas which it possessed at an earlier period. The defective state of the common law, both substantive and adjective, and the disturbed state of the country, which not only rendered its cumbersome procedure useless but even enabled litigants to abuse it to promote injustice, gave rise to a need for the growth of a set of equitable principles outside of and even opposed to the common law. In the second place, being thus developed outside the sphere of the common law and mainly by ecclesiastical Chancellors, its interference with the common law was more direct and avowed than it would have been if it had been developed in and through the common law courts. In the third place, the theory upon which the equity of these ecclesiastical Chancellors was based was somewhat different from the theory upon which the equity described by Bracton, and administered by the common lawyers of the thirteenth and early fourteenth centuries, rested. But this third difference needs a few words of explanation.

The common lawyers of the thirteenth and early fourteenth centuries used the term "equity" in a wide sense, and included under it such ideas as abstract justice and analogy. The ecclesiastical Chancellors, on the other hand, based their equity on the more restricted idea that the court ought to compel each individual litigant to fulfil all the duties which reason and conscience would dictate to a person in his situation.[1] Reason and conscience must decide how and when the injustice caused by the generality of the rules of law was to be cured. They were the executive agents in the work of applying to each individual case those dictates of the law of God and nature upon which the ecclesiastical Chancellors considered equity to rest. Therefore, their equitable jurisdiction was based on an application of the current ideas of the canonists of the fifteenth century regarding the moral government of the universe to the administration of the law of the state. The law of God or of nature or of reason must be obeyed; and these laws required, and, through the agency of conscience, enabled, abstract justice to be done in each individual case, even at the cost of dispensing (if necessary) with the law of the state. How far it could interfere with the law of the state was to be determined by drawing distinctions, in the light of this theory, between the various provisions of the laws which governed the state. Naturally equity administered on these lines was "loose and liberal, large and vague". But the popularity of the equity administered by the Chancellor on these lines was so great that, in the latter part of the fifteenth and in the sixteenth centuries, we begin to see the growth of a separate court of Chancery, with its own staff of officials and its own peculiar procedure. Naturally this development caused the growth of friction between this new court and the common law courts; and the literature of the period shows that this friction had become acute in the first quarter of the sixteenth century.[2]

This second stage in the history of equity ends with

[1] Sir Paul Vinogradoff, "Reason and Conscience in Sixteenth Century Jurisprudence", *L.Q.R.* xxiv, 379.
[2] Below, pp. 97–98.

the beginning of the Reformation in Henry VIII's reign. One of the indirect results of that movement was the beginning of a third stage, in which the ecclesiastical Chancellors of the preceding period gradually gave place to English lawyers.[1] Fortunately, however, the principles upon which the ecclesiastical Chancellors had acted had been summarized and rendered intelligible to English lawyers by St Germain's *Dialogues between the Doctor and the Student*[2]; and thus a greater degree of continuity between the second and third stages was secured than would otherwise have been possible. At the same time, the fact that English lawyers, educated at the Inns of Court, presided over the Chancery, tended to keep the equity administered by the court of Chancery in close touch with the development of the common law, and to improve the relations between common law and equity. At any rate an open conflict was avoided. But the root of the earlier differences was still present, and, at the beginning of the seventeenth century, the old conflict broke out with renewed vigour in the dispute between Coke and Lord Ellesmere. James I settled it in favour of the court of Chancery; with the result that from henceforth the court of Chancery was a court of equal, and in some respects of superior, authority to the courts of common law.[3]

These developments introduce us to a fourth stage in the history of equity. Equity tended to become less a principle or a set of principles which assisted, or supplemented, or even set aside the law in order that justice might be done in individual cases, and more a settled system of rules which supplemented the law in certain cases and in certain defined ways. We can see the beginnings of this change in the first half of the seventeenth century.

[1] Below, p. 98.   [2] For this book see below, pp. 95–97.
[3] Below, pp. 100–101.

Bacon, Ellesmere's successor, settled the procedure of the court on principles which lasted till the reforms of the nineteenth century; and that settlement of the court's procedure was a condition precedent to the settlement of the principles of equity. But till the latter part of the seventeenth century the development of settled principles was hindered by the victory of the Parliament and the common law, because Parliament suspected the equity administered by a Chancellor in close touch with the King, and the common lawyers still resented their defeat at the hands of Ellesmere and James I.

The equity administered by the ecclesiastical Chancellors in the Middle Ages was based to a large extent on the canon law: the equity administered by the lay lawyer Chancellors after the Reformation owed less to the canon law, but it still depended ultimately upon the view held by the canon lawyers as to the reason for the existence of a system of equity, and its place in a legal system. That this continuity was maintained between these two very different stages in the history of equity is due to the work of the first of the founders of the English system of equity—St Germain.

St Germain[1] was a barrister of the Inner Temple who was born about 1460, and lived till 1540. He was well read both in the English and the canon law, and interested in the religious controversies of the day. His knowledge of and interest in English and canon law led him to study the development of equity, because it had been developed under the influence of the ecclesiastical Chancellors and the canon law, and was directed to correcting and supplementing the rules of English law. He embodied his ideas in two dialogues between a Doctor of Divinity, who represents the canon law and the equitable standpoint, and a Student of the common

[1] Holdsworth, *H.E.L.* v, 266–269.

law who represents the standpoint of the common law. The book is generally known by the title of *The Doctor and Student*. The first dialogue was published in Latin in 1523, but no copy of it is known to exist. There was a second edition in 1528. The second dialogue was published in English in 1530, and the first dialogue was revised and published in English in 1531. These English editions were published with additions in 1532, and there have been many later editions of both dialogues.

That it was a very important book can be seen from the fact that it is cited by every writer on equity down to Blackstone's day. The reasons why it is so important are as follows: First, the English version of the first dialogue put into a popular and intelligible form the canonist learning as to the reason for the existence of a system of equity. According to that learning the reason for the existence of a system of equity was the generality of the law—"since the deeds and acts of men, from which laws have been ordained, happen in divers manners infinitely, it is not possible to make any general rules of law, but it shall fail in some case." But how was this injustice to be rectified? The canonists found the answer in conscience. Conscience must decide how and when the injustice caused by the generality of the rules of law was to be cured. It is the executive agent in the work of applying equity to the individual hard cases which were brought before the Chancellor.[1] St Germain's exposition of this theory made it the basis and starting-point of the English system of equity. Secondly, the time when the book appeared was very opportune. It came at the close of the period during which the court of Chancery had been presided over by the ecclesiastical Chancellors, and at the beginning of the period when its development was to be guided by the common lawyers. Thus it helped to promote a larger amount of continuity in the develop-

[1] See *L.Q.R.* xxiv, 378–379.

ment of equity than would otherwise have been possible. Thirdly, the popular form in which these canonist principles were expressed, and the manner in which they were applied in detail to many different rules of English law, facilitated the development of these principles on native lines. St Germain did for the principles of the canon law what Bracton did for the principles of the Roman civil law.[1] Both adapted foreign principles to an English environment. Both by this adaptation forwarded a native development of the law. In neither case was there any reception in detail of foreign law.

St Germain's book showed that the relations of law and equity must always be close. If equity was to redress the injustice caused by the generality of the rules of law, the Chancellor must be certain what the rules of law were. In fact the Year Books, from Henry VI's reign onwards, show that in doubtful cases the Chancellors were willing to hear the arguments of the serjeants and the judges as to the expediency of interfering with the law in particular cases.[2] At the end of the fifteenth century, though there may have been some professional dislike to the Chancellor's interference with the rules of the common law, the relations of law and equity were, on the whole, harmonious. But Cardinal Wolsey's somewhat high-handed proceedings disturbed this working arrangement. In the articles drawn up by the Council against him there are complaints of his encroachments upon the jurisdiction of the common law courts, and of his contemptuous treatment of some of the common law judges.[3] This growing hostility between equity and the common law is illustrated by the literary controversy which was aroused by the publication of *The Doctor and Student*. That book had stated and justified the need for equitable

---

[1] Above, pp. 20–23.
[2] Holdsworth, *H.E.L.* v, 220–222.
[3] *Ibid.* v, 219; for these articles see Coke, *Fourth Institute*, 89–95.

interferences with the law. It was replied to by a serjeant-at-law who set out to prove that no such interferences were necessary. To this reply there was a rejoinder, entitled *The Little Treatise concerning Writs of Subpoena*, in which these interferences are explained and justified.[1]

The common lawyers were a powerful body, and they were also an influential element in the House of Commons. Henry VIII knew very well that he could not pursue his matrimonial and ecclesiastical policy unless he could gain the support of the House of Commons. I think that it was to conciliate the common lawyers, and to secure their support, that he appointed as Wolsey's successor the second of the founders of the English system of equity—Sir Thomas More,[2] who was an eminent common lawyer, and the son of a common law judge. This appointment of Sir Thomas More as Chancellor marks an important turning-point in the history of equity. It marks the transition from the administration of equity by ecclesiastics and canonists to its administration by laymen and common lawyers. This change in the administration of equity provided a link between law and equity which made for the resumption of harmonious relations between them, and ensured that those relations would be relations of partnership. Except for the famous quarrel between Coke and Ellesmere, with which I shall deal later, their relations have been, as Maitland has pointed out,[3] harmonious.

Sir Thomas More's beautiful character would have made him an ideal Chancellor at any time. It was exactly fitted to the difficult position which he was called upon to fill. He was scrupulously pure and strictly impartial. He quickly cleared off the arrears of cases in his court.

---

[1] These tracts are printed by Hargrave, *Law Tracts*, 323–331, 332–355; see Holdsworth, *H.E.L.* v, 269–271.

[2] Holdsworth, *H.E.L.* v, 223–224.

[3] *Equity* (2nd ed.), 17.

He was easy of access, and made it a rule never to grant a subpoena till he was satisfied that the plaintiff had some real ground of complaint. When he heard that the common law judges were still complaining that injunctions were too frequently issued to stop litigants from proceeding in the common law courts, he invited them to dinner, and explained the principles on which he acted. He explained to them that if they would not mitigate the rigour of the law he must issue injunctions "to relieve the people's injury".[1] The result of his tenure of office was to restore harmonious relations between the court of Chancery and the common law courts for the next half century. It is for these reasons that he must be regarded as the second of the founders of the English system of equity.

The revival of the quarrel between the common law courts and the court of Chancery at the end of the sixteenth and the beginning of the seventeenth centuries was due partly to the claim made by Coke that the common law and the common law alone must decide the ambit of the jurisdiction of all rival courts; partly to the constitutional differences between common lawyers who asserted the supremacy of the common law, and other lawyers who asserted the supremacy of the prerogative; partly to the undoubted fact that equity could not function properly unless it could stop litigants who wished to make an inequitable use of their legal rights; and partly to the temper of the two principal disputants —Coke and Ellesmere. Ellesmere, by his victory over Coke, vindicated the right of equity to exist as an independent system, and settled the relations between it and the law. It is for this reason that Ellesmere must be regarded as the third of the founders of the English system of equity.

[1] Roper, *Life of More*, 31.

The chancellorship of Sir Thomas Egerton, Lord Ellesmere,[1] lasted for twenty-one years (1596–1617). Ellesmere was a great deal more than a mere lawyer. Elizabeth consulted him on matters of home and foreign policy; and in James I's reign his strong royalist proclivities ensured his continued influence at court. In his court of Chancery he would listen to no arguments against the prerogative. He would have liked to prevent Parliament from discussing the King's power to levy impositions, and he would have given a far greater authority to proclamations than the common lawyers allowed. Both on political and on professional grounds he was bound to oppose Coke's attempt to limit the competence of his court to issue injunctions to restrain litigants from suing at common law, or, if they had got judgment, from executing the judgment. He did much to organize the staff and the procedure both of the court of Chancery and the court of Star Chamber; and in his court he was a strict disciplinarian. That he was a very great lawyer was the opinion of his contemporaries. "All Christendom", says Fuller,[2] "afforded not a person which carried more gravity in his countenance and behaviour than Sir Thomas Egerton, in so much that many have gone to the Chancery on purpose only to see his venerable garb.... Yet was his outward case nothing in comparison of his inward abilities, quick wit, solid judgment, ready utterance." It is probable that the respect felt for him was no small factor in reconciling the professional opinion of the common lawyers to the King's decision in favour of the court of Chancery.

The controversy between Coke and Ellesmere as to the right of the court of Chancery to issue injunctions against proceedings in the common law courts, or against

---

[1] Holdsworth, *H.E.L.* v, 231–236, and the references there cited; see also *ibid.* i, 461–465.

[2] *Worthies of England* (ed. 1662), 176.

the execution of common law judgments, came to a head in James I's reign. James referred the matter to Bacon, then attorney-general, and other counsel. They advised that there was a strong current of authority since Henry VII's reign in favour of the issue of these injunctions, and that there were even cases in which the judges themselves had advised the parties to seek relief in Chancery. In accordance with this opinion James issued an order in favour of the Chancery. It is true that the common lawyers tried to reverse this decision by legislation, and it is true that the existence of equity was threatened when the outbreak of the Great Rebellion destroyed the constitution. But the decision of James was so obviously right; the need for a court of equity was so clear; the fact that the courts of common law and equity had, down to the outbreak of the Great Rebellion, worked well together to the advantage both of the litigant and the law was so evident—that even under the commonwealth it was impossible to dispense wholly with equity. At the Restoration it silently resumed the place which had been given to it by James I's decree. The objections which some few common lawyers continued to raise right up to the end of the seventeenth century have merely an academic interest.

It was fortunate even for the common law that this was so. If the common law had succeeded in reducing all its rivals to insignificance, it would have been in considerable danger of becoming as hide-bound as it was threatening to become in the fifteenth century. The development which the healthy rivalries of the sixteenth century had produced might have been stayed. It was still more fortunate for English law as a whole. Even if the common law had continued to develop, there were many proprietary relations, many social relations, many business relations, which the machinery of the common law could not have regulated adequately. We have only to think of such topics as the law of trusts, of mortgage, of guardianship, of partnership, of administration of assets, to see that this is obviously true. The growth of all these branches of law would have been hardly possible if they could only have been dealt with by the machinery of the common law; and their development by equity would have been stunted if the machinery of the court could only have been used under the supervision of the common lawyers.

Equity, then, was fortunate in securing its independent existence when it did. It was no less fortunate in securing, immediately afterwards, the guidance and direction of the friend and protégé of Lord Ellesmere, and the most philosophic lawyer in England—Francis Bacon. He consolidated the victory which Ellesmere had won, and gave to equity a great impulse along that path of definition, and co-ordination with the rules of the common law, which, since the advent of the lawyer Chancellors and until the late controversy, had been silently proceeding throughout the greater part of the sixteenth century. Bacon is the fourth and the greatest of the founders of the English system of equity.

Francis Bacon[1] was born January 22, 1561. He was the youngest son of Nicholas Bacon, who had been Lord Keeper during the first twenty-one years of Elizabeth's reign (1558–79). He was educated at Trinity College, Cambridge, and at Gray's Inn. He was the reader of the Inn in 1587 and 1599; and his reading on the statute of Uses is the best of the readings which have as yet been published. In 1584 he became a member of Parliament. By his conduct in Parliament he offended Elizabeth, and so failed to get any substantial promotion in her reign. But the fact that he was making his way in his profession is shown by his appointment as Queen's counsel extra-

[1] Holdsworth, *H.E.L.* v, 238–254.

ordinary—an appointment which was the origin of the order of King's Counsel.[1] As such he was employed in state prosecutions; and the part which he played in the prosecution of his friend and benefactor, the Earl of Essex, was then and has ever since been regarded as discreditable. In 1607 he became solicitor-general; and on the death of Salisbury he suggested that he should succeed him as Treasurer. But he failed to get this office. In 1613 he became attorney-general, and in 1617 Lord Keeper. In the following year he became Lord Chancellor and a peer. In 1622 he was impeached by the House of Commons for bribery, and confessed his guilt. The rest of his life was devoted to the philosophical work upon which he had been engaged throughout his life. In 1605 he had published *The Advancement of Learning*, and in 1620 the *Novum Organum*. In 1623 he published the *De Augmentis*. He died in 1626.

Bacon had great ideals. As a philosopher considering the welfare of mankind, as a statesman considering the solution of the political problems of the day, as a lawyer considering problems of law reform, he never lost sight of these ideals. His hopeful temperament never allowed him to despair of inducing his contemporaries to try to realize some of them. But these ideals were too high for the men who then ruled the state. The good advice which he gave them was generally rejected and never completely followed. But with all his idealism Bacon was no mere academic speculator. He had a very practical side to his intellect. His legal studies had enabled him to earn his living at the bar; and he hoped that his political speculations would give him the high place in the state which he was conscious that he could fill. But in Elizabeth's and James I's courts, such a place could only be won by flattery and intrigue. Bacon stooped to employ these arts, not seeing the fatal effect which their employment was having

[1] Holdsworth, *H.E.L.* vi, 472–476.

upon his character. This effect was the more fatal because
Bacon had a very unemotional nature, with the result
that, having no very keen sense of personal honour, he
was too ready to take his tone from the society in which
he was placed. But the moral tone of Elizabeth's court
was low, and that of James I's court was lower. Being
unprotected by a keen sense of honour, and absorbed in
the pursuit of his ideals, he was led to do acts which men
of less lofty ideals, but with a keener sense of personal
honour, would have instinctively avoided. That was the
secret of the actions which weigh heavily on his memory
and led to his ruin. In his eyes the service of the state
outweighed his great obligations to Essex, and led him
to press the charge of treason against his friend and
benefactor. He was unconscious of the corruption of
James I's court, and of the court of Chancery; and it
never seemed to have occurred to him that the presents
which he and other officers of his court took, and the
interferences of Buckingham with some of the cases
before the court, had an ugly look. And so he drifted
into questionable practices till the crash came. During
the course of the investigations which were being made
by the House of Commons into the actions of some of the
officials of the court of Chancery, accusations of corruption were made against the Lord Chancellor. He was
impeached, confessed his guilt, and was sentenced to fine
and imprisonment—which sentence the King remitted.
He acknowledged the justice of his sentence. But even
while making this acknowledgment he showed the same
moral insensibility that had caused his ruin. He maintained that he had always been a just judge, he could
never see that his condemnation was a bar to any further
public employment, and he could confidently leave his
name to the "next ages".

But it is Bacon's best side which survives in his
writings and arguments and achievement as Lord Chan-

cellor, and has given him his position as one of the Makers of English Law. In all the spheres that a lawyer can occupy he was pre-eminent—(1) as an advocate, (2) as Lord Chancellor, and (3) as a juridical thinker.

(1) As an advocate he combined two qualities which are rarely seen together. He was a master of eloquence and a master of law. Of his eloquence there can be no question. He was a *persona grata* both in the House of Commons and in the courts—and that is not very usual. The House of Commons on one occasion was considering whether the attorney-general ought to be a member of their House, seeing that he is summoned by a writ of assistance to the House of Lords. But, whatever was to be the rule for the future, they resolved to have Bacon. Ben Jonson's testimony of Bacon's eloquence as an advocate is decisive. Ben Jonson said,[1] "His hearers could not cough or look aside from him without loss. He commanded when he spoke, and had his judges angry and pleased at his devotion. The fear of every man that heard him was that he should make an end." Of his mastery of the law his arguments are a sufficient proof. He was a master of Year Books—of black-letter lore; and he marshalled his arguments and his instances with a logical force and in a literary form which no lawyer of his day could approach. Bacon's arguments and his other writings on English law are collected by Spedding in the seventh volume of his edition of Bacon's works.

(2) Of Bacon's judgments as Lord Chancellor Mr John Ritchie's collection of his decisions tells us something.[2] These decisions illustrate the need for a court with an equitable jurisdiction, which could stop unrighteous proceedings in the courts of common law.

[1] Cited Church, *Life of Bacon*, 265–266; cp. Spedding, *Letters and Life of Bacon*, i, 268 for another testimony.
[2] Reports of cases decided by Francis Bacon prepared from the records of the court; cp. *L.Q.R.* xlix, 61–69.

They also illustrate the fact that equity followed the law very closely, and that it acted very literally *in personam* —in one case Bacon modified his decree because *inter alia* the defendant was a "widow charged with eight children". At the same time some of his decisions show that the court was beginning to rely upon precedents, and that therefore some distinct bodies of equitable doctrine were beginning to emerge. But this collection of decisions is taken from the official records, and have the impersonal touch which characterizes official records. In Bacon's case, as in the case of other Chancellors of this period, we have no reports of the reasons by which he supported his decisions. But, from his own writings we do know a good deal more of his achievement than we know of the achievement of any other Chancellor before the beginning of the regular reports.

First, he restored a certain amount of harmony between the common law and the Chancery. No doubt the victory of the Chancery, to which he had contributed, had left the common lawyers rather sore. In the speech which he made on taking his seat in the court of Chancery he promised that the issue of injunctions should be carefully regulated. He imitated the example of Sir Thomas More, and invited the judges to dinner to discuss the matter. In the course of this discussion he pointed out to the judges that the controversy between Coke and Ellesmere had been largely personal—"The former discords", he said,[1] "were but flesh and blood; and now that the men were gone the matter was gone"; and he promised to reconsider any cases in which the judges thought that an injunction had been unjustly granted. He kept his word. In his orders he provided against the abuse by litigants of the power to get injunctions; and it is clear that his measures succeeded, since the courts of common law and Chancery ceased to

[1] Spedding, *Letters and Life of Bacon*, vi, 198.

quarrel. Secondly, he promised to reform some of the weaknesses in the procedure of his court. He fulfilled this promise by issuing a consolidated set of orders which, to a large extent, fixed the practice of the court till the reforms of the nineteenth century. Lastly, he fulfilled his promise to do speedy justice. A month after he had taken his seat in Chancery he could write to Buckingham, "This day I have made even with the business of the kingdom for common justice. Not one cause unheard. The lawyers drawn dry of all the motions they were to make. Not one petition unanswered."[1] And in December of the same year he was able to make the same boast.[2] Nor is there any evidence that the quality of justice dispensed was unsatisfactory. It is true that he was by his own confession too ready to take presents from suitors. It is true that in at least one case he allowed Buckingham's influence to pervert the course of justice.[3] But it is probable that the presents which he took did not prevent him from deciding as he would otherwise have decided. At least we do not hear that any large number of his cases were reversed by his successor.

It may be fairly said, therefore, that Bacon left his mark upon the court of Chancery. As attorney-general he had been largely instrumental in vindicating the independence of the court, and in thus securing the free development of equity. As Chancellor he helped to restore harmony between the Chancery and the courts of common law; and he created from the scattered orders of his predecessors a code of procedure, the formation of which was a condition precedent to the development of a system of equity. Thus he consolidated and completed the work of that school of lawyer Chancellors which had

[1] Spedding, *Letters and Life of Bacon*, vi, 208.
[2] *Ibid.* vi, 283.
[3] See Mr Heath's elaborate analysis of the case of Dr Steward, Spedding, *Letters and Life of Bacon*, vii, App. 579–588.

begun with the chancellorship of Sir Thomas More. That the development of a system of equity did not make rapid way till after the Restoration was due wholly to political causes.

(3) That he was a great juridical thinker his aphorisms on the law in the eighth book of the *De Augmentis* show. They were the first critical, the first jurisprudential, estimate of English law which had ever been made. And I think we can say that his powers as a juridical thinker were shown in two main directions. In the first place, he made valuable suggestions for the recasting of the rules of English law. Such schemes were then in the air, but in the existing state of politics they were impossible of realization. For all that, Bacon's suggestions show his prescience. He suggested a recasting of the statute law —his ideas on this subject have been to a great extent effected by the statute law revision Acts. He suggested a digest of case law—that is not yet realized. He suggested a book of Institutes for learners, to be composed on a plan which resembled that on which Blackstone composed his Commentaries more than a century later. He suggested the composition of three other books: a book *de antiquitatibus juris*—a book of legal history to be compiled from the records; a book *de regulis juris* explaining the general principles which underlie legal rules; and a book of *Terms of the Law*, i.e. a law dictionary. In the second place, he was a great teacher of law. He was a reader at Gray's Inn. And we are only just beginning to realize how good the readings of those old Inns of Court readers were, and the effective way in which they supplemented the defects of the system of case law by giving systematic surveys of various branches of law. Bacon's unfinished reading on the statute of Uses shows that he was a great teacher of law. In my opinion the only teacher of law who can be compared with him is Maitland—both were consummate lawyers, and in both

cases their law was illuminated by literature and philosophy.

Bacon once said that if his suggested recasting of the
law could have been carried out, succeeding ages would
have accounted him Coke's superior as a lawyer—
perhaps so. But those reforms were impossible then;
and because he took the losing side in the political controversies of his day, and because the influence of those
controversies has been large and lasting, Bacon's merits
as a juridical thinker have long remained unappreciated.
To have taken that side is no evidence of political incompetence or intellectual dishonesty. No doubt it is easy
for us to say that it was absurd to idealize James I—to
make of him a patriot King. No doubt it is easy for us
to say that he underrated the power and ability of Parliament. It is easy for us who know the end of the story.
It was not so easy for a man who had been brought up
in the traditions of the Tudor monarchy. This fact long
remained unrecognized, with the result that those who
took the losing side in seventeenth-century politics got
scant justice from the Whig historians of the last century
—I have sometimes thought that an interesting "Dialogue in the Shades" might be composed between Bacon
and Lord Macaulay, who, like Bacon, was a member of
Trinity College, Cambridge. But we who can at length
look at seventeenth-century politics through seventeenth-
century spectacles; we who can look at the great constitutional controversies of that century as matters of law;
we who can recognize that the law was often doubtful,
and that equally able and honest men could take
opposite sides—we can at length do justice to Bacon
as a statesman, as a lawyer, and as a juridical thinker.

If Elizabeth had been succeeded by a King who could
have appreciated Bacon, and if he had adopted his advice,
the issue of the constitutional and the jurisdictional con-

troversies of the seventeenth century would have been a great deal more doubtful. To many it would have seemed that the common lawyers and the Parliament, by rejecting the doctrine of sovereignty, and by trying to curtail the powers of the Crown, were rejecting the two great civilizing agencies, which had produced the modern state, and thereby ended medieval anarchy—to many it would have seemed that Parliament and the common lawyers wanted to get back to the anarchy of the time from which they drew their precedents. If James had been a statesman, and had allowed himself to be guided by men like Bacon, much might have been made of this sort of argument. But James was not a statesman. He antagonized all classes except a narrow clique of churchmen and the extreme royalists. The parliamentary opposition thus became what it had never been in Tudor times, a national opposition. Could it rise to this great opportunity? That it could and did do so—that Parliament and the common lawyers were able to show that a modern state could be constructed on lines which gave a share of power to Parliament, and admitted the supremacy of the law, is largely due to Bacon's great rival, Coke. Of Coke and of his great influence on the future history of English law I shall speak in my next lecture.

Lecture VI

SIR EDWARD COKE

THE first half of the seventeenth century is the turning-point in English constitutional and legal history, because it was then that it was decided that the government of England was to be by the King and Parliament, and not, as in most continental countries, by the King alone. This result was achieved by a Parliamentary opposition, which gradually made Parliament an integral and a permanent part of the government of the state, and compelled the Crown to submit to such modifications of its prerogatives as would leave Parliament free to exercise the powers which it had won. Hence, in later ages, political parties which have aimed at effecting constitutional changes designed to secure a larger measure of popular control over the executive government, have connected their struggles with these struggles of the seventeenth century, and have claimed as their ancestors the Parliamentary leaders who opposed the Stuart Kings. The Whig historians of the first half of the nineteenth century always regarded the struggle for Parliamentary reform, and for the many other changes which followed the Reform Act of 1832, as the sequel of these constitutional struggles of the seventeenth century. They represent the Parliamentary party as the party of progress, and the Royalist party as the party opposed to change. This picture is misleading. In the first half of the seventeenth century it was the Royalist party which was the party of progress, and the representative of modern ideas in politics: it was the Parliamentary party which resisted change, which drew its inspiration from a medieval past, which adopted as its central political idea the medieval conception of the rule of law. Abroad the medieval representative assemblies and medieval conceptions of government had disappeared; and modern experience seemed to prove that government by a sovereign King, backed by an army and a trained civil service, was the most effective means to secure, not only protection against lawlessness, but also the development of trade, the encouragement of learning, and the progress of all that made for an ordered civilization. Those who supported an enlarged prerogative and the subordination of Parliament to the King considered themselves to be the enlightened thinkers, who were supporting the most modern and up-to-date political theory, against opponents who were advocating a medieval conception of the state which experience had shown led to anarchy. It was by the prerogative that the Tudors had mastered this anarchy, and had made England a well-ordered state of the modern type. It followed that the prerogative of the King of England must be increased, as the prerogatives of continental Kings had been increased, if England were to keep her rank among the civilized states of Europe.

This contrast between the medieval political ideas of the supporters of the Parliament, and the modern political ideas of the supporters of the King, has its parallel in the contrast between the medieval legal ideas of the supporters of the common law and the common law courts, and the modern legal ideas of the lawyers who were making new law in the more recently established courts which were rivalling and competing with the common law courts. The fact that this contrast existed between these medieval ideas of the supporters of the common law and common law courts and the more modern ideas of the age of the Renaissance was pointed out for the first time by Maitland with his usual deftness and piquancy. He said:[1]

Perhaps we should hardly believe if we were told for the first time that in the reign of James I a man who was the contemporary of Shakespeare and Bacon, a very able man too and a learned, who left his mark deep in English history, said, not by way of paradox but in sober earnest, said repeatedly and advisedly, that a certain thoroughly medieval book written in decadent colonial French was "the most perfect and absolute work that ever was written in any human science". Yet this was what Sir Edward Coke said of a small treatise written by Sir Thomas Littleton, who, though he did not die until 1481, was assuredly no child of the Renaissance.... A lecturer worthy of that theme would—I am sure of it—be able to convince you that there is some human interest, and especially an interest for English-speaking mankind, in a question which Coke's words suggest: How was it, and why was it, that in an age when old creeds of many kinds were crumbling, and all knowledge was being transfigured, in an age which had revolted against its predecessor, and was conscious of the revolt, one body of doctrine and a body which concerns us all remained so intact that Coke could formulate this prodigious sentence and challenge the whole world to contradict it?

Coke not only "formulated this prodigious sentence", but by his writings and his career he succeeded in concealing its "prodigious" character from future generations of lawyers; he gave this medieval common law the victory over its rivals; and, without sacrificing the medieval legal and political ideas which it embodied, he made it fit to bear rule in a modern state. It is for this reason that, amongst all the many Makers of English Law, Coke is the most important.

In this lecture[2] I propose, in the first place, to deal very briefly with the events of Coke's life; in the second

---

[1] *English Law and the Renaissance*, 3–5.

[2] The authorities for most of the statements in this lecture will be found in my *History of English Law*, v, 425–493.

place, to say something of his writings; and, in the third place, to give some account of the great influence which his career and writings have had upon the future development of English law.

THE EVENTS OF COKE'S LIFE

Coke's career falls into three well-marked periods. The first extends to his appointment to the bench in 1606, the second to his dismissal from the bench in 1616, and the third to his death in 1634.

Coke was born February 1, 1552. He was educated at Trinity College, Cambridge, and the Inner Temple, and was called to the bar April 20, 1578. Owing to his own industry and learning and to the patronage of Burghley, his rise was rapid. On June 12, 1592, he became solicitor-general; on February 19, 1593, Speaker of the House of Commons, and on March 24, 1594, attorney-general, which post he held till 1606. As a law officer of the Crown he was an officer of state as well as a lawyer. The fact that he had been an officer of state during this period left a lasting mark upon his intellectual outlook. Hatred of Roman Catholics, reverence for the Crown, brutality to prisoners charged with treason or sedition, were characteristics which came naturally to many Englishmen who had lived through that period of national emergency; and more especially to those who, by reason of their official positions, knew the dangers to which the Queen and state were constantly exposed. In Coke, whose enthusiastic temperament often led him to unfortunate extremes in thought and action, these characteristics appeared in an exaggerated form, and resulted in so ferocious a treatment of the prisoners whom he was called upon to prosecute, that even his contemporaries were occasionally disgusted. On Raleigh's trial Cecil interposed to check Coke. "Good Mr Attorney," he said, "be not so impatient.

Give him leave to speak." To which Coke replied that he was encouraging traitors, and "sat down in a chafe, and would speak no more, until the Commissioners urged and entreated him".[1] His experiences as law officer also led him to approve of acts and doctrines which he later denounced as unconstitutional—such acts as the infliction of torture,[2] such doctrines as the validity of benevolences and impositions,[3] of commitments by the Council,[4] and of the practice of asking the judges to give extra-judicial opinions.[5] But neither then nor at any other period in his life did he waver in his belief that the common law was a wellnigh perfect system, upon which not only the public and private rights of Englishmen depended, but also the very being of the English state.

When, therefore, in 1606 he became chief justice of the Common Pleas, he obtained a post which was entirely congenial to him; for he could enforce from the bench his ideas as to the position of the common law. But these ideas assorted badly with the claims of rival courts, such as the Star Chamber, the court of Chancery, and the court of Admiralty; and they assorted even worse with the claim of James I to decide all conflicts of jurisdiction, and with his views as to the position of the prerogative in the state. According to Coke's view, the common law was the supreme law in the state, and the judges, unfettered and uncontrolled save by the law, were the sole exponents of this supreme law. According to James I's view the judges were, like other civil servants, the officers of the Crown. The Crown could supersede them if necessary and decide the matter for itself. The pre-

---

[1] (1603) 2 S.T. at p. 26.
[2] As attorney-general he had prepared documents to authorize its application: Spedding, *Letters and Life of Bacon*, v, 93 n., vii, 78, 79; cp. *Third Institute*, 35; Holdsworth, *H.E.L.* v, 185.
[3] *Ibid.* v, 427, nn. 4 and 5.
[4] *Ibid.* v, 450, n. 9.
[5] *Ibid.* v, 428, n. 1.

rogative was in the last resort supreme. It was inevitable, therefore, that Coke's tenure of the judicial office should be marked by a series of conflicts with the King, which defined the issues between them, and paved the way for Coke's alliance with the Parliamentary opposition. Between 1606 and 1613 there were conflicts on such subjects as the sphere of the jurisdiction of the ecclesiastical courts and of the Councils of Wales and the North, the claim of the King to withdraw cases from the courts and to decide them himself, the proper sphere of proclamations.

James I was angry with Coke; but he was conscious that he must be careful how he dealt with him. Personally Coke was not unpopular at court—Prince Charles is said to have delighted in his conversation. And it was clear that his fanatical reverence for the common law was the reflection of a deep-seated national feeling. The arguments used by the leaders of the Parliamentary opposition encouraged the belief that in the common law there was a store of principles, which demonstrated the illegality of such exercises of arbitrary power as the imposition of extra customs duties, and commitments to prison by orders of the King. Coke's conduct on the bench had, it seemed to many, proved the truth of this belief. Therefore the fact that he, the greatest master of the common law, had demonstrated from the bench that the common law was the greatest safeguard against arbitrary power had given him immense popularity.

In 1613 James I, on Bacon's advice, transferred Coke from the chief justiceship of the Common Pleas to that of the King's Bench. Probably Bacon thought that if he were removed from a court which was specially concerned with safeguarding the rights of the people, to a court where his special concern was to look after the rights of the King, his capacity for harm would be diminished. Bacon's advice showed some insight into

Coke's character. Coke had the mind of an advocate, and would fight with all his strength for a cause which he was retained to defend. But Bacon had not appreciated the fact that Coke's views as to the supremacy of the common law had become a settled belief not devoid of fanaticism. The result of his removal to the office of chief justice of the King's Bench was therefore very different from that which Bacon had expected. His three years' tenure of the office was marked by three quarrels with the King, the most famous of which was his dispute with Lord Ellesmere as to the jurisdiction of the court of Chancery, in which, as we have seen,[1] with James I's help, Lord Ellesmere came off victorious. On June 26, 1616, Coke was suspended from the Privy Council, forbidden to go on circuit, and ordered to spend his leisure in revising and correcting his reports; and on November 14, 1616, he was dismissed.

From 1616 to 1620 Coke had some hopes that he might be restored to favour. The marriage of his daughter to Sir John Villiers seemed to promise some help from Villiers's brother, the all-powerful Buckingham. But James was too conscious of the hopeless difference between his own and Coke's political views ever to trust him again with an important office. In the Parliament of 1620 Coke allied himself with the Parliamentary opposition. That was a momentous step, which had large consequences both for Parliament and for the common law. It cemented the old standing alliance between Parliament and the common law; it enlisted in favour of the Parliament that superstitious reverence which men felt for the common law; and it strengthened that note of legal conservatism which is the distinguishing characteristic of the constitutional struggles of the seventeenth century, and the secret of their successful issue. In the Parliaments of 1620, 1624,

[1] Above, pp. 100–101.

1625, and 1628 Coke was a leader of the Parliamentary opposition. It was in his last Parliament—the Parliament of 1628—that he did his most important work for the constitution; for it was in that Parliament that he took the largest part in framing and in carrying the Petition of Right—the first of those great constitutional documents since Magna Carta, which safeguard the liberties of the people by securing the supremacy of the law. Throughout his life Coke had held that the common law was supreme, and that it only needed to be clearly declared to be all sufficient to safeguard the rights of Englishmen. The placing on the Statute Book of a declaratory measure which embodied both these ideas was a fitting crown to his career.

The six remaining years of his life were spent in retirement. But he was naturally an object of suspicion to Charles I, who had embarked on his scheme of prerogative government. In 1631, Charles, hearing that he was about to publish a book, ordered the Lord Keeper to stop its publication. The reason which he gave for his action is the best evidence of the great reputation which Coke had acquired. "He is held", he said,[1] "too great an oracle amongst the people, and they may be misled by anything that carries such an authority as all things do that he either speaks or writes."

At first sight it may seem that there is a great inconsistency in Coke's career. At first sight it may seem that there is little in common between the attorney-general of Elizabeth and James I who was zealous in the defence of the prerogative, and the chief justice who lost his office on account of his attempt to limit the prerogative and became the leader of the Parliamentary opposition in James I's and Charles I's Parliaments. I think this inconsistency is resolved if we remember that Coke, throughout his life, had the outlook of a Tudor lawyer and statesman, and a Tudor lawyer and statesman of the

[1] *S.P. Dom* (1629–31), 490, clxxxiii, 18.

Elizabethan age. Bishop Gardiner tells us that Thomas Cromwell had once asked him in the presence of Henry VIII whether the maxim *quod principi placuit* did not apply to the King of England—an awkward question in such a presence; and that he had replied: "I had read indeed of Kings that had their wills always received for a law, but I told him the form of his reign, to make the laws his will was more sure and quiet, and by this form of government ye be established, and it is agreeable with the nature of your people."[1] This was the principle upon which both Henry VIII and Elizabeth acted; and it recognizes the supremacy of the law. Obviously much latitude could be allowed to a prince who recognized this principle, more especially in a time of national emergency. But equally obviously the same latitude could not be allowed to a prince in whose book—*The True Law of Free Monarchies*—is to be found, as Figgis has said, the doctrine of the divine right of the King "complete in every detail".[2] Coke was bound to resist an attempt by the King to enforce this theory, and to substitute the supremacy of the Crown for the supremacy of the common law; and his resistance inevitably led to an alliance with the Parliamentary opposition.

The character of the man and his age fully account for his vast influence upon the law and politics of the seventeenth century. But they do not account for the permanence of his influence upon the future development of English law. The permanence of that influence is due to the fact that his devotion to the common law led him to consider it to be his duty[3] to employ the scanty leisure of his busy career in restating all its principal doctrines. Therefore, in order to understand the reasons for Coke's permanent influence on the future development of English law, we must examine the character of his writings.

[1] 1 S.T. 588.   [2] *Divine Right of Kings*, 136.
[3] 8 Co. Rep. Pref. xxxiv, cited Holdsworth, *H.E.L.* v, 456, n. 2.

COKE'S WRITINGS

Coke was a master of the literature of the law in print and in manuscript; and his reading was not confined to law books. On points of medieval history he can cite Matthew of Paris;[1] and he had read Camden and Lambard[2]—the principal historians of his own day. He can contrast the civil and canon law with the common law;[3] he can enliven his text by references to Virgil,[4] Horace,[5] and Chaucer;[6] and he can illustrate a point by a citation from Tacitus,[7] Cicero,[8] or the Vulgate.[9] But it must be admitted that of non-professional books and of non-professional branches of knowledge he had no critical knowledge. He accepted the information which he derived from them with a credulity which is as medieval as his law. He was inclined to accept all the legends about Brut; he was convinced that the ancient Britons talked Greek;[10] and he accepted all the legends told by the author of the *Mirror of Justices*.[11] There is no doubt that Coke's credulity has been injurious to legal history, because succeeding lawyers did not distinguish between those parts of his work which rested on the solid authority of statute, record, Year Book, or report, and those which rested on his own uncritical acceptance of historical legends.

No one can contend that Coke's writings are literature. But they have some literary qualities. He was a skilful pleader; and to be a skilful pleader exactness of ex-

---

[1] Co. Litt. 43a; *Second Institute*, 15.
[2] 10 Co. Rep. Pref. xx; Co. Litt. 168a; *Fourth Institute*, 63.
[3] Co. Litt. 102a, 262a, 352b, 368a; 10 Co. Rep. Pref. xvii.
[4] Co. Litt. 165; *Fourth Institute*, 289.
[5] Co. Litt. 141.   [6] *Second Institute*, 123.
[7] *Fourth Institute*, 129, 244.
[8] *Ibid.* 129; *Foster's Case* (1615) 11 Co. Rep. 60a.
[9] *Second Institute*, 53, and many other passages.
[10] 3 Co. Rep. Pref. viii–x.   [11] 9 Co. Rep. Pref. i–v; above, 38–39.

pression was essential. He was a skilful advocate; and to
be a skilful advocate lucidity of expression was essential.
He could arrest attention by a pointed expression—
"good pleading", he said,[1] "is the heartstring of the
common law"; by a fine phrase—"the gladsome light of
jurisprudence";[2] or by a striking metaphor—"the laws
of England are the golden metwand whereby all men's
causes are justly and evenly measured".[3] Though his
style is often verbose, it is never obscure; and, when he
is fired by his theme, he rises to real eloquence—one
illustration is his summary of the manner in which the
Tudor statesmen had settled the vexed question of the
status of the copyholder:

But now copy-holders stand upon a sure ground, now they
weigh not Lord's displeasure, they shake not at every sudden
blast of wind, they eat, drink, and sleep securely; onely having
an especial care of the main chance (viz.) to perform carefully
what duties and services so-ever their Tenure doth exact, and
Custome doth require: then let Lord frown, the copy holder
cares not, knowing himself safe, and not within any danger. For
if the Lord's anger grow to expulsion, the Law hath provided
several weapons of remedy; for it is at his election either to sue
a *Subpoena* or an action of trespass against the Lord. Time hath
dealt very favourably with Copy-holders in divers respects.[4]

Coke wrote many books: *Readings*, a large book of
Entries, a little treatise on Bail and Mainprize, and, the
best of all his shorter works—his *Compleate Copy-Holder*.
By far the most important of his works, because they have
influenced the whole future development of English law,
are his *Reports* and his *Institutes*. The first part of Coke's
Reports was published in 1600, and the second and third
parts shortly afterwards. The remaining eight parts
appeared at short intervals between 1603 and 1615. The
twelfth and thirteenth parts were published after his

[1] Co. Litt. Pref.   [2] Co. Litt. Epilogue.
[3] *Fourth Institute*, 240.   [4] Coke, *Compleate Copy-Holder*, § 9.

death in 1655 and 1658. They were not prepared by him for the press and are, for the most part, simply notes of cases and other transactions in which he had been engaged. They are valuable as evidence of some of the facts of Coke's life, and of the evolution of his political views. But, though they contain some leading cases in constitutional law, e.g. *The Case of Proclamations*, they have never had the same authority as that possessed by the first eleven parts of the *Reports* which he himself published.

In Coke's day there was no agreement as to the form which a report should take. Coke's reports are written in all sorts of forms. Sometimes he makes the case a mere peg on which he hangs his summary of the law on a particular topic.[1] Sometimes he reports a series of cases on a particular topic very concisely.[2] Important cases he reports elaborately and at length.[3] He often intervenes to insert comments or advice of his own; and there is no doubt that he sometimes added much from his own reading. Bacon once said that in his reports there was too much *de proprio*;[4] and the writer of the *Observations on Coke's Reports* is even more severe.[5] The cases reported form a corpus of the common law, civil and criminal. All parts of the law are reviewed; the old learning is restated; and the manner in which it has been modified by more recent statutes and cases is explained. Thus, such new developments of the common law as the struggle against perpetuities, the development of the action of assumpsit,

---

[1] E.g. *Arthur Blackamore's Case* (1611) 8 Co. Rep. 156a; *Beecher's Case* (1609) 8 Co. Rep. 58a.

[2] E.g. 4 Co. Rep. 21a–32a (copyhold cases); *ibid.* 39b–48a (appeals and indictments).

[3] E.g. *Shelley's Case* (1579–1581) 1 Co. Rep. 88b.

[4] Spedding, *Letters and Life of Bacon*, v, 86.

[5] For this document, which has been attributed without much positive evidence to Lord Ellesmere, see Holdsworth, *H.E.L.* v, 478, n. 1.

the new practice of hearing actions on contracts made abroad, are noted and justified.[1]

The great developments of the common law, to which the *Reports* bear witness, had raised the problem of how this modern common law, which was arising on the foundations of the medieval common law, was to be taught to students. Since the older books had become inadequate, Coke set himself to supply the want of an up-to-date treatise by writing four books of *Institutes*.

The *First Institute*—Coke upon Littleton—is very different in character from the other three. It was meant to be Littleton brought up to date. But it is a great deal more than this. All matters mentioned by Littleton are explained and commented upon and a great many that are not; for all Coke's reading, and all his experience as counsel and judge, went to its making. It is in fact a legal encyclopaedia arranged on no plan except that suggested by the words and sentences of Littleton. Obviously it was not well suited to be a students' text-book—as Roger North said, the commentary was "much more obscure than the bare text without it".[2] The *Second Institute* is a commentary on some thirty-nine statutes, and deals mainly with public law. The *Third Institute* deals with criminal law, and the *Fourth Institute* with the jurisdiction of courts. Both the *Third* and *Fourth Institutes* are a good deal more elaborate than the books of Staunford, Lambard, and Crompton, which were the existing text-books on these subjects.

The *First Institute* was published in 1628. It was the only one of these four books published in Coke's lifetime. The others were not published till 1641. The reason is, I think, obvious. The *First Institute* dealt with topics very remote from the constitutional controversies of the day. The other three touched them at many points. In 1628, when the *Second* and *Third Institutes* were finished, Coke's

[1] Holdsworth, *H.E.L.* v, 465 nn. 1–4.   [2] *Lives of the Norths*, i, 17.

active career was over. When the *Fourth Institute* was finished Parliament had been dissolved, and the country was being governed by the Prerogative. We cannot blame Coke for not wishing to shorten his last years by a close imprisonment in the Tower. He had recorded his views: their publication could wait till a more favourable season. When they were published in 1641 it was the hour of the triumph of the Parliament and the common law; and so the *Institutes* and *Reports* were accepted without question as an accurate statement of the law. But in the last century Coke's writings have been attacked by two opposite schools of legal thought—by the historical school and by the analytical jurists.

Time has its revenges. Coke used to advise historians to be careful how they trespassed on to the domain of law;[1] and now the historians have turned upon Coke and shown that his history is often inaccurate, and that he has misrepresented the medieval law. There is some truth in these criticisms. Coke's excursions into the domain of history were all made for the purpose of proving some thesis; and there is no doubt that history written from this point of view is, as history, worthless. But, before we condemn Coke, we must, in the first place, distinguish between his treatment of cases of a political or semi-political kind, and his treatment of other cases; and, in the second place, remember that Coke's aim was to give an accurate presentation, not of medieval law, but of the law of his own day.

(1) There is no doubt that in cases of a political or semi-political kind Coke is sometimes inconsistent;[2] and that sometimes, in his eagerness to prove his case, he badly misrepresents his authorities. Thus in his *Second* and *Third Institutes*[3] he states that one of the counts in an

---

[1] 3 Co. Rep. Pref. xiii.   [2] Above, p. 115.
[3] *Second Institute*, 626; *Third Institute*, 208; Holdsworth, *H.E.L.* iv, 253, 257–258.

indictment of Wolsey contained an accusation that he had attempted to subvert the common law, and to substitute for it the civil and canon law. The fact is that the indictment in question was not an indictment of Wolsey, and the passage as to subverting the common law was merely the common form used in any indictment on the statute of Praemunire. The errors into which he fell in his attack on the court of Admiralty are well known, since they have been exposed by Prynne in the seventeenth century, and by Marsden in our own day. But in cases into which politics did not enter I do not think that a charge of inaccuracy is proved. His very able opponents, Bacon and Ellesmere, though encouraged by the King, found no serious errors in his reports except in these political or semi-political cases; and they knew the law of their own day more intimately than we know it. Bacon admitted that though Coke's *Reports* "may have errors, and some peremptory and extra-judicial resolutions more than are warranted, yet they contain infinite good decisions and rulings over of cases";[1] and the writer of the *Observations on Coke's Reports* made a similar admission. There are in them, he said, some things which are bad, some which are mediocre, but more things which are good.

(2) Coke was not writing legal history: he was stating modern law. There is no doubt that in some of the cases, in which he states a proposition which is at variance with a medieval authority, he has the authority of a later case. Thus Pike has accused Coke of misrepresenting the text of Littleton;[2] but in fact he had, as authority for his statement, a decision of Brian and Vavisor given after Littleton wrote.[3] No doubt we cannot justify all his statements in this way; but, having regard to Bacon and

---

[1] Spedding, *Letters and Life of Bacon*, vi, 65.
[2] *L.Q.R.* v, 36.
[3] Y.B. 5 Henry VII, Pasch. pl. 5, p. 3.

Ellesmere's verdict, probably a good many can be so justified.

Let us now turn to the exceptions taken by the analytical jurists. Though Coke's use of history was often unhistorical, he was a lawyer of the historical school; and he had all the defects of the historical lawyer in an exaggerated form. He could explain all the anomalies which disfigured the law; and it seldom occurred to him that there was a distinction between explanation and justification. On the other hand, he had all the good points of the historical lawyer. The analytical lawyer looks solely or mainly at the ideas current in his own day, and is inclined to reject as useless all that is not in accord with those ideas. His views, being founded merely on his own ideas of contemporary convenience, are apt to be superficial. But the historical lawyer preserves the ideas of past ages; and those ideas, and the rules and institutions founded on them, sometimes come into their own again in a future age. Coke preserved the medieval idea of the supremacy of the law, at a time when political speculation was tending to assert the necessity of the supremacy of a sovereign person or body, which was above the law; and the obscurity and indefinite character of some of the medieval rules which he states preserved for the common law the quality of flexibility.

Hobbes, one of Coke's younger contemporaries, was the greatest of all our analytical jurists. In his *Dialogue of the Common Laws* he attacks Coke with those analytical weapons which Bentham and Austin have made familiar to modern lawyers. Law is simply the command of a sovereign. It is no product of artificial reason. It should be so clear that every intelligent layman can understand it. Hobbes's criticisms were approved by Stephen[1]— though not altogether by Austin, who rightly said that Coke's mastery of the English legal system was equalled

[1] *History of Criminal Law*, ii, 206, n. 1.

only by that of the great Roman jurists.[1] And just as the theories of Austin and Bentham were replied to by Maine, so were Hobbes's criticisms replied to by Hale, whose mastery of the history of English law led him rightly to distrust the simple reasoning of the analytical philosopher.

In fact, Hobbes saw part of the truth but not the whole. At the beginning of the seventeenth century many lawyers and statesmen agreed that some restatement of English law was needed. But what form should that restatement take? Bacon, the man best fitted to answer such a question, saw that the construction of a logical code was impossible. He suggested, as we have seen,[2] a much more conservative measure of reform—the compilation of a digest of case law and a digest of statute law, and other books designed to facilitate the study of the law. But political events made the realization of Bacon's scheme impossible; and the outstanding merits of Coke's writings made the need for such a restatement less pressing. It is the outstanding merits of these writings which have given Coke his great and lasting influence over the future development of English law. The extent and character of that influence I must now endeavour to summarize.

COKE'S INFLUENCE ON THE DEVELOPMENT OF ENGLISH LAW

Coke's influence is apparent first upon the development of our private law; secondly, upon the form of our law; thirdly, upon our commercial law; and fourthly, upon our criminal law and our constitutional law.

(1) The sixteenth century—the century of transition from medieval to modern—had seen many changes in all branches of private law. Therefore a great deal of

---

[1] *Jurisprudence*, ii, 1130.   [2] Above, p. 108.

restatement was needed to bring the medieval and the modern rules of that law into harmony. In fact, in any age in which fundamental changes have taken place, the law will need reconsideration and restatement; and it is not one of the least of the advantages of our system of case law that it enables lawyers to adapt the law to a new environment. What a succession of eminent lawyers have done for the common law in the last century Coke accomplished for the common law of his own day. The manner in which he effected this work of restatement and adaptation can I think be summed up as follows:

First, he deduced from the scattered and often inconsistent dicta in the Year Books positive rules of law in harmony with the rules laid down by the modern reports; and he did his work so skilfully that later lawyers were content to accept his readings of the Year Books and the Abridgments of the Year Books. Secondly, in like manner, he brought the medieval literature of the common law into line with the modern literature. Glanvil, Bracton, Britton, and Fleta were made to explain and illustrate Perkins, Fitzherbert, Staunford, and Lambard. Thirdly, the information which his reports gave of the doings of the courts outside the sphere of the common law, such as the court of Chancery, the Star Chamber, and the court of Admiralty, familiarized common lawyers with the new ideas originating in those courts, which were giving rise to new legal developments. Therefore his reports made it easier for the common law to fill the great position which it acquired as the result of the constitutional conflicts of the seventeenth century.

In these three ways Coke's writings ensured the continuity of the development of the rules of English law amidst all the vast changes of this century of Renaissance, Reformation, and Reception of Roman law. This merit of Coke's writings was recognized in his own day by Bacon—"had it not been for Sir Edward Coke's reports", he wrote,[1] "the law by this time had almost been like a ship without ballast; for that the cases of modern experience are fled from those that are adjudged and ruled in former times". It was also recognized in the present century by Maitland—"Coke's books", he said in a letter to me, "are the great dividing line, and we are hardly out of the Middle Age till he has dogmatized its results." It is clear, therefore, that the great eighteenth-century conveyancer, Charles Butler, who with Hargrave produced a classical edition of Coke upon Littleton, was right when he said that, "the most proper point of view in which the merit and ability of Sir Edward Coke's writings can be placed, is by considering him the centre of modern and ancient law".[2]

(2) I turn to Coke's influence on the form of our law. The sixteenth century was a century in which many bodies of law, administered in separate courts, and rivalling the common law, were springing up. At the end of that century the Chancery, the Admiralty, the Star Chamber, the Ecclesiastical courts, were all putting forward claims to exercise a large jurisdiction. The only one of these courts which succeeded in making good all its claims was the court of Chancery. It succeeded in making good its claim to a jurisdiction independent of, and in some respects superior to, that of the common law courts; and the effect of its success has been to split the English legal system into two halves. If all the other rival courts had been equally successful the English legal system would have been split into many fragments. Coke saved English law from this fate. His success in asserting the supremacy of the common law, and his success in restating and adapting its principles to meet modern needs, made the English legal system a much more uniform system than it might otherwise have been; for

[1] Spedding, *Letters and Life of Bacon*, vi, 65.
[2] *Reminiscences*, i, 118.

it made the common law, as Holt C.J. once said, "the overruling jurisdiction in this realm".[1] But for Coke's efforts the common law might have become one among many equals. It would not have been the "overruling jurisdiction in this realm"; and if this had happened, our commercial law, our criminal law, and our constitutional law would have been very different.

(3) Coke's successful attack on the court of Admiralty secured for the common law control over the development of commercial law. This was one of the most valuable of all his services to the common law; for it gave to it a new and constantly expanding jurisdiction, which ensured its continued supremacy, and consolidated the victories which it had won in the constitutional controversies of the seventeenth century. If Coke's attack on the court of Admiralty had not succeeded English commercial law would have been developed in a court which applied Roman rules; and therefore it would have become a body of law which was very separate from the common law.

(4) Coke's influence upon our criminal law and our constitutional law has been very large. The Star Chamber had added much to our criminal law—much that the common law courts took over after its abolition. But it had borrowed something from the continental criminal procedure of the day; and one of the things which it had borrowed was the use of torture. Anyone who is familiar with the revolting character of the continental criminal procedure will, I think, agree that the elimination of torture from our criminal procedure, which was the consequence of the victory of the common law, by itself outweighs all the disadvantages which that victory may have entailed.[2] It made the English criminal procedure the model which was followed by France and other European countries after the French Revolution. Esmein

---

[1] *Shermoulin* v. *Sands* (1697) 1 Ld. Raym. at p. 272.
[2] Holdsworth, *H.E.L.* v, 170–176, 185–187.

tells us that in the seventeenth and eighteenth centuries the inquisitorial procedure—the procedure which involved the use of torture—prevailed; but that one European country—England—had escaped the contagion, and served as a model for the legislation of the French Revolution.[1]

We have seen that one of the most decisive events in the history of our constitutional law was the fact that Coke, after his dismissal from the bench, became a leader of the Parliamentary opposition.[2] It was a decisive event because it cemented the old standing alliance between Parliament and the common law. In the Middle Ages and in the sixteenth century the lawyers had helped to make the English Parliament an efficient representative assembly.[3] In the seventeenth century Parliament handsomely repaid this debt by helping Coke to maintain the medieval conception of the supremacy of law, and to apply it to the government of a modern state. In this matter also England became a model both to the framers of the constitution of the United States and to the framers of constitutions in continental states. The Supreme Court of the United States is a body which safeguards, more effectually than any other tribunal in the world, Coke's ideal of the supremacy of the law. As to the debt owed by the framers of constitutions in continental states, Esmein is again a witness. After pointing out that the supremacy of the law was what Voltaire most admired in the government of the English state, he tells us that the framers of the French Constitution of 1791 made it its central principle.[4]

Both these achievements—the elimination of torture from criminal procedure, and the establishment of the rule of law—were due mainly to Coke's insistence on the

---

[1] *History of Continental Criminal Procedure* (Continental Legal History Series), 322–332.   [2] Above, p. 117.
[3] Holdsworth, *H.E.L.* ii, 430–434; iv, 174, 188–189; above, pp. 55, 84.   [4] *Essays in Legal History* (1913), 214.

supremacy of the common law; and their acceptance by later generations of lawyers, as fundamental principles of English law, was due to the manner in which he had stated and enforced them in his writings. Queen Elizabeth once boasted that she was "mere English". But her statecraft had large effects upon the course of European history. Coke was the most English of our great common lawyers. But seeing that these two achievements have made themselves felt whenever and wherever men have had the will and the power to establish constitutional government, we may claim that these large results of his work entitle him to a place amongst the great jurists of the world.

This is a large claim; but not I think too large. Intellectually Coke was a statesman of the Tudor period; and his work has all the characteristics of Tudor statesmanship. In fact it was its complement; for just as the Tudor statesmen succeeded in adapting the medieval institutions of the English state to modern needs, without any appreciable sacrifice of the medieval ideas contained in them, so Coke succeeded in remoulding the medieval common law in such a way that it was made fit to bear rule in the modern English state. As a lawyer and a statesman he belonged to the greatest period of the Tudor dynasty—the Elizabethan age; and so, like many of the other great leaders of thought and action in that age, he was the author of much in our national life that we still rightly treasure. What Shakespeare has been to literature, what Bacon has been to philosophy, what the translators of the authorized version of the Bible have been to religion, Coke has been to the public and private law of England. He was one of those great Elizabethans whose genius and enthusiasm enabled them, as Kipling has finely and truly said in his Elizabethan poem,

> Lightly to build new world, or lightly loose
> Words that shall shake and shape all after time.

Lecture VII

HALE AND NOTTINGHAM

COKE had begun the work of modernizing the common law. That this work had been proceeding throughout the seventeenth century is shown by Rolle's Abridgment which was probably compiled before 1640;[1] and that it had made still further progress in 1668, when that Abridgment was published by Hale, is shown by Hale's preface. The abolition of the military tenures by the Act of 1660,[2] the disappearance of the status of villeins, the disuse of the real actions and the rise of the action of ejectment, were modernizing the land law. The growth of actions on the case was modernizing the law of contract and tort, was rendering obsolete much old law, and was simplifying the law of procedure. During the period of the Commonwealth many more reforms in the law had been advocated, some of which would have been beneficial, and were at length made during the nineteenth century. In the land law, for instance, there were proposals for a simplified mode of barring entails, the registration of conveyances, and the abolition of general occupancy; and in the criminal law there were proposals for the abolition of the benefit of clergy, of the peine forte et dure, and of the rule which denied counsel to persons accused of felony.[3] It was proposed that choses in action should be assignable;[4] and in the law of procedure and pleading changes were proposed which would have secured many of the objects which have been secured by such Acts as the Uniformity of Process Act, the Common Law Procedure

---

[1] Holdsworth, *H.E.L.* v, 376. [2] 12 Chas. II, c. 24.
[3] Holdsworth, *H.E.L.* vi, 416–417.
[4] *Ibid.* vi, 418.

Acts, and the Judicature Act.[1] Very few of these far-reaching changes became law under the Commonwealth; and little more is heard of them after the Restoration. But a considerable number of the Ordinances actually made during the Commonwealth period foreshadow changes made by the Legislature in the latter part of the seventeenth century.[2] It was inevitable that they should do so. The Great Rebellion had introduced both in law and in politics the modern atmosphere and the modern outlook, so that both the enactments of the Legislature and the reported decisions show the emergence of modern rules and doctrines stated in a modern way.

Hale and Nottingham were the two great lawyers of the early part of Charles II's reign who played the principal part in this work of modernizing English law. Sir Matthew Hale's work has had a large influence upon many different branches of the common law. Lord Nottingham began the work of systematizing the substantive rules of equity and settling its relations to the law. Hale can be regarded as the first of our great modern common lawyers: Nottingham has always been called, and rightly called, "the Father of Modern Equity".

SIR MATTHEW HALE

Hale was born in 1609. He was a pupil of Noy, Charles I's attorney-general, and he acquired his taste for historical studies from Selden. It was his friendship with Selden which, Burnet tells us,[3] "first set him upon a more enlarged pursuit of learning". In fact he not only studied subjects akin to English law such as Roman law and English history, but also mathematics, natural science, and philosophy; and the depth and sincerity of his religious beliefs led him also to study theology. He

[1] Holdsworth, *H.E.L.* vi, 419.   [2] *Ibid.* vi, 426–427.
[3] *Life and Death of Sir Matthew Hale*, 23.

soon made his name at the bar. But, though he had advised Strafford, Laud, and Charles I, he made his peace with the Commonwealth, and in 1654 accepted, as his royalist friends advised, the post of judge of the Common Pleas. But he refused to take a commission from Richard Cromwell, and actively forwarded the Restoration. In 1660 he was made chief baron of the Exchequer; and in 1671 he was made chief justice of the King's Bench. In 1676 failing health compelled him to resign, and he died the same year.

The opinion of Hale's contemporaries makes it clear that Hale's deep religious convictions had so directed his great natural abilities, that they had produced a beautiful character, comparable amongst English judges only to that of Sir Thomas More. It was an age in which the standard of professional honour was not high. But of Hale it was said that

in his pleading he abhorred those two common faults of mis-reciting evidences, quoting presidents or books falsely, or asserting things confidently; by which ignorant juries or weak judges are too often wrought on. He pleaded with the same sincerity that he used in the other parts of his life, and used to say that it was as great a dishonour as a man was capable of that for a little money he was to be hired to say or do otherwise than as he thought.[1]

He was charitable in the widest sense of the word. He left but a small estate considering the practice that he had had at the bar and the high judicial posts that he had filled; and Baxter tells us that he had never known any man "more free from speaking evil of others behind their backs".[2] Though he thought and wrote much on theological questions, there was no intolerance in his disposition. He befriended royalists in the days of the

[1] Burnet, *Life and Death of Sir Matthew Hale*, 144–145.
[2] Baxter, *Additional Notes on the Life and Death of Sir Matthew Hale*, 36.

Commonwealth, and protestant dissenters in the days of Charles II.

It is true that he had the defects of some of his qualities. His charity was apt to be indiscriminate; and he sometimes pushed to absurd lengths his fear of influencing his judgment by taking gifts. His dread of ostentation and vanity led him to go so shabbily clothed that even Baxter remonstrated with him. It is probable, too, that his sincere religious beliefs led him to see no harm in the act which posterity, and more especially the Whig historians of the last century, have most condemned— the sentencing of two witches to death, at a time when the rationalizing and sceptical spirit of the day was beginning to cause the more enlightened to doubt the existence of witchcraft. But we should remember that the sentence was in accordance with the law, and that the existence of witches was vouched for by the Bible. Therefore a man of Hale's mind and temper could hardly be expected to doubt. And these are, after all, small matters. When all deductions have been made, there is no doubt that Hale was a man of a really saintly character, who, by his genuine goodness, attracted the affection of all—even of those with whom he came into merely passing contact.

Hale's character and talents made him the greatest English lawyer of his day. His association with Selden's school of historical lawyers made him, with the exception of Francis Bacon, the most scientific jurist that England had yet seen. At the same time his active life as a barrister and a judge during the troubled period of the Rebellion and the Commonwealth made him an acute political thinker. It is for this reason that he was able to write books some of which have always been regarded as books of authority, and all of which are historically of the greatest importance. Let us look at him from these four different points of view—as a lawyer, as a jurist, as a political thinker, and as a writer of classical books about law.

(1) As a barrister no one was his superior. "He might", says Burnet,[1] "have had what practice he pleased." As a judge it was said of him by an eminent lawyer, probably Lord Nottingham, that "he hath sat as judge in all the courts of law, and in two of them as Chief, but still wherever he sat, all business of consequence followed him, and no man was content to sit down by the judgment of any other court, till the case were brought before him, to see whether he were of the same mind. And his opinion being once known, men did readily acquiesce in it."[2] As chief baron of the Exchequer he had an equitable jurisdiction; and as a judge in equity his authority was equally great—indeed he has some claims to be considered Lord Nottingham's teacher. Even Roger North, who, to justify his brother's political career, thought it necessary to pick holes in Hale's character,[3] admitted that under his presidency the court of King's Bench was a veritable school of law. North says:

I have known the court of King's Bench sitting every day from eight to twelve, and the Lord Chief Justice Hale's managing matters of law to all imaginable advantage to the students, and in that he took a pleasure or rather pride; he encouraged arguing when it was to the purpose, and used to debate with counsel, so as the court might have been taken for an academy of sciences as well as the seat of justice.[4]

(2) Hale's pre-eminence as an English lawyer was due to the fact that the wide range of his legal studies had made him a jurist. He was a student of Roman law, and "often said that the true grounds and reasons of law were so well delivered in the Digest, that a man could never understand law as a science so well as by seeking

---

[1] *Life and Death of Sir Matthew Hale*, 179.   [2] *Ibid.* 174.
[3] *Lives of the Norths*, i, 79–91; iii, 93–102.
[4] *Discourse on the Study of the Laws*, 32–33.

it there".[1] He was a student of constitutional law and legal history; and he studied these subjects in the original authorities. He spent forty years, he tells us in his will, in making his magnificent collection of MSS to help him in his studies; and his treatises published and unpublished show that he knew well how to use it. Both his studies in Roman law and his studies in constitutional law and legal history gave him the power to look at English law as a whole, to set it out in orderly form, and to criticize its rules.

(3) Hale's learning as an English lawyer and a jurist made him an acute political thinker. In the first place, he had definite views as to the theory which underlay the government of the English state. Secondly, he could offer sound criticism of parts of its mechanism. Thirdly, he could see through the fallacies both of the ultra-radical and ultra-conservative political thinkers. First, the fact that he had definite views as to the theory which underlay the government of the English state is shown by his reply to Hobbes's *Dialogue of the Common Laws.*[2] In the first part of that reply he answers Hobbes's *a priori* analytical criticism of the common law, in somewhat the same way as Maine has criticized the *a priori* analytical reasoning of Bentham and Austin. He points out that as law is designed to settle the infinitely various affairs of men, something more was needed to make a good lawyer than sound general principles and a capacity to reason correctly. Experience and training were far more important qualities; and the rules which long experience had approved were more likely to do justice than the untried fancies of philosophers. In the second part of his reply he set out to controvert Hobbes's theory of sovereignty. But his criticism of Hobbes shows that he had not grasped Hobbes's theory. In his view the

---

[1] Burnet, *Life and Death of Sir Matthew Hale,* 24.
[2] Printed Holdsworth, *H.E.L.* v, 500–513.

King is sovereign; but he is not sovereign in the sense in which Hobbes used the word; for he asserts that upon the King's powers as sovereign there are limitations. In fact by the sovereignty of the King, Hale meant a supremacy in certain spheres of government, which was not incompatible with the supremacy of Parliament or the law in other spheres.[1] But, looking at the constitutional facts and law of the second half of the seventeenth century, it is difficult to see to what other conclusion he could come. Secondly, Hale offered sound criticism of parts of the mechanism of the English state. Both in his short *History of the Common Law* and in his tract on *The Amendment or Alteration of Lawes*[2] he made valuable suggestions for reforms in the law as to pleading and evidence, for reforms in the machinery for the collection of the revenue, and for reforms in the offices of the court of Common Pleas; and he suggested the establishment of an efficient system of county courts. Thirdly, Hale could see through the fallacies both of the ultra-radical and ultra-conservative political thinkers. In the disturbed times through which he had lived he had had experience of both varieties. Of the first variety he said that some of them were inspired by a personal grievance, and that others thought the law foolish because they did not understand it.[3] Of the second variety he said that many, especially those that were aged legal practitioners, attached a superstitious reverence to old forms.[4] His knowledge of history taught him that unless law changed with the times it would be unable to guide the activities of the state and its subjects in the new conditions of a changing world.[5]

[1] Holdsworth, *H.E.L.* vi, 204–207.
[2] Hargrave, *Law Tracts*, 253–289.   [3] *Ibid.* 257, 261.   [4] *Ibid.* 264.
[5] "The matter changeth the custom; the contracts the commerce; the dispositions educations tempers of men and societies change in a long tract of time; and so must their lawes in some measure be changed, or they will not be usefull for their state and condition", *ibid.* 269–270.

(4) A lawyer with these qualifications was well fitted to write classical books about law. His most important books are upon constitutional law and criminal law.

The most important of his books on constitutional law is his *Jurisdiction of the Lords' House* published by Hargrave with an elaborate preface in 1796. This topic comprised some of the most controverted political questions of the day; and Hale had written much upon it in the early days of the Long Parliament, during the Commonwealth, and after the Restoration. This essay— the last of three written after the Restoration—represents his final judgment on the matter; and he himself tells us that the MS was complete, and only needed his final revision. Upon certain points his views have not prevailed—e.g. his view of the inability of the House to hear appeals from the courts of equity, and his view that its jurisdiction to hear cases in error depends rather upon a commission from the King than upon inherent right. But generally he lays down the law which has prevailed. The whole book is a striking testimony to Hale's mastery of records, to his impartiality, and to his statesmanlike qualities.

Another considerable treatise, which touches constitutional law at many points, was published in the Hargrave *Law Tracts*.[1] It is in three parts. The first part deals with the right of the King and private persons to the rivers and foreshore, the second with sea ports, and the third and longest with the customs duties upon goods imported and exported. It is the first systematic treatise upon all these topics; and Hale was especially well fitted to deal with them, by reason both of his mastery of records, and of his practical knowledge of the law upon these matters, which he had acquired as chief baron of the Exchequer. The third part of this treatise is especially interesting because the question of the King's imposing

[1] At pp. 1–248.

power had not long been settled. An impartial account
of this branch of the law, by a man who had lived during
the time when the right to impose customs duties had
been one of the most fiercely controverted political
questions of the day, is invaluable. In his short work on
"Sheriffs' Accounts", written for the Lord Treasurer
and the Chancellor of the Exchequer, he deals with
another branch of the revenue. It shows Hale's mastery
of the early history of the Exchequer, and of the history
of, and seventeenth-century practice as to, the financial
relations of the sheriffs and the Crown; and it contains
some valuable suggestions for improvements in the
existing practice. Another paper published in the
Hargrave *Law Tracts* deals with the rivalry of the courts
of King's Bench and Common Pleas.[1] It gives us an
interesting account of the process, organization, and
jurisdiction of the King's Bench, and of the devices used
by the Common Pleas to compete with the King's
Bench. All these treatises and tracts illustrate Hale's
wide historical and legal knowledge, and his political
wisdom.

Hale's most important work on the criminal law is his
unfinished *History of the Pleas of the Crown*. Hale had
designed a work in three books. The subject of the first
was to be capital offences—treasons and felonies; and it
was to be divided into two parts—the kinds of treasons
and felonies, and the method of procedure upon them.
The subject of the second was to be non-capital crimes;
and of the third, franchises and liberties. Only the first
book was completed. But it was left in the most perfect
state of any of his works. The whole had been tran-
scribed; and a large part of it had received the author's
final revision. In 1680 the House of Commons ordered
it to be printed; but the first edition was not published
till 1736. It was edited with great care by Sollom Emlyn.

[1] At pp. 359–376; cp. Holdsworth, *H.E.L.* i, 200, 221–222.

The subject had been carefully studied by Hale all through his professional career; and we shall see that he had summarized it at an earlier period. This book, so far as it extends, gives a complete presentment of this branch of the law, both in its development and in its condition at Hale's own time. It was a branch of the law which could not then be adequately described without a very complete knowledge of its history; and, partly because it contained very ancient ideas and rules, partly because it had been added to, and in many details modified, by very many statutes, it greatly needed systematic treatment. Coke, Staunford, and Pulton had summarized it in a somewhat unsystematic form. Hale, because he was a competent historian, jurist, and lawyer, did the work which they endeavoured to do infinitely better. Ever since its first publication it has been regarded as a book of the highest authority.

Hale wrote many other shorter books and tracts—an *Analysis of the Civil Part of the Law* which was said by Blackstone to be the most scientific and comprehensive that had yet appeared; a *Summary of the Pleas of the Crown* which was a first attempt to introduce some order into this branch of the law; notes upon Fitzherbert's *Natura Brevium* and upon Coke's *First Institute*. The only other one of his books which it is necessary to notice is his *History of the Common Law*. This, the first history of the common law ever written, is only a fragmentary sketch, and Hale did not mean it to be published. It consists of twelve chapters, the titles of which indicate the contents of the book, and illustrate its fragmentary character.[1]

---

[1] I. Concerning the distribution of the laws of England into Common and Statute law. And first, concerning the Statute law, or Acts of Parliament. II. Concerning the *Lex non Scripta*, i.e. the Common or Municipal Laws of this Kingdom. III. Concerning the Common Law of *England*, its use, excellence, and the reason of its denomination. IV. Touching the original of the Common Law of *England*. V. How

But, in spite of its fragmentary character, it has very considerable merits. It gives us a clear statement of the development of the most important external features of the common law—the difference between common and statute law; the relation of the common law to other bodies of law recognized by it, such as ecclesiastical law, the law merchant, maritime law, and martial law; the characteristics and advantages of trial by jury; the main features of the system of pleading recognized by the common law at different periods; the relations of English law to Welsh, Irish, and Scotch law, and to the law observed in the Channel Islands and the Isle of Man. The author throughout bases his text on the best authorities accessible to him. The fact that its weakest part is the pre-Conquest history is no fault of his. From the Conquest onwards he shows that he is a master of the principal original authorities and authors. In his chapters on Norman law, and in other parts of his book,[1] he shows acquaintance with foreign bodies of law; and a capacity to compare the development of English with foreign law, without which, as Maitland has said, no complete or critical legal history is possible. No doubt current controversies caused him to give an unduly large space to a question which, in our eyes, is a purely academic discussion—the question in what sense, if at

the Common Law of *England* stood at and for some time after the coming of King *William I.*   VI. Concerning the parity or similitude of the Laws of *England* and *Normandy*, and the reasons thereof.   VII. Concerning the progress of the Laws of *England* after the time of King *William I* until the time of King *Edward II.*   VIII. A brief continuation of the progress of the laws from the time of King *Edward II*, inclusive, down to these times.   IX. Concerning the settling of the Common Law of *England* in *Ireland* and *Wales* and some observations touching the Isles of *Mann*, *Jersey*, and *Guernsey*, etc.   X. Concerning the communication of the laws of *England* into the Kingdom of *Scotland.*   XI. Touching the course of descents in *England.*   XII. Touching trials by jury.

[1] E.g. at various points in Chaps. ix–xii.

all, William I could be said to be a conqueror.[1] Then too there is a very meagre account of the history of legal doctrine—the history of the law of inheritance is the only body of legal doctrine adequately treated; and the treatment of the period from Edward II to his own day is so sketchy that it is hardly even an outline. The book is really a series of essays, some of which are united to others by a chronological thread. But, when all deductions have been made, it is, in my opinion, the ablest introductory sketch of a history of English law that appeared till the publication of Pollock and Maitland's volumes in 1895.

Hale was the greatest common lawyer since Coke. Though his influence upon the history of English law has not been so great as that of Coke, he was, as a lawyer, Coke's superior. The position which they respectively occupy in our legal history is as different as their character and mental outlook. Coke, as we have seen, stands midway between the medieval and the modern law. Hale is the first of our great modern common lawyers. Coke was essentially a fighter both in the legal and political arena: when Hale was on the bench the legal contests about the jurisdiction of courts had been settled, and there was a lull in political strife. He was what Coke never was—a true historian; and, like Bacon, he had studied other things besides law, and other bodies of law besides the English common law. He possessed a judicial impartiality which Coke never possessed, even when he was dealing with matters of public law. This impartiality was not shown by any other lawyer of his day,

[1] Chap. v; Maitland, *Materials for English Legal History, Collected Works*, ii, 5, says, "Unfortunately he was induced to spend his strength upon problems which in his day could not permanently be solved, such as the relation of English to Norman law, and the vexed question of the Scottish homage; and just when one expects the book to become interesting, it finishes off with protracted panegyrics upon our law of inheritance and trial by jury."

or by the post-Revolution lawyers who, as a general rule, adopted without criticism the legal and historical views upon controverted points of public law which the Revolution had caused to prevail. It is not till almost our own day that appreciation of the historical value of the public records has enabled us to reach anything like the standard of knowledge which Hale applied to the elucidation of the public law of the seventeenth century; and that the cessation of the practical influence of seventeenth-century politics has enabled us to attain anything like his standard of impartiality. Hence, until quite modern times, it has been impossible to appreciate fully his true greatness as an historian and a lawyer.

HENEAGE FINCH, LORD NOTTINGHAM

Heneage Finch came of a famous legal family. He was born in 1621, and, during the Commonwealth, acquired a reputation as a lawyer and an orator. At the Restoration he was made solicitor-general, and, in that capacity, conducted the trials of the regicides. In 1670 he became attorney-general and in 1673 Lord Keeper. In 1675 he was made Lord Chancellor, and in 1681 Earl of Nottingham. He died in 1682. He was a royalist in politics. But, because he was a moderate royalist, he refused to be a party to obviously unconstitutional acts. He refused, for instance, to seal the pardon which Danby got to shelter himself from impeachment. In an age in which only too frequently the judges displayed on the bench the prejudices of the political party which they favoured, Nottingham brought into politics something of the impartiality which should characterize a judge. He was almost the only politician of the period who retained throughout his career the confidence of both King and Parliament.

As a lawyer, he was distinguished by the fact that his technical mastery of English law had in no wise narrowed his intellectual outlook. He was the patron and friend of learned and literary men of many different shades of political opinion;[1] and he took a conspicuous part in the promotion of some of the legislative reforms of the period —while solicitor-general he introduced the bill for the abolition of the military tenures;[2] and as Chancellor he drew and took a leading part in passing the statute of Frauds.[3] The breadth of his intellectual outlook made him not only an able lawyer and a distinguished judge, but also, if I may coin an expression, a legal statesman. He was a lawyer who had mastered the technical learning of the law without being mastered by it; and a statesman who was in close touch with the political conditions and the intellectual ideas of his age. Hence he was able so to mould the technical development of scattered and nebulous equitable rules and conceptions, that they gained a precise meaning and a definite place in our legal system; and so to fashion their contents, that they harmonized with those political conditions and intellectual ideas. He was always anxious that his decisions should be not only technically sound, but also that they should commend themselves to the common sense of laymen at home or abroad;[4] and that, on questions of public law, they should harmonize with existing political conditions. It is because he was so keenly sensible to the necessity of thus harmonizing legal rules with the public opinion of the day, that, in so many of his decisions, familiar rules of modern private law take for the first time their modern shape; and this characteristic can also be illustrated from

---

[1] Foss, *Lives of the Judges*, vii, 96–97; Burnet, *History of the Reformation*, ii, Pref. p. 4, acknowledges assistance both pecuniary and literary.

[2] *D.N.B.*   [3] Holdsworth, *H.E.L.* vi, 380–384.

[4] Thus, even in considering such a question as the construction of a devise, he has an eye to the opinion of the laymen—"this kind of rigorous construction is against natural and universal justice, and would be laughed at in any other part of the world", *Nurse* v. *Yerworth* (1674) 3 Swanst. at p. 620.

some of his rulings upon points of international or constitutional law, which came before him as Chancellor. Thus, the rules which he laid down as to the effect to be given by English courts to a foreign judgment, and as to the recognition which these courts should give to rights conferred by foreign law,[1] contain the germs of some of the principles of our modern private international law. Similarly, he was one of the first, if not the first, of English lawyers to recognize clearly the distinction between the rights given to a state by treaty, which fall wholly outside the sphere of municipal law and municipal courts, and the rights conferred upon individuals by municipal law, with which municipal courts can deal.[2]

Nottingham's decisions show that he had all the qualities of a great judge. His analyses of complicated facts are masterly, both for their minuteness, and for the clearness with which the results of his analyses are stated.[3] He can enunciate a principle, and reason from it closely and logically; and this power enables him to distinguish between different principles, and to define the spheres of their application. Two very good illustrations of these qualities are to be found in the *Duke of Norfolk's Case*,[4] and the case of *Cook* v. *Fountain*.[5] In the first case he settled the true principle which should govern the law against remoteness of limitation; and this enabled him to enunciate a rule which not only settled what limitations

---

[1] "It is against the law of nations not to give credit to the judgment and sentences of foreign countries, till they be reversed by the law, and according to the form, of those countries wherever they were given. For what right hath one kingdom to reverse the judgment of another? And how can we refuse to let a sentence take place till it be reversed? And what confusion would follow in Christendom, if they should serve us so abroad, and give no credit to our sentences", 2 Swanst. at p. 326.

[2] *Blad* v. *Bamfield* (1674) 3 Swanst. 605.

[3] See e.g. *Salsbury* v. *Bagott* (1677) 2 Swanst. 603; *Cook* v. *Fountain* (1672) 3 Swanst. 586.

[4] *Howard* v. *Duke of Norfolk* (1681) 2 Swanst. 454.

[5] (1672) 3 Swanst. 586.

were illegal because they infringed the rule, but also what limitations were permissible. In the second case he analysed the various kinds of trust; and his statement of the conditions under which the court should permit the existence of constructive trusts is in substance that adopted by our modern law. These powers enabled him to deal successfully with cases which involved the consideration of the limits of equitable interference with legal rules. A good illustration will be found in the case of *Nurse* v. *Yerworth*,[1] in which he considers the manner in which equity should treat the legal doctrine of merger, and regulate the use of attendant terms.

These and many other of his decisions were beginning to settle the doctrines of equity. This settlement of equitable doctrine modified the character of equity itself, and placed it and its relation to the common law upon its modern basis.

Throughout the seventeenth century, and especially since the Restoration, equity had been developing into a regular system. But the process had been proceeding so silently that lawyers still sometimes spoke of equity as if it depended on the conscience of the Chancellor, in the same way as it depended upon his conscience in the earlier part of the sixteenth century. And to some extent it still did depend on his conscience. Lord Nottingham, differing in the *Duke of Norfolk's Case* from the opinions of some of the judges, could say, "I must be saved by my own faith, and must not decree against my own conscience and reason";[2] and that case showed that the elasticity still retained by equity, in consequence of the survival of the older idea, sometimes gave a great Chancellor larger opportunities of moulding the rules of his court to meet modern needs than were open to the common law judges. In Hale's opinion a

---

[1] (1674) 3 Swanst. 608.
[2] The *Duke of Norfolk's Case* (1681) 3 Ch. Cases at p. 47.

much slighter technical equipment fitted a man to practise in the Chancery than was necessary to enable him
to practise in the common law courts.[1] But the con-
ventional language used about equity was becoming
more and more untrue. Lord Nottingham said of Hale
that,

> He did look upon equity as a part of the common law, and one
> of the grounds of it; and therefore as near as he could, he did
> always reduce it to certain rules and principles, that men might
> study it as a science, and not think the administration of it had
> anything arbitrary in it.[2]

And he himself laid it down that,

> With such a conscience as is only *naturalis et interna*, this
> Court has nothing to do; the conscience by which I am to
> proceed is merely *civilis et politica*, and tied to certain measures;
> and it is infinitely better for the public that a trust security or
> agreement, which is wholly secret, should miscarry, than that
> men should lose their estates by the mere fancy and imagination
> of a Chancellor.[3]

This change in the character of equity is partly the
cause and partly the effect of a change in the relations of
law and equity. It had become clear that law and equity
must recognize the fact that they were not rival but
complementary systems, and that, consequently, common lawyers and equity lawyers must work together in
partnership, as, for the most part, they had done before
the dispute between Coke and Ellesmere.[4] This development was made the easier by the fact that many Chancellors had served as chief justices in the common law

---

[1] Runnington in his *Life of Hale* (prefixed to Hale's *History of the
Common Law*, p. x) tells us that Hale is reported to have said, "A little
law, a good tongue, and a good memory, would fit a man for the
Chancery."

[2] Burnet, *Life and Death of Sir Matthew Hale*, 176.

[3] *Cook* v. *Fountain* (1672) 3 Swanst. at p. 600.

[4] Above, pp. 97, 98.

courts, and by the fact that there was no hard and fast separation between the common law and equity bars. Therefore the ideas and modes of thought of the common lawyers were becoming ever more in evidence in the court of Chancery. Both common law and equity were becoming settled systems; and when, at the close of the century, equity accepted the common law view of the binding force of precedents, and reports of equity cases began to appear in increasing numbers, its systematization proceeded apace. Since it was now being developed by a method similar to that of the common law, a new and important link between the two systems was added.

Nottingham takes his place as the equal of his two great predecessors Ellesmere and Bacon. His work was different from, and yet a continuation of, theirs. They had organized and systematized the court of Chancery, its practice, and its procedure. He began the work of organizing and systematizing the principles upon which the court acted; and, as a result of his work, equity began to assume its final form. His success was due partly to his own industry and genius, and partly to the fact that the time was ripe for the beginning of such a settlement. The man and the opportunity happily coincided; and so, whether we look at his influence upon the principles of equity, or upon the character of equity itself, we must admit that he deserves his traditional title of "the Father of Modern Equity".

My next two lectures will show how two great common law judges and two great Lord Chancellors completed the work, begun by Hale and Nottingham, of modernizing law and equity and of settling the relations between them.

Lecture VIII

HOLT AND MANSFIELD

THE violence of the political controversies which marked the close of Charles II's and the whole of James II's reigns had a disastrous effect upon the bench, and, consequently, retarded the development of English law. Such chief justices as Scroggs and Jeffreys lowered the tone of the bench; and the political reasons which led to their appointment lowered it still further, because it involved the dismissal of many other judges. Those who took their places were notoriously incompetent, and some were men of no character. Jeffreys, in spite of Lord Keeper Guildford's opposition, got Charles II to make Robert Wright a judge, although he was not only an incompetent lawyer, but a man of immoral life and guilty of fraud and perjury.[1] James II's determination to get twelve judges of his mind lowered still further the quality of the bench. The least opposition to his wishes was the signal for dismissal. The effect upon the bench was described by the Marquis of Halifax in his *Character of a Trimmer*.[2] He says:[3]

The authority of a King, who is head of the law, as well as the dignity of public justice, is debased when the clear stream of law is puddled and disturbed by bunglers, or conveyed by unclean instruments to the people. Our Trimmer would have them appear in their full lustre, and would be grieved to see the day when, instead of their speaking with authority from the seats of justice, they should speak out of a grate with a lamenting voice, like prisoners that desire to be rescued. He wisheth that the Bench may ever have a natural as well as a legal superiority to

[1] *Lives of the Norths*, i, 324–327.
[2] Printed by Foxcroft, *Life and Works of Halifax*, ii, 280–342.
[3] At pp. 285–286.

the Bar; he thinketh men's abilities very much misplaced when
the reason of him that pleads is visibly too strong for those who
are to judge and give sentence.... If ever such an unnatural
method should be introduced, it is then that Westminster Hall
might be said to stand upon its head.

That Westminster Hall was indeed standing "upon its
head" is illustrated by the list of the counsel who
appeared for the Seven Bishops. They included the late
chief justice Pemberton, the late judge Levinz, the late
attorney-general Sir Robert Sawyer, the late solicitor-
general Heneage Finch (Lord Nottingham's son),
Pollexfen (William III's first chief justice of the Common Pleas), Sir George Treby (Pollexfen's successor), and
the future Lord Chancellor Somers. It did not include
Sir John Holt, the future chief justice of the King's
Bench, but only because he was one of the King's
serjeants, and so could not appear against the Crown.

The Revolution rescued the bench from this deplor-
able position, and so made possible the resumption of
that work of modernizing the law, and adapting it to a
changing society, which had been begun by Hale and
Nottingham in the earlier years of Charles II's reign.

From the beginning of William III's reign the judges
ceased to be appointed "durante bene placito"; and the
Act of Settlement gave statutory stability to their tenure
of office. From the point of view both of our constitutional and of our legal history, this new independence of
the bench was one of the most important results of the
Revolution. From the point of view of constitutional
history its effect has been to establish finally that rule of
law for which Coke had contended. Though the judges
still attended at Whitehall to receive instructions as to
the conduct of business on circuit, it was now wholly
impossible for the government to use them, as they had
been used in the seventeenth century, to support the
legality of government measures. From the point of view

of legal history its effect has been to guarantee an orderly development of the law free from all governmental interference, and to raise the tone of the legal profession. From henceforth, as Foss puts it,[1] "the judges succeeded each other in quiet independence, scarcely ever leaving the seats they occupied till incapacitated by infirmity or removed by death".

Of all William III's judges the most eminent was Sir John Holt. His work at the end of the seventeenth and the beginning of the eighteenth centuries, and Lord Mansfield's work in the second half of the eighteenth century, not only put the common law on its modern basis, but fitted it to deal with the problems arising from the vast economic, social, and political changes which, at the end of the eighteenth and the beginning of the nineteenth centuries, came with the Industrial Revolution, with the ideas propagated by the French Revolution, and with the ideas propagated by Bentham.

SIR JOHN HOLT

Holt[2] was born in 1642. He was called to the bar in 1663, and at the latter part of Charles II's reign he had acquired a large practice. He appeared for the Crown in some of the state trials of the period; but at the end of the reign he was more generally retained for the defence. He was a Whig—but a Whig of such moderate views that he was knighted by James II in 1686 and made recorder of London and King's serjeant. He was dismissed from his recordership because he refused to take the view that a soldier convicted of desertion was guilty of felony. In 1689 he was made chief justice of the King's Bench. He was offered and refused the office of

---

[1] *Lives of the Judges*, vii, 291.
[2] *Ibid.* vii, 386–395; *D.N.B.*; Campbell, *Lives of the Chief Justices*, ii, 118–178; Holdsworth, *H.E.L.* vi, 516–522.

Lord Chancellor in 1700. His office of chief justice was renewed by Anne, and he held it till his death in 1710.

The Revolution had created a new set of political conditions; and expanding trade was creating a new set of commercial conditions. Under these circumstances, the common law had need of a judge, who was sufficiently conversant with modern needs and modern thought to appreciate the nature of the problems demanding solution; who had sufficient statesmanship to see the best solutions; who was a sufficiently good lawyer to put those solutions into a form which harmonized with the principles and technical rules of the common law. Holt satisfied all these needs. He was a learned common lawyer; but he fully appreciated the modern political and commercial conditions under which he administered justice. Consequently he used his legal learning so to develop the rules of the common law that they could do substantial justice under these new conditions. He carried on Hale's work of making and developing the modern common law.

His greatest work was done in the three departments of constitutional law, criminal law, and commercial law.

(1) *Constitutional Law.*

Many of the most fundamental of the modern rules of constitutional law depend on cases decided after the Revolution; and in Holt's decisions we can see the original authorities for some of them. But since the outstanding constitutional question of the day—the relations of King and Parliament—had only just been settled, we cannot expect that all the consequences of that settlement would at once be appreciated. Consequently, though Holt's decisions in many cases lay down the modern rules, in some cases they have been overruled either by the Legislature or by the decisions of his successors.

Some of Holt's decisions upon the following five topics of constitutional law rank as leading cases: the remedies open to the subject against the Crown or its servants for wrongs committed against him; the relation of privilege of Parliament to the law; the right to personal liberty; the right to freedom of discussion; colonial constitutional law.

(i) *The remedies open to the subject against the Crown or its servants for wrongs committed against him.* In the *Bankers' Case*[1] Holt and the House of Lords decided that the subject can sue the Crown by petition of right for breach of contract. This decision is very important because it took a long step towards adapting the medieval remedy of the petition of right to modern needs. In the case of *Lane* v. *Cotton*[2] Holt, differing from his brethren, held that the head of a government department—the Postmaster-General—was liable for the misdeeds of one of his subordinates. In this case Holt's views have not been upheld.[3] As the other judges pointed out, the doctrine of employer's liability cannot be applied in such a case both for technical reasons and on grounds of public policy. For technical reasons, because such employees are servants, not of the head of the department, but of the Crown; and on grounds of public policy, because it would be unfair to make the head of a department liable to satisfy such claims. Holt thought that the Postmaster-General was in the same position as sheriffs or gaolers who were liable for the misdeeds of their subordinates, and also that, since he exercised a public calling like that of a carrier, he ought, like the carrier, to be liable for any failure in the performance of his duties. His reasoning

---

[1] (1700) 14 S.T. at pp. 32–39; for the importance of this case in the history of the remedy of the petition of right see Holdsworth, *H.E.L.* ix, 32–39.

[2] (1701) 1 Ld. Raym. 646.

[3] *Whitfield* v. *Lord le Despencer* (1778) 2 Cowp. 754; *Bainbridge* v. *Postmaster-General* [1906] 1 K.B. 178.

is an instance of a strain of legal conservatism which characterizes some of his other decisions and dicta.

(ii) *The relation of privilege of Parliament to the law*. This was a much controverted question upon which the courts and Parliament had been disputing for the greater part of the century. Holt laid down the modern law in three cases—*R.* v. *Knollys*,[1] *Ashby* v. *White*,[2] and *Paty's Case*.[3] In the first of these cases he held that the House of Lords could not extend its privileges at its will, and in the two other cases he negatived a similar claim by the House of Commons. In substance those cases decide that if the point at issue is the existence of a privilege, the court must decide it as a matter of law, for privilege of Parliament is part of the law; and that a resolution of the House must be disregarded, since a resolution of the House cannot change the law. This view of the law was dissented from by the other judges in the two last-named cases. But it was upheld by the House of Lords in *Ashby* v. *White*, and it was followed in 1839 in the case of *Stockdale* v. *Hansard*.[4] On the other hand, if the existence of the privilege is not in dispute, but only the mode of its exercise, the courts cannot interfere, because on this matter the House is the sole judge.[5]

(iii) *The right to personal liberty*. Holt in several cases[6] anticipated Lord Mansfield's decision in *Sommersett's Case*,[7] and held that slavery is not a status recognized by the law of England. In one case he said that "by the common law no man can have a property in another";[8] and in another case he said that "as soon as a negro comes to England he is free; one may be a villein in England

---

[1] (1695) 1 Ld. Raym. 10.   [2] (1704) 2 Ld. Raym. 938.

[3] (1705) 2 Ld. Raym. 1105.   [4] 9 Ad. and E. 1.

[5] *Case of the Sheriff of Middlesex* (1840) 11 Ad. and E. 273; *Bradlaugh* v. *Gosset* (1884) 12 Q.B.D. 271.

[6] *Chamberlain* v. *Harvey* (1698) 1 Ld. Raym. 146; *Smith* v. *Browne* (1701) Holt K.B. 495; *Smith* v. *Gould* (1707) 2 Ld. Raym. 1274.

[7] (1771) 20 S.T. 1.   [8] 2 Ld. Raym. 1274.

but not a slave".[1] On the other hand he thought that a member of the Privy Council could commit to prison on any charge[2]—a decision overruled by Lord Camden who held that this power was confined to the case of high treason.[3]

(iv) *The right to freedom of discussion.* As yet the law on this topic was not settled on its modern basis. The refusal of Parliament to renew the Licensing Act in 1694 had left the extent of the right to freedom of discussion to be determined by the common law. By the rules of the common law discussion was free, except in so far as it was restrained by the law of libel as administered by the common law courts. But the common law courts had inherited their law of libel from the Star Chamber. The Star Chamber regarded any criticism of the government as libellous, because the government, being the superior of the subject, must be treated with respect; and this idea continued to prevail throughout the seventeenth century. It is for this reason that Holt laid it down, in *R. v. Tutchin,*[4] that any criticism of the government amounted to a seditious libel. There are many precedents which show that this ruling was good law in Holt's day. But the idea upon which it was founded gradually became obsolete in the course of the eighteenth century, because, as the result of the new political conceptions which the Revolution had introduced, there was a fundamental change in men's ideas as to the relations of rulers to their subjects. The government, instead of being regarded as the superior of the subject, was regarded as his agent or servant, so that criticism of it was not only legitimate but laudable.

(v) *Colonial constitutional law.* The growth of Eng-

---

[1] Holt K.B. 495.
[2] *R. v. Kendal and Row* (1696) 1 Ld. Raym. 65.
[3] *Entick* v. *Carrington* (1765) 19 S.T. 1030.
[4] (1704) 14 S.T. 1095.

land's colonies raised some fundamental questions as to the position of English subjects residing in these colonies. What was their position as against the Crown? Could they claim all the rights which English subjects had in England? In the case of *Blankard* v. *Galdy*[1] Holt answered this question by distinguishing settled from conquered colonies. In the former "all laws in force in England are in force there": in the latter, "the laws of England do not take place there until declared by the conqueror". If an infidel country is conquered, "their laws by conquest do not entirely cease, but only such as are against the law of God; and that in such cases, where the laws are rejected or silent, the conquered country shall be governed according to the rule of natural equity". Holt, thus, in substance anticipated Lord Mansfield's more famous judgment in the case of *Campbell* v. *Hall*.[2]

(2) *Criminal Law*.

Holt introduced the modern attitude of the judge to the criminal. His predecessors had sometimes defended the rule which denied the help of counsel to prisoners accused of treason or felony, by saying that the judge was counsel for the prisoner. Holt was the first judge to put this theory into practice. He allowed and even invited interruption if the prisoner thought that he was not stating his case fairly;[3] and he stopped the practice of keeping prisoners in irons during their trial.[4] It was this revolution which he effected in the conduct of criminal trials which most impressed the public. Steele wrote of him in *The Tatler*:[5]

Wherever he was judge, he never forgot that he was also counsel. The criminal before him was always sure he stood before

[1] (1694) 2 Salk. 411.   [2] (1774) 20 S.T. 239.
[3] Campbell, *Lives of the Chief Justices*, ii, 143, 145.
[4] *Trial of Cranburne* (1696) 13 S.T. 222.
[5] No. 14 (May 12, 1709).

his country, and, in a sort, the parent of it. The prisoner knew, that though his spirit was broken with guilt, and incapable of language to defend itself, all would be gathered from him which could conduce to his safety; and that his judge would wrest no law to destroy him, nor conceal any that could save him.

(3) *Commercial Law.*

In the sixteenth century it looked as if the court of Admiralty would be the tribunal through which the commercial law of England would be developed. But Coke's successful attack on the court of Admiralty, and the constitutional results of the Great Rebellion, had crippled that court and had given the common law courts a large commercial jurisdiction,[1] with the result that commercial cases came with increasing frequency before them. Holt was the first judge to appreciate the modern conditions of trade, and the importance of moulding the doctrines of the common law to fit them. Instances of his work in thus developing the doctrines of the common law are his invention of the modern principle of the employer's liability for the torts of his employee;[2] his settlement of very many of the rules relating to negotiable instruments;[3] and his settlement in the case of *Coggs* v. *Bernard*[4] of the various forms of the contract of bailment. But Holt was not, like Mansfield, learned in those foreign systems of commercial law which, relatively, were more advanced than English law. In his work of developing English commercial law to fit it to meet modern needs he relied mainly on the evidence of the merchants. He was essentially a common lawyer, and he had many of the conservative instincts of a common lawyer. For instance, he was averse to extending the action of assumpsit in such a way that it could enforce quasi-contracts;[5] he once

---

[1] Above, pp. 125, 130; below, pp. 212, 220–221.
[2] Holdsworth, *H.E.L.* viii, 474–477.   [3] *Ibid.* viii, 161–170.
[4] (1704) 2 Ld. Raym. 909.   [5] Holdsworth, *H.E.L.* viii, 93–96.

described the archaic appeal of murder as "a noble remedy";[1] and he refused to admit the negotiability of promissory notes.[2] Holt's legal conservatism prevented him from developing commercial law as quickly as it might have been developed. But it is arguable that a slow development meant a more thorough incorporation of these new principles into the common law. No doubt to complete that settlement the cosmopolitan learning of a jurist like Mansfield was needed.[3] But the fact that a lawyer like Holt, who combined an appreciation of modern commercial conditions with an almost exclusive training in the common law, had begun that settlement, helped Mansfield at a later date to effect a much more thorough incorporation of the principles of commercial law with the common law than would otherwise have been possible.

LORD MANSFIELD

The development of the common law during the first half of the eighteenth century was slow. Its procedure was very technical; and its rules of pleading were tending to become more and more subtle and rigid. It was developing and expanding less rapidly than the parallel system of equity. But though the common law of this period has serious shortcomings, it ought not to be unreservedly condemned. Just as Walpole's policy of "quieta non movere" was of considerable service to the state in that it established firmly the Revolution settlement, so the routine work of the common law courts, though it did not develop the common law rapidly, was of considerable service to it. In the first place, this routine work established firmly the principles of that modern common law which had emerged in the earlier part of the seventeenth century, and had been developing

[1] *R. v. Toler* (1701) 1 Ld. Raym. at p. 557.
[2] Holdsworth, *H.E.L.* viii, 172–176.   [3] Below, pp. 162, 168.

since the Restoration and the Revolution. In the second place, it gave fixity and coherence to its principles.

But at the beginning of the second half of the eighteenth century there were signs of changes and developments in many directions. The colonies were developing, and industry and commerce were expanding. These developments and expansions were giving rise to new problems, which called for new developments in the law, and a new intellectual approach by the lawyers. It was fortunate for the common law that in 1756 the new chief justice of the King's Bench was a man who was not only the greatest lawyer of the century, but also a legal statesman, who was fully cognizant of the need to infuse new ideas into the administration and principles of the common law, if it was to remain adequate to solve the new problems to which changing commercial and industrial conditions were giving rise; and it was fortunate for the common law that he held office for almost thirty-two years. Lord Mansfield, because he was familiar with other systems of law besides English law, was able to apply to its principles a criticism which was at once learned and detached. His extensive practice had made him as great an equity as a common lawyer; and he was impressed with the capacity for expansion which equity was showing, and convinced of the need to import some of its principles into the common law. Because he was the chief justice of a court which exercised a wider jurisdiction than the other two common law courts, he was able to make his influence felt throughout the whole sphere of common law jurisdiction. Though, as we shall see, he failed to persuade his contemporaries and successors to adopt all his views as to the manner in which it was possible and desirable to develop certain of the branches of English law,[1] and notably his views as to the relations of law and equity,[2] he succeeded in putting the

[1] Below, pp. 167, 173–175.   [2] Below, p. 173.

commercial law of England on its modern basis; and, what was equally important, he succeeded in infusing a new spirit into the common law, substantive and adjective, the influence of which was felt outside his own court.

William Murray, the future Lord Mansfield,[1] was born at Scone in Scotland March 2, 1705. He left Scotland in 1718, and was educated at Westminster School and Christ Church, Oxford. He was called to the bar by Lincoln's Inn in 1730. In his student days he laid the foundations of his legal learning. He studied Roman law, international law, and Scottish law; and the study of Scottish law led him to study those French and Dutch authorities upon which the leading writers on that law relied. His rise at the bar was rapid. Nor is this surprising, for it is clear from his decisions as chief justice of the King's Bench that he had completely mastered the rules and principles of English law; and all his contemporaries agree that he was as eminent as an orator and an advocate as he was as a lawyer. In 1742 Murray became solicitor-general and a member of the House of Commons. In the House of Commons he was as successful as he had been in the courts. His only rival was the elder Pitt. In 1756 the death of Ryder, the chief justice of the King's Bench, enabled him to claim his reward for his services to the government. Though tempting offers were made to him if he would stay in the House and continue to defend the government, he refused them, and demanded and obtained the chief justiceship of the King's Bench and a peerage.

Mansfield remained a member of the government till 1763. He performed his greatest service to the state when, in 1757, he persuaded the King not to put Henry

---

[1] Fifoot, *Lord Mansfield*; Campbell, *Lives of the Chief Justices*, ii, 302–584; Foss, *Lives of the Judges*, viii, 335–348; Holliday, *Life of Lord Mansfield*; Holdsworth, *H.E.L.* xii, 464–560.

Fox at the head of the government, and so made it possible for Hardwicke to negotiate the famous coalition between Pitt and Newcastle which changed the course of European history. For many years he continued to be a leading member of the House of Lords. But as he grew older he devoted all his time and talents to his legal work in the King's Bench and the House of Lords. The value of that work was appreciated not only by English lawyers but by the lawyers of other countries. Blackstone tells us that his conduct of prize cases "was known and revered by every state in Europe";[1] and Park said, in his dedication to him of his book on Insurances, that his conduct of commercial cases had made his name "the boast of Britain and the admiration of Europe". He resigned his chief justiceship in 1788. On his resignation he retired to his house at Kenwood where he spent his remaining years, in full possession of all his faculties, improving his estate, reading the classics, and entertaining, with the social charm for which he was famous, his friends old and young. He died in 1793, and was buried in Westminster Abbey. The expense of his monument by Flaxman was defrayed by the legacy of a Mr Baillie—a grateful client for whom he had recovered a large estate.

The breadth of Mansfield's legal learning, and his perception of the changing economic conditions of the age, led him to be more acutely conscious than any other lawyer or statesman of his day of the deficiencies of the common law. At the same time he had all the common lawyer's traditional reverence for the common law, all his traditional belief in the need to maintain its supremacy, and, consequently, all his traditional consciousness of the sanctity and responsibility of the judicial office. Having this consciousness of the deficiencies of the common law, having the learning and the statesmanship to perceive the appropriate remedies, and holding this traditional

[1] *Commentaries*, iii, 70.

creed, it was natural that he should think that the best way of adapting the common law to the needs of a changing age was by means of the decisions of the courts; and it is not surprising that his attempt thus to adapt the common law to new needs should have had a large measure of success. His readiness to import new ideas was seconded by his skill in adapting them to the technical environment of the common law, and by an astonishing foresight of the future trends of legal thought. But it was also natural that, in seeking to accomplish this object, he should have sometimes disregarded settled principles, have gone beyond his authorities, and, in effect, have usurped the functions of the Legislature. That was a fault; but it was a fault on the right side; for it meant that his mind was directed to the task of fitting the common law to face the problems of the future. So successfully did he accomplish this task that he gave the common law a capacity to adapt itself to new conditions, which enabled it to cope successfully with the problems set by the age of reform which was opening at the end of the eighteenth century. Therefore, in order to understand the nature and extent of Mansfield's influence upon the future development of the common law, we must examine his work from these different points of view.

The views of the lawyers and statesmen of the eighteenth century as to the conditions under which developments of and reforms in the law should be made were very different from the views of the lawyers and statesmen of the nineteenth century. Bentham was as yet only a precocious youth, and the age of extensive law reforms effected by the Legislature on *a priori* principles was yet to come. On the other hand, a purely historical school of lawyers, who aimed at explaining, and sometimes at justifying, the apparently unreasonable rules of past ages had not yet arisen. These eighteenth-century lawyers and statesmen had some of the characteristics of both these schools. They had some affinities to reformers of the Benthamite persuasion in that, being firmly convinced of the superiority of their own to past ages, they were very ready to reform archaic and barbarous rules in the light of principles of natural reason and justice, upon the discovery of which they prided themselves. It is for this reason that they were ready to welcome the abolition or the reform of proved abuses and archaisms, provided that the fundamental principles of the law and the constitution were left untouched. "Blackstone, though an optimist, was not opposed to reasonable changes; Pitt, Burke, and Fox were all of them in different ways reformers."[1] They had some affinities to thinkers of the historical school, in that many of them, being conscious of the need to preserve the heritage of the past, insisted that the developments needed to meet new circumstances ought to be made, not by sweeping statutory changes, but by adaptations of, and small changes in, existing law as and when the need was proved. This was the attitude of Burke and Blackstone and Mansfield. All of them were opposed to large legislative changes in the law; all of them supported the legislative reform of proved abuses; and all of them were in favour of the adaptation of the law to the needs of the time by the judicial manipulation of old rules and principles to meet new circumstances.

Both Burke and Blackstone would have been prepared to go farther in the path of legislative reform than Mansfield. Mansfield, it is true, supported the abolition of the hereditary jurisdictions in the Highlands, Hardwicke's Marriage Act, the abolition of the right of the servants of peers to the protection of the privilege of Parliament, and the Act for the relief of the Roman Catholics. But, in general, he opposed legislative changes in the law. In one of his greatest speeches he opposed the

[1] Dicey, *Law and Opinion* (1st ed.), 123.

Habeas Corpus bill of 1758; and when he was solicitor-general he said, in his argument in the case of *Omychund* v. *Barker*, that "a statute can seldom take in all cases, therefore the common law that works itself pure by rules drawn from the fountain of justice is for this reason superior to an Act of Parliament".[1] But he was very ready—more ready than any of the great lawyers of his day—to reform the law and to adapt it to the needs of the time through the agency of the courts.

Mansfield had, in spite of many temptations to devote himself to a political career, remained faithful to the law. He had an immense reverence for the law, founded upon a thorough knowledge of all that its impartial and enlightened administration meant to the state and the individual. Therefore he had very high ideals as to the duty and conduct of a judge. In this respect, indeed, he was in line with the tradition of the common law from medieval to modern times. But that reverence for the law and those ideals as to the duty and conduct of a judge were never more eloquently expounded than in his famous judgment in which he reversed the outlawry of Wilkes.[2]

A man who held these views as to the conduct of a judge and the administration of justice, a man, who, at the same time, was fully conscious of the need to develop the law in accordance with the needs of his age, would be likely to think that the best way of effecting these developments was by means of the decisions of the courts. He always insisted that the cases must be interpreted in the light of principles; and he held that, though rules of law established by a series of cases could not be over-

[1] (1744) 1 Atk. at p. 33. This statement naturally roused the ire of Bentham, *Works*, vii, 311.
[2] (1768) 19 S.T. at pp. 1111–1114; "he leaned back in his chair", says Bowring, "and made the speech which won for him, at the time, so much applause and admiration", Bentham, *Works*, x, 45.

turned, the cases must if possible be so interpreted as to
bring them into conformity with those principles. Moreover, he held that if the rules established by the older
cases were based upon reasons which no longer applied
to modern conditions, those rules could and ought to be
disregarded. He acted on this principle in the case of
Taylor v. *Horde*, when he tried to prove that since the
terms seisin and disseisin, tenure, freehold, and feoffment had lost their old significance, the old reason for
allowing a feoffment to have a tortious operation had
ceased, so that it could not now have this operation.[1] He
acted on it in the case of *Perrin* v. *Blake* when he tried
to reduce the rule in *Shelley's Case* to the level of a rule of
construction.[2] He acted on it in the case of *Corbett* v.
Poelnitz when he held that a married woman, living
apart from her husband and having a separate maintenance, could be sued as a *feme-sole*.[3]

It was the application of these principles to many
branches of the common law, by a man who had a profound knowledge of its rules and principles, which
enabled Mansfield to develop English law, and to bring
it into harmony with modern conditions. By acting on
these principles, he effected great and salutary changes
in the practice of his court. He was always ready to
mould the rules of practice and pleading so as to save
litigants time and expense; and he was skilful in moulding
the fictions and conventions which governed the procedure of the courts, notably the fictions which centred
round the action of ejectment, so as to produce substantial justice. He helped to develop the law of evidence
on rational lines. Some of his decisions on points of
constitutional law, and notably colonial constitutional
law, lay down the basic principles of our modern law.

[1] (1757) 1 Burr. at pp. 107–108, 113–114; cp. Holdsworth, *H.E.L.*
vii, 43–44.
[2] (1770) Collect. Jurid. i, 283–322.   [3] (1785) 1 T.R. 5.

His decisions on many questions relating to the criminal law, the land law, contract, and tort helped to develop or to give precision to existing rules. But the most notable of all his services to English law was his settlement of the main principles of our modern system of commercial and maritime law. It was this last achievement which was his most important contribution to the development of the law. Buller J.'s well-known appreciation of it[1] has been indorsed by Campbell[2] and Foss,[3] and by all who have studied the history of mercantile law. Mansfield was able to do this great work more skilfully than it could have been done by any of his contemporaries because he had mastered the learning of the continental lawyers. It is for this reason that he was able, in the first place, to survey critically the decisions of his predecessors; and, in the second place, to follow to a larger extent and with greater knowledge than his predecessors the policy of adapting continental rules to an English environment. For these reasons he was able to base his decisions on a solid background of principles which were acceptable both to English and to continental lawyers.

[1] "We find in *Snee* v. *Prescott* [(1743) 1 Atk. 245] that Lord Hardwicke himself was proceeding with great caution, not establishing any general principle, but decreeing on all the circumstances of the case put together. Before that period we find that in courts of law all the evidence in mercantile cases was thrown together; they were left generally to a jury, and they produced no established principle. From that time we all know the great study has been to find some certain general principles, which shall be known to all mankind, not only to rule the particular case then under consideration but to serve as a guide to the future. Most of us have heard these principles stated, reasoned upon, enlarged, and explained, till we have been lost in admiration at the strength and stretch of the human understanding. And I should be very sorry to find myself under a necessity of differing from any case on this subject which has been decided by Lord Mansfield, who may be truly said to be the founder of the commercial law of this country", *Lickbarrow* v. *Mason* (1787) 2 T.R. at p. 73.

[2] *Lives of the Chief Justices*, ii, 403–405.

[3] *Lives of the Judges*, viii, 342.

It was Mansfield's readiness to reform and develop many branches of English law by these methods which won the praise of three such diverse characters as Burke, Charles Butler, and the youthful Bentham. Burke, alluding to his argument in the case of *Omychund* v. *Barker*, said:[1]

His ideas go to the growing melioration of the law, by making its liberality keep pace with the demands of justice, and the actual concerns of the world; not restricting the infinitely diversified occasions of men, and the rules of natural justice, within artificial circumscriptions, but conforming our jurisprudence to the growth of our commerce and of our empire.

Charles Butler said:[2]

Considering his decisions collectively they will be found to form a unique code of jurisprudence on some of the most important branches of our law; a system founded on principles equally liberal and just, admirably suited to the genius and circumstances of his age, and happily blending the venerable doctrines of the old law with the learning and requirement of modern times.

Bentham tells us that:[3]

From the first morning on which I took my seat on one of the hired boards, that slid from under the officers' seats in the area of the King's Bench...at the head of the gods of my idolatry, had sitten the Lord Chief Justice.... Days and weeks together have I made my morning pilgrimage to the chief seat of the living idol.

So impressed was he that he began a poem to him which never got farther than the first two lines:

> Hail noble Mansfield! chief among the just,
> The bad man's terror, and the good man's trust.[4]

---

[1] Report of a Committee to inspect the Lords' Journals relative to the impeachment of Warren Hastings, *Works* (Bohn's ed.), vi, 481.

[2] *Reminiscences*, i, 130–131.

[3] *Works*, i, 247. [4] *Ibid.* x, 46.

It was because Mansfield was learned in other systems of law besides the common law, that he was able by his decisions to develop and modernize many of the rules and principles of the common law. His knowledge of other systems of law helped him to come to right conclusions as to the correct legal principle to apply to the case before him; and his knowledge of English law helped him to give to that legal principle a technical form which was in accordance with authority. Where authority was scanty or conflicting it was not difficult to do this: where the ground was more completely covered by authority it was more difficult. But it is not always easy to draw the line between these two classes of cases. It is not always easy to distinguish between cases where authority is so scanty and conflicting that the judge's opinion as to what is the ideally correct rule can have full scope, and cases where authority is so abundant and uniform that it must be followed, although it is contrary to the judge's own opinion. Mansfield was aware of this difficulty—"My dear Garrick," he once said, "a judge on the bench is now and then in your whimsical situation between tragedy and comedy; inclination drawing one way, and a long string of precedents the other."[1] He wished to decide cases upon ideally right principles, but he recognized that established rules ought not to be overturned. As we might expect, he did not always succeed in balancing these conflicting ideals. His knowledge of other bodies of law outside the common law, his knowledge of the history of and authorities for the common law, and his view that it was possible to disregard old rules if the reason for them had ceased, made it the more difficult for him to strike this balance. It is not therefore surprising that in several instances he gave decisions which were based on principles which he considered, not unjustly, to be right and reasonable, although

[1] Holliday, *Life of Lord Mansfield,* 211.

the weight of authority was in favour of an opposite conclusion. His knowledge of other bodies of law outside the common law enabled him to come to a conclusion as to the right and reasonable principle. His knowledge of the history of and authorities for the common law enabled him so to explain the cases that he was able to satisfy himself that they were not inconsistent with this principle. His view that old rules, the reason for which had ceased, could be disregarded, enabled him to dismiss as worthless the authority upon which those rules rested.

It will I think be found that in these instances he discovered what he considered to be the right and reasonable principle in two bodies of law of which he was a master —Scottish law and the principles of equity.

Mansfield was a learned Scottish lawyer. His earliest practice had been in Scottish appeals to the House of Lords; and in later life his knowledge of Scottish law had been matured by his experience in hearing these appeals in the House of Lords. The fact that he was a learned Scottish lawyer affected his mind in two ways. In the first place, it made him familiar with the sometimes more reasonable rules of Scottish law. In the second place, it helped to give him that distinctive Scottish outlook upon law—that outlook which led Scottish lawyers to look, as Lord Macmillan has pointed out, not for the appropriate writ, but for the appropriate legal principle, which led them to build up their system by logical and deductive methods, and not by the empirical inductive English method of decided cases.[1] Mansfield always attempted to find the principle appropriate to the decision of the case before him, and he considered that attention should be paid, not so much to the actual decision in any given case, as to the principle underlying that decision. To a man with this mental outlook it was tempting sometimes to disregard cases which laid down principles which

[1] *L.Q.R.* xlviii, 482.

appeared to him to be unreasonable, and sometimes to wrest the meaning of cases so as to justify the establishment of reasonable principles. Thus, he found in Scottish law a theory of contract which he considered very much more reasonable than the English theory based on consideration. In the case of *Pillans* v. *Van Mierop*[1] he disregarded the English decisions, and put forward a theory of contract which was in substance identical with the theory of Scottish law; and in other cases he wrested the meaning of the cases to justify his view that a moral obligation was a sufficient consideration. In the case of *Taylor* v. *Horde*[2] he gave a definition of seisin and disseisin which had affinities to the doctrines of Scottish law, but which was demonstrably not English law.

Mansfield was also a learned equity lawyer. While he was a law officer of the Crown he had had the leading practice in the court of Chancery. We shall see that during the greater part of the eighteenth century the question of the relations of law and equity to one another was an open question.[3] Most lawyers thought with Hardwicke that law and equity must be kept distinct and separate, and that the courts of law and the court of Chancery, though they must work in partnership, must work each on their separate lines. On the other hand, Mansfield and a few other lawyers thought that it would conduce to the ease of litigants if this separation could as far as possible be broken down, and some sort of fusion between the principles of law and equity could thereby be effected. Here again he was probably influenced to some extent by Scottish law, where law and equity were administered in the same tribunals. In fact the question whether the English system of separate tribunals, or the Scottish system of identical tribunals, was the better, had been the subject of a correspondence between Hardwicke

[1] (1765) 3 Burr. 1663.   [2] (1757) 1 Burr. 60; above, p. 167.
[3] Below, pp. 201–208.

and Kames,[1] of which Mansfield was probably not un-
aware. Mansfield stated his view on this question in the
case of *Burgess* v. *Wheate*,[2] in which the line of division
between the two schools of thought on this matter was
clearly marked; and he tried to give effect to it, not only
in his treatment of quasi-contract, but also in several
cases in which he recognized and gave effect to equitable
rights.[3] It was these decisions which gave some point to
the invective of Junius, and led his successors Kenyon
and Eldon to depreciate his services to English law. In
fact, there is no doubt that in these cases Mansfield went
beyond the province of the judge and usurped the province of the Legislature. On this matter Bentham, who
was, when a young man, an admirer of Mansfield,[4] spoke
truly when, in his *Comment on the Commentaries*, he said:[5]

> Should there be a judge who, enlightened by genius, stimu-
> lated by honest zeal to the work of reformation, sick of the
> caprice, the delays, the prejudices, the ignorance, the malice, the
> fickleness, the suspicious ingratitude of popular assemblies, should
> seek with his sole hand to expunge the effusions of traditionary
> imbecility, and write down in their room the dictates of pure and
> native justice, let him but reflect that partial amendment is
> bought at the expense of universal certainty; that partial good
> thus purchased is universal evil; and that amendment from the
> judgment seat is confusion.

There is no doubt that Mansfield laid himself open to
this sound criticism. But, in estimating his services to

---

[1] Below, pp. 200–201.   [2] (1757–9) 1 Eden, at pp. 215–239.
[3] *Atkins* v. *Hill* (1775) 1 Cowp. 284; *Weakly* v. *Bucknell* (1776)
1 Cowp. 473; *Eaton* v. *Jaques* (1780) 2 Dougl. 455; *Hawkes* v. *Sanders*
(1782) 1 Cowp. 289.
[4] Above, p. 169.
[5] At p. 214. This work, from which the *Fragment on Government*
was detached and separately published by Bentham, has been edited by
C. W. Everett. Bentham does not refer to Mansfield by name, but I
think Mr Everett is clearly right in thinking that Bentham had Mansfield
in mind when he wrote this passage.

English law, we should not allow too great a weight to this one defect in his conduct as a judge. Let us remember, in the first place, that the decisions open to this criticism are few in number by comparison with the large number of decisions in which he succeeded, with universal approval, in modernizing and developing English law. In the second place, let us remember that the reasonableness of the principles underlying some of his heresies has been endorsed by the Legislature in the nineteenth and twentieth centuries and by later generations of lawyers—feoffments have ceased to have a tortious operation,[1] the rule in *Shelley's Case* has been abolished,[2] and many lawyers prefer the theory of contract which he outlined in *Pillans* v. *Van Mierop* to the theory of modern English law.[3] In the third place, let us remember that though he failed, and fortunately failed, to effect a fusion between the principles of law and equity, he did succeed in introducing certain equitable principles into the common law. Three important principles which he or his fellow judges helped to introduce into the common law are the doctrine of estoppel by conduct,[4] the doctrine of stoppage *in transitu*,[5] and the rule that there is no right of stoppage *in transitu* against the assignee of the consignee.[6] So too some of the limitations upon the generality of the principle *in pari delicto potior est conditio defendentis*, which were imported by Mansfield into the common law, were equitable in their origin.[7] In

[1] 8 and 9 Vict. c. 106, § 4.

[2] The Law of Property Act, 1925, 15 Geo. 5, c. 20, § 131.

[3] Holdsworth, *H.E.L.* viii, 46–48; cp. Lord Wright's paper in *Harv. Law Rev.* xlix, 1225–1253.

[4] Holdsworth, *H.E.L.* ix, 161–162.

[5] *Lickbarrow* v. *Mason* (1787) 2 T.R. at p. 75.

[6] *Lickbarrow* v. *Mason* (1793) 6 East at p. 36.

[7] *Smith* v. *Bromley* (1760) 2 Dougl. at p. 697; cp. *Bosanquet* v. *Dashwood* (1734) Cases T. Talbot 38 cited 2 Dougl. at p. 698; also *Ward* v. *Lant* (1701) Prec. in Chy. 182, and *Hastelow* v. *Jackson* (1828) 8 B. and C. at pp. 226–227 *per* Littledale J.

the fourth place, let us remember that though his attempt to extend the sphere of *indebitatus assumpsit* to remedy equitable and moral obligations failed,[1] his decisions helped to develop the law of quasi-contract; and that his familiarity with equitable principles helped him to create our modern system of commercial law. It was inevitable that Mansfield should have the defect of those unique and remarkable qualities which enabled him to perform such great and lasting services to the law and its administration.

English law has been fortunate in securing, at important turning-points in its history, great judges, who have so moulded its development that it has been made fit to solve the problems of a new age, without any appreciable sacrifice in the continuity of its principles. This continuity has been no small gain to the state and to the law. To the state, because it has helped to preserve the Englishman's traditional reverence for the law, which is a condition precedent to a law-abiding habit. To the law, because it has ensured a logical and scientific development of its principles, which is a condition precedent for the creation of a stable and permanent system. Just as Coke's decisions and books ensured the continuity of the development of the common law amidst all the great changes of the age of Renaissance, Reformation, and Reception of Roman law; so Mansfield's decisions ensured the continuity of its development amidst all the great changes produced by the Industrial Revolution, by the ideas propagated by the French Revolution, and by the ideas propagated by Bentham. The fact that English law was able to adapt its principles to the needs of the new age of reform, and yet remained a stable and steadying influence in the life of the nation, was due principally to Mansfield's work.

[1] See *Sinclair* v. *Brougham* [1914] A.C. at pp. 455–456 *per* Lord Sumner.

Lecture IX

HARDWICKE AND ELDON

DURING the period from the death of Lord Nottingham in 1682 to the appointment of Lord Hardwicke to the Lord Chancellorship in 1737 the principles and rules of equity were being rapidly developed. This development is summed up in Ballow's *Treatise of Equity*, which was published anonymously in 1737.[1] These principles and rules continued to be rapidly developed throughout the eighteenth century, and during the first three decades of the nineteenth century. But, because Ballow's *Treatise* comes at the end of the earlier part of this period of rapid development, we can see in his book both the connection between the later fixed principles and rules of equity and the original bases upon which equitable modifications of and additions to the law rested, and the manner in which these principles and rules were developed from isolated modifications of and additions to the law in particular cases on grounds of fairness and justice. Ballow's acquaintance with all the authorities ancient and modern, and his philosophical turn of mind, which led him to try and reduce to some principle the scattered and often nebulous principles and rules of equity, made him an admirable exponent of this phase of the development of equitable doctrine.

In the first place, Ballow bases the need for a system of equity on the reason stated by St Germain in *The Doctor*

---

[1] The book was published anonymously, but it is almost certain that Ballow, who held an office in the Exchequer, was its author, Holdsworth, *H.E.L.* xii, 191–192; for an account of the book and of Fonblanque's edition of it, see *ibid.* xii, 192–193.

and Student[1] and accepted by Ellesmere[2]—the unfairness
sometimes caused to particular persons in particular
cases by the generality of the rules of law. It followed
that, unless an unfairness of this kind could be proved,
equity must follow the law. Just as St Germain helped
to carry over this reason for the existence of equity from
the medieval period, when equity was administered by
ecclesiastical Chancellors, into the period when equity
was administered by laymen and English lawyers,[3] so
Ballow helped to carry it over into the period when
equity was rapidly becoming a definite system of fixed
principles and rules. In the second place, Ballow admits
that there are limitations upon the power of equity to
modify legal rules. It cannot interfere if the law has
specifically forbidden its interference;[4] and the manner
of its interference must be determined in many cases by
the practice of the court. As we have seen, Lord Nottingham had said that the conscience by which he must
be directed was not *naturalis et interna*, but *civilis et
politica*.[5] But, in the third place, because the development of a system of equity was as yet in an initial stage,
Ballow can still lay down some very loose doctrines which
were later repudiated—for instance he lays it down that
mere inadequacy of price is a ground for rescinding a
contract[6]; and it is clear that as yet many of the doctrines
of equity are more flexible and less fixed than they afterwards became. In fact some of the early decisions of the
Chancellors are like some of the dicta to be found in the
Year Books. They contain the germs of modern principles and rules, but they also contain rulings which have
been rejected by modern lawyers.

This wide and flexible jurisdiction was being used by

---

[1] Above, p. 96.
[2] *Earl of Oxford's Case* (1616) 1 Ch. Rep. at p. 6.
[3] Above, pp. 94, 96–97.   [4] Treatise 3.   [5] Above, p. 149.
[6] Treatise 11; cp. Holdsworth, *H.E.L.* xii, 229.

the court all through this period to enforce high standards of fairness; and as yet the court was very free to use
it to strike at courses of conduct of which it disapproved,
or to adjust the equities arising out of the often complicated states of fact which were brought before it. But
it was inevitable that the exercise of this wide and flexible
jurisdiction should give rise to definite bodies of equitable
doctrine upon certain types of these cases. As yet this
process has not gone far; but some of the cases indicate
some of the lines which it will pursue. Thus it is clear that
the determination of the court not to allow even a statute
to be made an instrument of fraud will give rise to the
equitable rules as to secret trusts; and that the interference of the court to prevent equitable waste will
modify the position of the tenants for life without impeachment of waste. The rules laid down by the court as
to the remedies which it will give against fraudulent
dealings by infants will add to the law a gloss which will
make this branch of the law complex and uncertain.[1] Its
interference to prevent "catching bargains" with heirs
and reversioners will make the rules on this point a very
distinct branch of equity. Its interference to prevent
undue influence had already added a much needed supplement to the common law rules as to duress; and in the
distinction which it was drawing between cases where it
would and where it would not presume this influence,[2]
and between the different considerations which it would
apply to deeds and wills alleged to have been obtained by
this influence,[3] we can see some of the outlines of the
modern law.

[1] See Lord Sumner's judgment in *Leslie* v. *Sheill* [1914] 3 K.B. at
613–618.
[2] *Manners* v. *Banning* (1709) 2 Eq. Cas. Ab. 282.
[3] Gilbert, *Lex Praetoria*, 295–296; *James* v. *Greaves* (1725) 2 P.
Wms. 270; for this distinction, which is now grounded upon different
and sounder reasons than those assigned in this case, see *Parfitt* v. *Lawless*
(1872) 2 P. and D. at pp. 468–470.

Ballow's book and the reported decisions of the Chancellors from 1682 to 1737 show that equity had reached a stage at which it needed as a Chancellor a first-rate lawyer whose tenure of office was sufficiently lengthy to make his influence felt. Fortunately for equity these conditions were fulfilled by Hardwicke. Next to Mansfield he was the greatest lawyer of the eighteenth century, and he held his office for nearly twenty years.

LORD HARDWICKE[1]

Philip Yorke, Lord Hardwicke, was born in 1690. He was the son of an attorney; but when he was quite young his ability was so marked that his father determined to send him to the bar. In 1706, at the age of sixteen, he went to the office of Salkeld, the clerk of the papers in the court of King's Bench, where he met three other pupils all of whom attained judicial rank.[2] He became a member of the Middle Temple[3] in 1708, and was called to the bar in 1715. During these years he had worked so hard that he was ready to practise as soon as he was called. His progress at the bar was rapid. In 1719 he became a member of the House of Commons, and in 1720, at the age of twenty-nine, he was made solicitor-general. In 1724 he became attorney-general. As attorney-general he showed that he was a good common lawyer, and that he was learned also in ecclesiastical law, Roman law and international law. He showed, too, that he could defend effectively the government measures in the House of

[1] Holdsworth, *H.E.L.* xii, 237–297; Yorke, *Life of Hardwicke*; Foss, *Lives of the Judges*, viii, 178–197; Campbell, *Lives of the Chancellors*, v, 1–173.

[2] Parker C.B., Strange M.R., and Jocelyn Lord Chancellor of Ireland.

[3] When he became attorney-general he joined Lincoln's Inn, of which he became treasurer in 1725, *Black Books of Lincoln's Inn*, iii, 269, 270; he remained a bencher of the Middle Temple, Yorke, *Life of Hardwicke*, i, 107.

Commons. In 1733 he became chief justice of the King's Bench and a peer. In 1737 Talbot, the Lord Chancellor, died, and Hardwicke began his long tenure of that office. He resigned it November 19, 1756; but he remained a member of the government till 1762. He died in 1764.

As a minister of state he exercised a steadying and a harmonizing influence. It was because he was respected by all parties that he was able to negotiate the famous alliance between the elder Pitt and Newcastle, which, as I have said,[1] changed the course of European history. His Marriage Act, and his Acts which settled the Highlands of Scotland after the rebellion of 1745, are proofs of his sound statesmanship. Like Blackstone, he had an unbounded admiration for the balanced eighteenth-century constitution; and a keen sense of the need to maintain the supremacy of the law. There was no doubt some danger that his admiration for the constitution and the law would lead him to oppose salutary reforms. To some extent he avoided this danger; but not altogether. We shall see that his neglect to make much needed reforms in the procedure of the court of Chancery had some important and permanent effects upon the later history of equity.[2] As a judge he won universal approval. "Multitudes", said Lord Camden,[3] "would flock to hear Lord Hardwicke as to hear Garrick"; and Lord Mansfield, Burke, and Wilkes all agreed that when he pronounced his decrees "wisdom herself might be supposed to speak".[4]

But the most eloquent as well as the truest estimate of Hardwicke as Chancellor was pronounced, on November 8, 1756, by the only lawyer of the eighteenth century whose fame rivals his own—Lord Mansfield. The date

---

[1] Above, p. 163.   [2] Below, pp. 189–190.
[3] Hardinge's *Life*, cited Campbell, *Lives of the Chancellors*, v, 361.
[4] Butler, *Reminiscences*, i, 133.

and the occasion on which that estimate was given were very memorable. Hardwicke was just about to resign and, as we have seen, resigned a few days later.[1] Charles Yorke, his son, had been made solicitor-general two days previously, and was then treasurer of Lincoln's Inn. As treasurer he presided at the farewell dinner given by the Inn to Mansfield, who was taking the degree of serjeant-at-law preparatory to his becoming chief justice of the King's Bench. Mansfield used this occasion to pronounce a panegyric on the father, whom he took the opportunity to recognize as his master in the law, and to congratulate the son, with the eloquence and felicity for which Mansfield was famous. He said:[2]

If I have had in any measure success in my profession, it is owing to the great man, who has presided in our highest Courts of Judicature the whole time I attended at the bar. It was impossible to attend him, to sit under him every day, without catching some beams from his light....If we can arrogate nothing to ourselves, we may boast the school we were brought up in; the scholar may glory in his master, and we may challenge past ages to show us his equal....It is a peculiar felicity of the great man I am speaking of to have presided very near twenty years, and to have shone with a splendour, that has risen superior to faction and that has subdued envy. I did not intend to have said, I should not have said, so much upon this occasion, but that, in this situation, with all that hear me, what I say must carry the weight of testimony rather than appear the voice of panegyric. For you Sir [addressing the treasurer] you have given great pledges to your country; and large as the expectations of the country are concerning you, I dare say you will answer them.

Succeeding ages have ratified Lord Mansfield's opinion that his words carried the weight of testimony, and were not merely the voice of panegyric.

Hardwicke gave to many of the principles of equity their final form. When he began his work many of these principles had been established, and the ground was to

[1] Above, p. 180.   [2] Holliday, *Life of Lord Mansfield*, 105–106.

some extent covered by precedents, which, though in many cases conflicting, indicated both the problems which awaited solution and alternative methods of solving them. The fact that he was a consummate lawyer, both industrious and capable of clear and rapid thought, and the fact that he had an exceptionally long tenure of office, enabled him to solve satisfactorily many of these problems, and thus to make his chancellorship as distinctive a landmark in the history of equity as the chancellorship of Nottingham.[1] He failed to do much to reform the abuses in the practice and procedure of his court. It is true that those abuses were not so great as they became at the end of the eighteenth and the beginning of the nineteenth centuries. It is true that he did something to alleviate them by the orders which he made. It is true that his capacity for quick and sound decision made them less noticeable during his tenure of office. But, after allowing for all these circumstances, the fact remains that he failed to arrest the steady deterioration of that practice and procedure, with the result that, under his less gifted successors, it went from bad to worse. I shall deal first with Hardwicke's influence upon the substantive principles of equity and secondly with his influence upon its adjective rules.

(1) *Substantive principles.*

Hardwicke never lost sight of the fundamental principle that equity follows the law. He said:[2]

This is to be understood respectively according to the different laws to which the constitution of this kingdom subjects that kind of property which happens to be in question. If it is a legatary or testamentary matter the king's ecclesiastical law; if a maritime matter the Admiralty law; if a matter concerning a real estate the common law of the land.

---

[1] For Nottingham see above, pp. 145–150.
[2] *Harvey* v. *Aston* (1738) West t. Hard. at p. 425.

But if necessary equity would modify and develop the rules of law—one instance is the development of the doctrine of equitable waste. As Hardwicke explained in his letter to Kames,[1] new commercial conditions, new modes of dealing with property, new forms of property, had compelled equity to make new rules. His success in developing these new doctrines was due to the fact that he combined respect for established principles and rules with a recognition of the fact that his court was a court of conscience. He would never make a decree contrary to an established principle though personally he did not agree with it;[2] and yet, as he said in his letter to Kames,[3] he must not be so strictly bound by rules as the common law judges; for, if he were, "he must sometimes pronounce decrees which would be materially unjust", and "this might lay a foundation for an equitable relief, even against decrees in equity, and create a kind of super foetation of courts of equity". Thus he claimed a wide power to deal with frauds and sharp practices of all kinds. His analysis, in the case of *Chesterfield* v. *Janssen*,[4] of many different varieties of sharp practice has helped courts of equity from that day to this[5] to give relief in cases in which no relief could be got at common law.

Hardwicke's decisions lay down the fundamental principles which underlie many bodies of equitable doctrine. Thus he settled the nature and characteristics of equitable as compared with legal estates, many of the rules relating to the doctrine of notice, the position of a volunteer as compared with a purchaser for value; and the many questions arising out of the need to construe wills and settlements gave opportunities for the settle-

[1] Cited Yorke, *Life of Hardwicke*, ii, 555.
[2] *Prowse* v. *Abingdon* (1738) 1 Atk. at p. 485.
[3] Yorke, *Life of Hardwicke*, ii, 554.
[4] (1750) 1 Atk. at pp. 351–353.
[5] See *Lancashire Loans* v. *Black* [1934] 1 K.B. at pp. 403–404 *per* Scrutton L.J.

ment of such bodies of equitable doctrine as satisfaction, ademption, election, and conversion. As the result of his decisions, such bodies of doctrine as Trusts, Family Law, Mortgages, and Administration of Assets attained, to a large extent, their final form. It is true that under Hardwicke the boundaries of equity were not fixed in quite the same ways as they came to be fixed in the nineteenth century. Then and later the Chancellor had a large jurisdiction in bankruptcy; and equitable rules and principles have had some influence on the development of that branch of the law. During his time many commercial cases came before the court. But its procedure was not well adapted to the trial of these cases, and Hardwicke's method of trying them prevented him from making any great contribution to commercial law, for the reasons given by Buller J.[1] But, subject to these modifications, it would be true to say that equity attained during Hardwicke's chancellorship almost its final form. The merits of his great constructive work were recognized by his contemporaries. As Daines Barrington said,[2] "nearly twenty years of well considered decrees... have now established so clear, consistent, and beneficial a system of equity, that ignorance only can reproach it with being *jus vagum aut inconditum*."

(2) *Adjective rules.*

There is no doubt that the system of equity procedure and pleading suffered from very grave defects. It was lengthy, technical, and inordinately expensive. The words which Gibbon used of the procedure of Roman law under Justinian[3] apply to the procedure of the court of Chancery under Hardwicke and his successors. "It was a mysterious science and a profitable trade", and

[1] Above, p. 168, n. 1.
[2] *Observations on the Statutes* (4th ed.), 558.
[3] *Decline and Fall of the Roman Empire*, chap. xliv.

"the innate perplexity of the study was involved in tenfold darkness by the private industry of the practitioners"—with the result that "the expense of the pursuit sometimes exceeded the value of the prize, and the fairest rights were abandoned by the poverty or prudence of the claimants". The causes for these defects can be summed up as follows:

First, the manner in which many of the officials of the court were recruited was medieval. Some of the offices were patent offices, the holders of which drew large revenues from the fees paid by the suitors, whilst the work was done by poorly paid deputies.[1] Other offices were filled by persons who drew large fees from the suitors for work not very adequately performed,[2] or for services or for copies of documents which were unnecessary.[3] The clerks in these offices, who generally did the greater part of the work, were, as in other government offices, employed by the head of the office; and they often tried, not unsuccessfully, to extract new fees from the suitors.[4] These characteristics were common to the official staffs of the courts of law and the court of Chancery;[5] but they produced worse consequences in the court of Chancery than in the courts of law, by reason of the peculiar characteristics of the Chancery procedure and pleading, and of the administrative character of its business.[6] Secondly, the fact that a cumbersome and irrational system of pleading was being developed on strictly logical lines;[7] the fact that all the evidence in Chancery proceedings was written evidence obtained and presented to the court in a particularly ineffective way;[8] the fact that the court set out, not to try issues between

---

[1] Holdsworth, *H.E.L.* i, 424–425, 441.   [2] *Ibid.* i, 440.
[3] *Ibid.* i, 426, 441.   [4] *Ibid.* i, 427, 441.
[5] *Ibid.* i, 424–425; ix, 371–372; for the official staffs of the common law courts see *ibid.* i, 246–262.
[6] *Ibid.* i, 426; ix, 373–375.   [7] *Ibid.* ix, 393.
[8] *Ibid.* ix, 354–358.

two parties, but to do complete justice as between many persons;[1] and the fact that, in order to do this complete justice, it was necessary to take accounts, to make enquiries and to administer estates,[2] aggravated the evil effects of the employment of a staff recruited and paid by medieval methods. Thirdly, the judicial staff of the court of Chancery was inadequate. As compared with the courts of common law, the court of Chancery was under-staffed; and that meant that the Chancellor and the Master of the Rolls had no time to supervise adequately the doings of the officials of the court.[3] Therefore all the abuses which followed from the two first-mentioned causes were able to increase and multiply. These were the reasons why the system of equity procedure and pleading deteriorated throughout the eighteenth century. It is, I think, the one defect in Hardwicke's otherwise admirable achievement—a defect which is even more apparent in the achievements of all the other Chancellors of this century—that he made no effective attempt to arrest this deterioration.

In 1733 the report of a committee of the House of Commons called attention to some of these defects, and as a result an enquiry was made into the personnel of the court and the fees charged. The facts elicited by it caused Hardwicke to make a long order on these matters.[4] But he initiated no other reform of the abuses existing in the practice and procedure of his court. That he initiated no other reform is due partly to his innate conservatism, partly to the difficulty of overcoming the opposition of the vested interests of officials, partly to the fact that he was overburdened with work. It is regrettable that he took no action. In his day the abuses were not so bad as they afterwards became; and he was the only Chancellor of the century who had sufficient skill and authority to

---

[1] Holdsworth, *H.E.L.* ix, 348.   [2] *Ibid.*

[3] *Ibid.* i, 423–424, 437; ix, 373–374.   [4] *Ibid.* xii, 286–288.

initiate such a reform with any prospect of success. He was not, however, indifferent to these abuses, and, not being able or willing to carry legislative reforms, he tried by his own industry and skill to mitigate some of them.

Both P. C. Yorke in his life of Hardwicke,[1] and Twiss in his life of Eldon,[2] have tried to demonstrate that their heroes were not answerable for the admitted defects in the practice and procedure of the court of Chancery, and that they did their best to obviate the evils which flowed from the faulty system of procedure and pleading. There is considerable force in their arguments. Twiss succeeds in showing that Eldon tried very hard to keep abreast of his work; that he directed all his great talents to the work of settling on lines, which were technically correct and substantially just, the doctrines of his court; and that all the delays of his court were not due to him. Yorke proves that the same assertions can be made of Hardwicke; and in one respect there is no doubt that Yorke's defence of Hardwicke is more conclusive than Twiss's defence of Eldon. Twiss is obliged to admit that Eldon's habit of delaying his decrees aggravated the evils which flowed from the defects in the procedure and practice of the court.[3] But Yorke is able to prove that no such charge can be made against Hardwicke.[4] He is able to prove also that, whilst Eldon's habit of relying upon his own researches into the facts of the case, and of paying little attention to the arguments of counsel, increased his delay in coming to a decision,[5] Hardwicke's habit of listening attentively to the argument and of relying on the industry

---

[1] Yorke, *Life of Hardwicke*, ii, 500–509, 514–520.
[2] Twiss, *Life of Lord Eldon*, iii, 327–408.
[3] *Ibid.* iii, 323–327; Holdsworth, *H.E.L.* i, 437–438.
[4] Yorke, *Life of Hardwicke*, ii, 508.
[5] *Ibid.* i, 142; ii, 525–526; this habit was defended by Eldon, see *Ruscombe* v. *Hare* (1817–1818) 6 Dow at p. 16, cited Twiss, *Life of Lord Eldon*, iii, 353; and he told this story: "Lord Abergavenny told me he once compromised a suit, because his attorney had told him there was in

of counsel, both helped to shorten the argument, and enabled him to come to much more speedy decisions.[1] No doubt Hardwicke sometimes took a considerable time to consider his judgments. The case of *Casborne* v. *Scarfe* was heard on January 28 and March 4, 1737, and judgment was not given till March 25, 1738;[2] and there are other cases in which there was a delay of two or even three years between the hearing and the decree.[3] But whilst Eldon in many cases delayed his decision for many years,[4] it was very unusual for Hardwicke to delay his decision for longer than a few days.[5] Daines Barrington, a contemporary, said that

> when a cause is once brought to a hearing, nothing can be more expeditious; the Lord Chancellor or the Master of the Rolls sits 5 or 6 hours in court most days of the year, and 19 suits out of 20 receive an immediate determination.[6]

At the beginning of the nineteenth century, some of those who attacked Eldon's habit of delaying his decrees contrasted his procrastinations with Hardwicke's rapidity in decision.[7]

In fact, paradoxical as it may seem, it can be contended that the efforts which Hardwicke made to minimize the defects of the machinery of his court were almost too successful. His ability and industry were so successful

his case a weak point, which, though the opposing parties were not aware of it, *that old fellow* would be sure to find out if the case came before him", *ibid.*

[1] Yorke, *Life of Hardwicke*, ii, 525; in the case of the *Duke of Marlborough* v. *Lord Godolphin* (1750) 2 Ves. Sen. at p. 83, having given judgment, he said next morning that "he had forgot to take notice of the cases cited for the defendants", but that there was one answer to them all.

[2] 1 Atk. at pp. 603, 605.

[3] See Yorke, *Life of Hardwicke*, ii, 505 n. 2.

[4] Holdsworth, *H.E.L.* i, 437–438.

[5] Yorke, *Life of Hardwicke*, ii, 505.

[6] *Observations on the Statutes* (4th ed.), 559.

[7] Yorke, *Life of Hardwicke*, ii, 508.

in palliating these deep-seated defects, that the demand for reform was less urgent than it might otherwise have been; and so the opportunity for arresting the growing deterioration was lost. None of his immediate successors had the same ability or industry; and, at the end of the century, the terror excited by the French Revolution, and the need to concentrate the energies of the nation on the prosecution of the war with France, put an end to all chance of reform. And so the system of procedure and pleading was allowed to go from bad to worse, until its own vices, and the increase of the business of the court which followed upon the commercial prosperity of the country, caused it to become the worst of all the many abuses of the English judicial system.

Hardwicke's great and enduring work was the settlement of the substantive principles of equity on the sound lines upon which they had been developing from the time of Nottingham. The result of that work, and the result of his failure to effect any substantial reforms in the practice and procedure of his court, were the continued development of the substantive principles of equity on the sound lines upon which he and his predecessors had placed them, and the continued deterioration of its adjective principles. The same assertion can also be made of the development of the substantive and adjective principles of the common law during this century—though in the case of the common law the procedural defects were not so grave as they were in the case of equity.[1] Consequently when the era of reform came, the reformers concentrated their attention mainly on the procedural defects in the systems of the common law and equity. We shall see that this phenomenon, coupled with the manner in which the relations between law and equity had come to be fixed during this century, is the key to the shape taken by the series of reforms

[1] Holdsworth, *H.E.L.* ix, 371–375.

which culminated in the Judicature Act.[1] Hence it may
be said that both the strong and the weak points in the
development of the common law and of equity during
this century have left their marks upon both the substantive principles and the procedural rules of the
English law which governs us to-day.[2]

Lord Hardwicke's chancellorship ends the formative
period in the history of equity. But there were still some
gaps to be filled, some obscurities to be elucidated, some
contradictions to be eliminated. This work was begun
by the Chancellors who succeeded Hardwicke. Their
decisions paved the way for the achievement of Eldon,
just as the decisions of the Chancellors between the death
of Nottingham and the accession of Hardwicke paved the
way for the latter's work. Eldon's work was the complement of Hardwicke's; and so in the sphere of equity, as in
other legal spheres, the eighteenth century was a creative
century, which fixed the conditions in which the lawyers
of the nineteenth century did their work of adapting the
law to the needs of a rapidly changing society.

LORD ELDON[3]

John Scott, the future Lord Eldon, was born at Newcastle on June 4, 1751. He was educated at the Royal
Grammar School at Newcastle, and throughout his life
he was grateful to Hugh Moises the master of that school
—as soon as he had become Lord Chancellor he made
him one of his chaplains, and at a later period he acknowledged his obligations to him and offered him high
preferment in the church. His elder brother William,

---

[1] Below, p. 208.   [2] Below, pp. 208–210.
[3] Twiss, *Life of Lord Eldon*; Townsend, *Lives of Twelve Eminent
Judges*, ii, 366–520; Foss, *Lives of the Judges*, ix, 39–52; Campbell,
Lives of the Chancellors, vol. vii; W. E. Surtees, *Lives of Stowell and
Eldon*.

the future Lord Stowell,[1] who had become fellow and tutor of University College, Oxford, persuaded his father to send him to that College. He was elected to a fellowship by his College in 1767, took his degree in 1770, and in 1771 gained a university prize for an English essay. In 1772 there occurred the most romantic event in his life —his elopement with the daughter of Aubone Surtees, a banker of Newcastle, and his marriage in Edinburgh. His brother William deplored the folly of this step. But in fact it was the wisest step he ever took; for it was the beginning of a happy union which lasted till his wife's death in 1831, and it was the foundation of his future success. John Scott was a model husband, and acted up to his dictum that "the only reparation which one man can make to another for running away with his daughter is to be exemplary in his conduct to her".[2] But for his marriage and the consequent loss of his fellowship he might have entered the church. George III told Eldon, on his becoming Chancellor, that he wished to be remembered to his wife because, said the King, "I know that you would have made yourself a country curate, and that she has made you my Lord Chancellor".[3]

Between the years 1774 and 1776 Scott deputized for Robert Chambers, who had been one of his tutors at University College, and had succeeded Blackstone as Vinerian Professor of English law. Chambers had been appointed a judge of the high court at Calcutta, and the University had allowed him to keep his chair for three years, in case he found that he could not live in India.

During these years Scott followed his maxim that a man who wished to succeed as a lawyer must "live like a hermit and work like a horse". The result was that when he was called to the bar by the Middle Temple in

---

[1] Below, pp. 223–232.
[2] Twiss, *Life of Lord Eldon*, iii, 189–190.
[3] Townsend, *Lives of Twelve Eminent Judges*, ii, 375–376.

1776 he was a very learned lawyer. He soon made his way at the bar; and his famous argument in *Ackroyd* v. *Smithson*[1] in 1779, which established his fame as the finest equity lawyer of his day, shows that he was as able an advocate as he was a lawyer. It is a fine piece of clear, close, terse, and logical reasoning which revolutionized some generally held opinions on the doctrine of conversion, and put the law on its modern basis. Its effect on contemporary legal opinion is illustrated by the following tale told by Eldon himself:[2] In the Chancellor's court of Lancaster he was briefed to support the opposite conclusion to that which he had supported in *Ackroyd* v. *Smithson*. The judge, who was Dunning afterwards Lord Ashburton, on hearing the point which he proposed to argue, said,

"Sit down, young man." As I did not immediately comply, he repeated, "Sit down, Sir, I won't hear you." I then sat down. Dunning said, "I believe your name is Scott, Sir." I said it was. Upon which Dunning went on: "Mr Scott, did you not argue that case of *Ackroyd* v. *Smithson*?" I said that I did argue it. Dunning then said, "Mr Scott, I have read your argument in that case of *Ackroyd* v. *Smithson*, and I defy you or any man in England to answer it. I won't hear you."

In 1783 he entered Parliament, and was a strong supporter of Pitt against the coalition ministry of Fox and North. In 1788 he became solicitor-general, and in 1793 attorney-general. As such he prosecuted the leaders of the party who wished to spread in England the French revolutionary ideas, and to make radical changes in the constitution. In the prosecutions of Hardy, Horne Tooke, and Thelwall he pressed for more than it was worth the doctrine of constructive treason. It was fortunate for the liberty of the subject that the jury, by acquitting the accused, prevented this extreme

---

[1] (1779) 1 Bro. C.C. at pp. 505–514.
[2] Twiss, *Life of Lord Eldon*, i, 119–120.

application of that doctrine. As the result of these acquittals he introduced and carried through the House of Commons bills designed to strengthen the government against revolutionary agitators. This legislation succeeded in its object; and there can be no doubt that the war with France and the conditions of the country made it necessary.

In 1799 he became chief justice of the Common Pleas, and Lord Eldon. He was not sorry to leave the House of Commons; for he was too much the lawyer and the pleader ever to shine as a debater. He was far more at home in the dignified atmosphere of the House of Lords, where he exercised an increasing authority during the many years of his chancellorship.[1] In 1801 he became Lord Chancellor. He left the Common Pleas with real regret. "I there sat", he said,[2] "in an honourable, independent, and reasonably profitable situation for life.... Of politics I had had more than enough before I got there. No man, therefore, ever said 'Nolo episcopari' with more sincerity than I did." But he felt himself bound to obey the King's commands; and so he began his career as Chancellor, and his work upon equity, which puts him amongst the Makers of English Law. He held office from 1801 to 1806, and from 1807 to 1827. He resigned in 1827; but he still continued to hear cases in the Privy Council and the House of Lords. The last case which he heard there was that of *White* v. *Baugh* in 1835.[3] He died of old age in 1838.

Throughout the Napoleonic wars Eldon was a tower of strength to the government. But he had one great defect as a statesman. He was unable to move with the times, and could not see that after 1815 great legislative

---

[1] Townsend, *Lives of Twelve Eminent Judges*, ii, 473–477.

[2] Twiss, *Life of Lord Eldon*, i, 388.

[3] *Ibid.* iii, 243; the case is reported 9 Bligh N.S. 181, and 3 Cl. and Fin. 44, but Eldon's presence is not mentioned.

reforms were needed. "His mind", as Townsend says,[1] "seems to have been moulded between 1788 and 1798, and to have subsequently undergone no material alteration—mistrusting the most specious improvement, considering any organic change as synonymous with confusion; and satisfied that audacity in reform was the principle of revolution." It is true that he caused the bankruptcy law to be consolidated, that he helped to draw the Act which created a vice-chancellor, that he helped to frame a bill to improve the administration of justice in court of Chancery founded upon the inadequate recommendations of the Chancery commission of 1826, that he did not oppose the Act which abolished appeals of felony and trial by battle. But all important reforms he opposed. As Bagehot has said:[2]

He believed in everything which it is impossible to believe in —the danger of Parliamentary Reform, the danger of Catholic Emancipation, the danger of altering the Court of Chancery, the danger of altering the Courts of Law, the danger of abolishing capital punishment for trivial thefts, the danger of making landowners pay their debts, the danger of making anything more, the danger of making anything less;

and, it may be added, the danger of interfering with the slave trade. And his opposition was unfortunately successful; for till 1827 he was an influential member of the government. He appealed successfully both to the prejudice in favour of things established felt by ordinary men in an age of revolutions, and to the scepticism felt by more enlightened men of the efficacy of any suggested change and their feeling that the smallest change might be the beginning of a series of undesirable reforms. Bagehot says:[3]

We read occasionally in conservative literature alternations of sentences, the first an appeal to the coarsest prejudice—

---

[1] *Lives of Twelve Eminent Judges*, ii, 457.
[2] *Literary Studies*, i, 6–7.   [3] *Ibid.* i, 11–12.

the next a subtle hint to a craving and insatiable scepticism. You may trace this even in Vesey junior. Lord Eldon never read Hume or Montaigne, but sometimes, in the interstices of cumbrous law, you may find sentences with their meaning, if not in their manner: "Dumpor's case always struck me as extraordinary; but if you depart from Dumpor's case, what is there to prevent a departure in every direction?"

It is not surprising that Eldon resigned when the advent of Canning to power made it certain that changes would be made. It is not surprising that he opposed Catholic Emancipation to the last, and so helped to create that split in the Tory party, which gave the Whigs power in 1831, and produced reforms which were revolutionary largely because his opposition had prevented more gradual changes.

But it is Eldon's character as a lawyer and not as a statesman with which we are concerned. He had all the qualities of a great judge—a subtle mind, great sagacity, great learning, much patience. His pleasant manners made him a favourite with the bar, the solicitors, and the officers of his court. His opponent Brougham said that of all the judges before whom he had practised his "amenity of manners" and "quickness of mind" made him the most generally popular.[1] As chief justice of the Common Pleas his decisions were learned, and quickly given. The common law system of pleading which ensured a clear definition of the issue, and the fact that he sat with other judges, helped to prevent delays. But when as Chancellor he was set to decide cases by himself, and by means of a system of pleading which made his decision depend, not on a single issue, but on the effect of many complicated transactions and the conduct of many parties, his great knowledge of the law and his extreme conscientiousness led him to delay his decisions for years, and so to aggravate the effects of the faulty

[1] Townsend, *Lives of Twelve Eminent Judges*, ii, 436.

procedure of his court. These delays were really un-necessary; for he was capable of quick decision, and, as Romilly said, his first impression of the merits of a case was rarely varied by the months and years which he gave to its study.[1] It is true that he sometimes discovered facts which had escaped the notice of both parties, and put a new complexion on the case.[2] It is true that his long consideration produced judgments which, as he pointed out, settled the rule of equity for all time, and so saved future litigation.[3] But these considerations do not out-weigh the evil results which flowed from that habit of procrastination which grew upon him with age. This fault, and the fact that he was unwilling to take any effective steps to arrest the growing deterioration of the practice of his court, and its growing incapacity to meet the new needs of the age, are his two great defects. But, in spite of these defects, his merits as a lawyer and a judge make his chancellorship an important epoch in the history of equity.

Of his merits as a lawyer and a judge the famous conveyancer Charles Butler has, I think, given the truest account. He says:[4]

In profound extensive and accurate knowledge of the prin-ciples of his court, and the rules of practice by which its proceedings are regulated—in complete recollection and just appreciation of former decisions—in discerning the just inference to be drawn from them—in the power of instantaneously applying this immense theoretical and practical knowledge to the business immediately before the court—in perceiving almost with intuitive readiness, on the first opening of a case, its real state, and the ultimate conclusion of equity upon it, yet investigating it with the most conscientious, most minute, and edifying industry—in all or any of these requisites Lord Eldon, if he has been equalled, has assuredly never been surpassed by any of his predecessors.

[1] Twiss, *Life of Lord Eldon*, iii, 337–338.
[2] *Ibid.* iii, 351–353; above, p. 187, n. 5.
[3] Twiss, *Life of Lord Eldon*, iii, 358.   [4] *Reminiscences*, i, 135–136.

This praise was echoed by Jarman in his dedication to him of his edition of Powell on Devises,[1] by Sugden in his dedication to him of his book on Powers,[2] by Lyndhurst,[3] and by his political opponents Romilly[4] and Brougham.[5] Greville[6] truly said of him that "he has lived to see his name venerated and his decisions received with profound respect, with the proud assurance that he has left to his country a mighty legacy of law and secured to himself an imperishable fame". It is true that his judgments are sometimes overloaded with subtle distinctions; and it is true that they are wholly destitute of literary grace. But, in spite of these defects, it is true to say that no lawyer of his day was as learned and as experienced as Eldon; and no lawyer worked harder in his court of Chancery, and in the House of Lords. Of his capacity for hard work in his court of Chancery a tale told by Wilberforce is a good illustration. He says:[7]

I remember coming to speak with Romilly in court, and seeing him look fagged, and with an immense pile of papers before him. This was at a time when Lord Eldon, having been reproached for having left business undischarged, had declared that he would get through all arrears by sitting on till the business was done. As I went up to Romilly, Lord Eldon saw me, and beckoned to me with as much cheerfulness and gaiety as possible. When I was alone with Romilly, and asked him how he was, he answered, "I am worn to death, here have we been sitting on in the vacation from nine in the morning till four, and when I leave this place I have to read through all my papers to be ready for tomorrow morning; but the most extraordinary part of all is, that Eldon, who has not only mine but all the other business to go through, is just as cheerful and untired as ever."

---

[1] Twiss, *Life of Lord Eldon*, iii, 418.
[2] *Ibid.* iii, 323.   [3] *Ibid.* iii, 89–90.
[4] *Autobiography*, ii, 186.
[5] Twiss, *Life of Lord Eldon*, iii, 324; below, p. 198.
[6] *Memoirs*, ii, 388.
[7] Townsend, *Lives of Twelve Eminent Judges*, ii, 417–418.

To his hard and successful work in the House of Lords Brougham testifies. He said in the House of Commons in 1823 that,

the Noble Lord decided on the cases which came before him with a degree of skill and penetration—and in appeal cases from Scotland and Ireland with a degree of wisdom—which was most extraordinary, considering that to the law of the latter countries, and especially Scotland, the Noble and Learned Lord was in some sort a foreigner. Their law, however, he had reformed; inveterate abuses he had corrected; and the Scotch lawyers, however averse they at first were to the suggested reformations, soon perceived their value, acknowledged their expediency, and ultimately adopted them.[1]

The two great contributions to the system of equity made by Eldon were first his settlement of a very large number of the leading principles of equity, and secondly his final settlement of the relations between law and equity. Of these two contributions I must now say something.

His settlement of the principles of equity.

Many of the leading principles of equity had been settled by Lord Hardwicke. Lord Eldon's decisions completed this settlement. He elaborated some of the settled doctrines of equity; and he fixed the final form of other doctrines. His large knowledge both of the law and the practice of his court, and the careful attention which he gave to all the more important cases, enabled him to settle and define the ambit of equity, the contents of its principles and rules, and their relations to one another. The following are a few of the more important cases in which he effected this settlement and this definition:

We have seen that it was his argument in the case of *Ackroyd* v. *Smithson* which settled on logical lines the

[1] Twiss, *Life of Lord Eldon*, iii, 431–432.

operation of the doctrine of conversion.[1] In the case of
Ellison v. *Ellison*[2] he stated the rules as to when the court
would assist a volunteer. The case of *Howe* v. *Earl of
Dartmouth*[3] is a leading case as to the duties of trustees in
relation to wasting and reversionary property which has
been settled to be enjoyed in succession. In the case of
Aldrich v. *Cooper*[4] he stated the principle which underlies
the doctrine of the marshalling of assets. The case of
Murray v. *Lord Elibank*[5] settled the principles regulating
a wife's equity to a settlement—a very important doctrine before the Married Women's Property Acts. *Ex
parte Garland*[6] laid down some very fundamental principles of the law relating to the rights and duties of an
executor who has been given a power to trade by his
testator. The case of *Brice* v. *Stokes*[7] is a leading case on
the question when a trustee may be held to be liable for
breaches of trust committed by his co-trustee. These are
a very few instances of the many cases in which Lord
Eldon fixed the doctrines of equity. It is true that some
nineteenth-century decisions have made important additions. As Jessel M.R. said in *Re Hallett's Estate*[8] the
main doctrines of equity are, as compared with the main
doctrines of the common law, modern—"we can name
the Chancellor who first invented them, and state the
date when they were first introduced into equity jurisprudence." Such branches of equitable doctrine as the
right to follow trust property expounded in *Re Hallett's
Estate*, and the development of the rules as to covenants
running in equity with the land, which started with the
case of *Tulk* v. *Moxhay*,[9] are post-Eldon. But, when all
deductions have been made, there is no doubt that

---

[1] (1779) 1 Bro. C.C. 503; above, p. 192.
[2] (1802) 6 Ves. 656.   [3] (1802) 7 Ves. 137.
[4] (1802) 8 Ves. 381.   [5] (1804) 10 Ves. 84.
[6] *Ibid.* 110.   [7] (1805) 11 Ves. 319.
[8] (1879) 13 C.D. at p. 710.   [9] (1848) 2 Ph. 774.

Eldon's work succeeded in attaining the result which, in the case of *Gee* v. *Pritchard*,[1] he said that he had aimed at attaining:

The doctrines of this court ought to be as well settled, and made as uniform, almost, as those of the common law, laying down fixed principles, but taking care that they are to be applied according to the circumstances of each case. I cannot agree that the doctrines of this court are to be changed by every succeeding judge. Nothing would inflict on me greater pain in quitting this place, than the recollection that I had done anything to justify the reproach that the equity of this court varies like the Chancellor's foot.

As Kerly has said in his very able *History of Equity*,

Equity, when Lord Eldon retired, was no longer a system corrective of the common law: it could only be described as that part of remedial justice which is administered in Chancery, while, taken generally, its work was administrative and protective, in contrast with that of the common law, which was remedial and retributive.[2]

We shall now see that the fact that this verdict can be passed on Lord Eldon's work is partly due to the manner in which he helped to settle finally the relations between law and equity.

His final settlement of the relations between law and equity.

The growing systematization and elaboration of the rules of equity raised the question of the relation of these rules to the rules of the common law. In the first place, lawyers were beginning to ask whether the English system of administering law and equity in separate tribunals was the best possible system. Henry Home, Lord Kames, a Scotch judge who had published a book on equity in 1760,[3] had some correspondence with

[1] (1818) 2 Swanst. at p. 414.   [2] At p. 167.

[3] *Principles of Equity*; for an account of this book see *Sources and Literature of Scots Law* (Stair Society), i, 252–254.

Hardwicke upon this matter. He advocated the Scottish system, under which law and equity were administered by the same tribunals.[1] Hardwicke replied to him, and gave reasons for preferring the English system of separate tribunals.[2] In the second place, legislation giving courts of law power to give relief against penalties,[3] and power to give lessees relief against forfeiture,[4] and legislation as to the rights of mortgagors and mortgagees,[5] had effected a slight fusion of legal and equitable rules. If the Legislature had pursued this policy, the separation between the rules of law and equity would have been weakened, and some sort of a fusion between some of these rules might have been effected. But these are the only instances in which it pursued this policy. It did nothing to settle the larger question of the relations of law and equity, so that this question was left to be settled by the lawyers.

Upon this question there were, during a considerable part of the eighteenth century, two schools of thought. One school of thought approved the existing system, under which the administration of law and equity was entrusted to separate tribunals acting upon different principles, but working in partnership with one another —equity scrupulously following the law, and then, having ascertained the legal rights of the parties, compelling them to use their legal rights in accordance with its notions of fairness and justice. The other school of thought emphasized the delays, the expense, and the technical complications which resulted from the separation of tribunals and the divergence of the principles upon which they acted; and it considered that, in the

---

[1] His view was that the objections to the administration of law and equity by the same tribunals could be obviated by an Institute or Digest in which the boundaries of law and equity were clearly marked out; his book on the *Principles of Equity* was intended to supply such an Institute, A. F. Tytler, *Memoirs of Lord Kames*, i, 327–328.

[2] Yorke, *Life of Hardwicke*, ii, 553.   [3] 4, 5 Anne c. 16, § 13.

[4] 4 Geo. II, c. 28, §§ 3 and 4.   [5] 7 Geo. II, c. 20.

interest of the harmonious development of English law, and in the interest of the litigant, some fusion of the principles and rules applied by these separate tribunals ought to be effected.

The Chancellors and the majority of the judges favoured the first of these schools. But the second was favoured by Lord Mansfield, by some of his puisne judges, and by Blackstone. The division of opinion was clearly marked in the case of *Burgess* v. *Wheate*,[1] in which Mansfield held, contrary to the opinion of the majority of the court, that the incidents of equitable estates ought to be assimilated to the incidents of legal estates, and, consequently, that, on the death of a c.q. trust of real property without heirs and intestate, his interest escheated. On the other hand the majority of the court held that escheat was a purely legal result of the fact that the land had been left without a tenant, and that as there was an existing tenant, to wit the trustee, no escheat could take place. Lord Mansfield in several cases acted on the principle that the rules of law and equity ought to be assimilated, and, consequently, that it was advisable to give effect to equitable interests and rights in courts of law;[2] and Blackstone, in his description of equity in the third Book of his *Commentaries*, argued that the differences between law and equity were not substantial but procedural. They consisted, he said, in the mode in which the courts of common law on the one hand, and the court of Chancery on the other, administered justice —"in the mode of proof, the mode of trial, and the mode of relief".[3]

But the premises upon which the reasoning of Lord Mansfield and Blackstone was based were fallacious. In the first place, both Lord Mansfield and Blackstone

---

[1] (1757–9) 1 Eden 177.
[2] Holdsworth, *H.E.L.* xii, 588–589; above, pp. 172–173.
[3] *Commentaries*, iii, 429–442; Holdsworth, *H.E.L.* xii, 593–594.

ignored the fundamental difference between the point of view of the courts of law and the courts of equity, which is apparent from the very earliest period in the history of the equity administered by the court of Chancery. Equity, from the first, had always acted *in personam*.[1] It always took all the circumstances of the case and the conduct of the parties into consideration; and its remedies were and are, for that reason, always discretionary. The courts of law gave, as they were bound to give, the judgment to which the parties were entitled, taking into consideration only the facts pleaded and proved by the evidence. They could not travel out of the record. In the second place, both Lord Mansfield and Blackstone underrated the effect upon substantive rules of the working, for several centuries, of the differences "in the mode of proof, the mode of trial, and the mode of relief". These procedural differences had accentuated the fundamental difference between law and equity. They had thus given rise to many substantial differences, which tended to grow more fundamental, as the variant effects of the two procedures were worked out in detail.

It did not follow that because, for instance, equity would say that a power was validly executed, there was a good execution in law,[2] or, conversely, that because a court of law insisted on the strict performance of a condition, equity could not give relief against non-performance.[3] In fact, as Lord Eldon pointed out, the

---

[1] "*Doctor.* But in case where a subpoena lieth, to whom shall it be directed, whether to the judge or the party? *Student.* It shall never be directed to the judge, but to the party plaintiff or his attorney; and thereupon an injunction commanding them by the same, under a certain pain therein to be contained that he proceed no further at the common law, till it be determined in the king's *chancery*, whether the plaintiff had title in conscience to recover, or not", *The Doctor and Student*, bk. I, chap. xvii; see Holdsworth, *H.E.L.* iv, 279–283.

[2] *Wykham* v. *Wykham* (1811) 18 Ves. at p. 415.

[3] *Clarke* v. *Palmer* (1812) 19 Ves. at pp. 21–22.

adoption of equitable rules by courts of law, without the safeguards with which equity hedged those rules about, might do substantial injustice. Thus, the fact that in the case of *Pasley* v. *Freeman*[1] the common law had sanctioned an action for deceit ought not to oust the equitable jurisdiction over fraud, because to oust it would be unfair to a defendant, since it would deprive him of safeguards which the rules of equity gave to him:

A Defendant in this Court has the protection arising from his own conscience in a degree, in which the law does not affect to give him protection. If he positively, plainly, and precisely, denies the assertion, and one witness only proves it as positively, clearly, and precisely, as it is denied, and there is no circumstance, attaching credit to the assertion overbalancing the credit due to the denial, as a positive denial, a Court of Equity will not act upon the testimony of that witness. Not so at Law. There the Defendant is not heard. One witness proves the case; and, however strongly the Defendant may be inclined to deny it upon oath, there must be a recovery against him.[2]

The common law judges were conscious of the truth of these facts. They realized that they had not got the machinery for dealing with the personal equities which may arise from trusts and other matters falling under the jurisdiction of the court of Chancery. They therefore agreed with the Chancellor that the established boundaries between the courts of law and equity must be maintained.[3] The clearest statement of this point of view was made by Lord Kenyon C.J., in the case of *Bauerman* v. *Radenius*.[4] He said:

Our courts of law only consider legal rights: our courts of equity have other rules, by which they sometimes supersede those

[1] (1789) 3 T.R. 51.

[2] *Evans* v. *Bicknell* (1801) 6 Ves. at p. 184.

[3] See e.g. *Goodtitle d. Jones* v. *Jones* (1796) 7 T.R. 43, 46; *Marshall* v. *Rutton* (1800) 8 T.R. 545, 547; *Tucker* v. *Tucker* (1833) 4 B. and Ad. at pp. 748–749 (argument by Erle to which the court assented).

[4] (1798) 7 T.R. 663.

legal rules, and in so doing they act most beneficially for the subject. We all know, that if the courts of law were to take into their consideration all the jurisdiction belonging to courts of equity, many bad consequences would ensue. To mention only the single instances of legacies being left to women who may have married inadvertently: if a court of law could entertain an action for a legacy, the husband would recover it, and the wife might be left destitute: but if it be necessary, in such a case, to go into equity, that court will not suffer the husband alone to reap the fruits of the legacy given to the wife; for one of its rules is, that he who asks equity must do equity, and in such a case they will compel the husband to make a provision for the wife before they will suffer him to get the money. I exemplify the propriety of keeping the jurisdictions and rules of the different courts distinct by one out of a multitude of cases that might be adduced. If the parties in this case had gone into equity, and that court had directed an issue to be tried, they might have modified it in any way they thought proper. One of the rules of a court of equity is, that they cannot decree against the oath of the party himself on the evidence of one witness alone without other circumstances: but when the point is doubtful, they send it to be tried at law, directing that the answer of the party shall be read on the trial; so they may order that a party shall not set up a legal term on the trial, or that the plaintiff himself should be examined; and when the issue comes from a court of equity, with any of these directions, the courts of law comply with the terms on which it is so directed to be tried. By these means the ends of justice are attained, without making any of the stubborn rules of law stoop to what is supposed to be the substantial justice of each particular case; and it is wiser so to act, than to leave it to the judges of the law to relax from those certain and established rules by which they are sworn to decide.[1]

This reasoning was accepted by the judges in the nineteenth century, when they were faced by the problem of interpreting section 83 of the Common Law Procedure Act of 1854,[2] which had given the courts of common law power to give effect to certain equitable

---

[1] At pp. 667–668.   [2] 17 and 18 Vict. c. 125.

defences. But if those principles still held good in 1854, they were still more true of the unreformed common law of the middle of the eighteenth century; and they afford an abundant justification for the rejection of Lord Mansfield's views by the judges and Chancellors of the latter part of that century.

And I think that it may be maintained that, in the then existing condition of the procedure of the courts of law and equity, the separation of law and equity was necessary for both. On the one hand, the common law system of procedure, pleading, and evidence fitted it to deal only with single issues defined by the pleadings of the parties, and made it quite unable to deal with those questions of the personal conduct of the parties upon which the decisions of the Chancellors were based. On the other hand, all equitable interference with the law must, as was long ago pointed out in *The Doctor and Student*, be based upon a correct appreciation of the law applicable to the particular case.[1] If conflicts between the courts of law and equity, as to what the law was, were to be avoided, if the equitable modifications of the law were to be saved from starting from false premises, it was advisable that the courts of law should be able to lay down the law applicable to the particular case or cases stated by the court of Chancery in the manner described by Lord Kenyon C.J.[2] The separation of law and equity was needed if equity, by means of its more flexible procedure, was to be able to modify and supplement the legal rights of the parties in accordance with its ideas of justice, and, at the same time, to avoid the danger of evolving a set of equitable rules and principles which directly contradicted

---

[1] "Conscience must always be grounded on the law", bk. I, chap. xxvi; "to search conscience upon any case of the law it is in vain, but where the law in the same case is perfectly known", bk. II, Introduction; Holdsworth, *H.E.L.* iv, 279–283.

[2] Above, pp. 204–5.

the rules of the common law. Paradoxical as it may appear, the preservation of the boundaries of the jurisdiction of the separate courts of law and equity was, in the then existing circumstances, necessary to preserve the free and the harmonious development both of law and of equity.

The judges who rejected the views of Lord Mansfield and Blackstone would not have disagreed with Blackstone's statement that

there cannot be a greater solecism, than that in two sovereign independent courts established in the same country, exercising concurrent jurisdiction, and over the same subject-matter, there should exist in a single instance two different rules of property, clashing with or contradicting each other.[1]

But they differed entirely from Lord Mansfield and Blackstone as to the best means of avoiding this solecism. Their solution of the problem of the relation of law to equity was not a fusion, but a partnership, based upon a division of the jurisdiction of the court of Chancery under the well-known three heads of auxiliary, concurrent, and exclusive. That classification, implicit in the equitable jurisdiction all through the eighteenth century, was made explicitly by Fonblanque in his *Treatise of Equity*, the first edition of which was published in 1793–4.[2] The principles of equity coming under these three heads were so developed that a conflict between the rules of law and equity was avoided. There was no doubt a conflict between the rights and duties of citizens as defined by the rules of law and equity: there was no conflict between the rules themselves. As Maitland puts it, "Equity had come not to destroy the law, but to fulfil it. Every jot and every tittle of the law was to be obeyed, but when all this had been done something might yet be needful, some-

---

[1] *Commentaries*, iii, 441.
[2] Fonblanque, *Treatise of Equity* (5th ed.), i, 9.

thing that equity would require."[1] Something, that is, which equity would require of all citizens, in order to enforce duties or protect rights which were outside the ken of the common law. The rules of equity operated not on the law, but *in personam* on the litigants who came before the court of Chancery. The correctness of Maitland's assertion that there was little conflict between the actual rules of law and equity is proved by the small effect of the provision of the Judicature Act[2] that, in case of conflict between the rules of law and equity, the rules of equity should prevail.[3] So skilfully had the relationship between law and equity been regulated by the Chancellors and judges who had rejected Lord Mansfield's policy of fusion for the historic policy of partnership.

When, in the nineteenth century, reform came, it did not take the shape outlined by Lord Mansfield and Blackstone. It was then thought, and rightly thought, that what most required reform was, not the substantive rules of law and equity, but the procedure of the court of Chancery and the courts of common law. Consequently the energy of these reformers was principally concentrated on these systems of procedure. Their reforms culminated in the Judicature Act. It fused the courts of law and equity; it created an almost uniform system of procedure and pleading; and it provided that, in cases of conflict between the rules of law and equity, the rules of equity should prevail; but it did not fuse the two systems of rules.

It is sometimes said that Lord Mansfield attempted to anticipate the Judicature Act. That is to some extent true. It is true in so far as that Act fused the jurisdiction of the courts which administered law and equity; and it

[1] Maitland, *Equity*, 17.
[2] 36, 37 Vict. c. 66, § 25.
[3] Maitland, *Equity*, 151–155.

is true in so far as it got rid of conflicts between law and equity by providing that, in case of conflict, the rules of equity should prevail. But it is not wholly true. If the views expressed by Lord Mansfield and approved by Blackstone had become established, there would have been a fusion of many of the substantive rules of law and equity, and not merely a fusion of jurisdiction, procedure, and pleading. The adoption of their views as to the relations of law and equity would have meant that the Judicature Act, when it came, would have completed a fusion between the substantive rules of law and equity which had long been in progress. It would not have been merely a first step in the direction of fusion.

What will be the nature of the agencies by which the further steps in the direction of complete fusion will be taken? No doubt the chief agency will be in England, as it was at Rome, the Legislature. Acts like the Property Acts of 1925 have gone far to substitute uniform statutory rules for the distinct and supplementary rules of law and equity. Another agency is the action of a uniform Supreme Court. But the action of these agencies will take time. The statutory rules of the Property Acts are derived both from the rules of equity and the rules of law. But it must not be forgotten that they have increased the number of purely equitable interests; that very many of their provisions are simply restatements, with or without modification, of equitable principles; and that they contemplate that the powers and discretions which they give to the Court will be exercised in accordance with those principles. The High Court, for convenience of business, is split into Divisions; and the traditions of the separate courts of law and equity are to a large extent inherited by these separate Divisions. Blackstone noted the fact that the "distinction between law and equity, as administered in different courts, is not at present known, nor seems to have ever been known, in any other country at any time".[1] But he had no idea of the fundamental importance of this fact. He had no idea that it made a fusion between law and equity impossible in his day, and that it would continue to operate long after the separation between the courts of law and equity had been abolished. The fact that the two courts had evolved distinct procedures, distinct modes of pleading, and distinct rules of evidence, was fatal to the scheme of fusion which he advocated; and though these differences have now, for the most part, disappeared, the different genesis of the rules evolved in these jurisdictions, the different technical approach to these rules, and the different points of view of the lawyers who, in the several Divisions of the High Court, administer them, will long militate against complete fusion.[2] What Maitland said of the forms of action is true of the differences between law and equity. The separate courts of law and equity and their separate systems of procedure and pleading and evidence are dead. But they "rule us from their graves", because they still live in the two separate systems which they have created, and, consequently, in the separate intellectual cast which they impose upon those who study and apply them.[3]

[1] *Commentaries*, iii, 49.
[2] A good illustration of this fact is the judgment in *In re Wait* [1927] 1 Ch. 606; see Sir Frederick Pollock's Note on that case, *L.Q.R.* xliii, 293–295.
[3] See *L.Q.R.* li, 159–161.

Lecture X

LEOLINE JENKINS, STOWELL, AND THE CIVILIANS

W E have seen in the last lecture that the fact that law and equity were, before the Judicature Act, administered in separate courts, and by means of different systems of procedural rules, caused so deep a line of cleavage between them, that, after the Judicature Act, it was necessary to entrust their administration to separate Divisions of the High Court. But the King's Bench Division and the Chancery Division are not the only Divisions of the High Court. There is also a Probate, Divorce, and Admiralty Division which administers bodies of law which, before the Judicature Act, were more separate from the common law than the system of equity. These bodies of law were administered in the ecclesiastical courts, the court of Admiralty, and the Prize court; and, since they were administered by the civilians, their substantive rules were partially, and their procedural rules were principally, based on the Roman civil and canon law.

In the sixteenth century it seemed probable that the sphere of the civilians' practice would be large. It seemed likely that the court of Admiralty would guide the development of maritime and mercantile law; that the court of High Commission and the other ecclesiastical courts would exercise an exclusive jurisdiction not only over all ecclesiastical cases, but also over marriage and divorce and over all matters connected with the administration of the estates of deceased persons; that the Star Chamber and the Councils of Wales and the North would administer a criminal law which owed something to Roman ideas, and by means of a procedure which

14-2

owed more to them.[1] But, by the middle of the seventeenth century, these prospects had faded. Coke and his brother judges had begun their successful struggle with the court of Admiralty, the result of which was to give to the common law the control over the development of mercantile and large parts of maritime law; and they were insisting on their right to control the ecclesiastical courts and the Councils of Wales and the North.[2] The legislation of the Long Parliament suppressed the Star Chamber, the jurisdiction exercised by the Council in England, the similar jurisdiction of the Councils of Wales and the North,[3] and the court of High Commission[4]—thus, as Charles I said when he assented to these Acts, "altering in a great measure those fundamental laws, ecclesiastical and civil, which many of my best governing predecessors have established".[5] The Parliamentary opposition acted in close alliance with the common lawyers, so that it appeared very likely that the prophecy of Sir Henry Martin, the judge of the court of Admiralty, that the Long Parliament was likely to prove "the funeral of his profession",[6] would be a true one.

But that prophecy was not completely fulfilled. Though the sphere of the civilians' practice was curtailed, something was still left. The court of Admiralty still retained some part of its jurisdiction over maritime law, and it had an exclusive jurisdiction in Prize, which the wars of the succeeding centuries and the growth of inter-

---

[1] Above, pp. 85–86, 116.   [2] Above, pp. 129–130.

[3] 16 Chas. I, c. 10; it was only if these Councils exercised a regular common law or equity jurisdiction besides the jurisdiction similar to that exercised by the Star Chamber, that they survived; it is for this reason that the Council of Wales survived, Holdsworth, *H.E.L.* i, 126–127, 515 n. 3.

[4] 16 Chas. I, c. 11.

[5] *S.P. Dom.* (1641–43), 44, cccclxxxii, 17.

[6] Above, p. 89.

national law were making of ever increasing importance. An Act of 1661[1] restored the criminal and corrective jurisdiction of the ecclesiastical courts, and they retained their matrimonial jurisdiction, and their jurisdiction over probate and grants of administration to the estates of deceased persons. The civilians did their best to exploit the jurisdiction which was left to them; and their efforts were successful, for, by their writings and by the decisions of their courts, they laid the foundations of the bodies of law which are to-day administered in the Probate, Divorce, and Admiralty Division of the High Court.

That their efforts were successful was largely due to the fact that early in the sixteenth century they had become an organized profession. In 1511 an "association of doctors of law and of the advocates of the church of Christ at Canterbury" had been formed; in 1565 it had begun to inhabit the premises then known as Mountjoy House, and afterwards known as Doctors' Commons; it had been incorporated in 1767 under the name of "the College of Doctors of Law exercent in the Ecclesiastical Courts";[2] and in 1783 it had bought the freehold of these premises from the Dean and Chapter of St Paul's.[3] The conditions laid down in the charter for becoming a fellow of Doctors' Commons, and for becoming an advocate, embody the practice which had been worked out in the preceding centuries. A candidate must be a doctor of Civil Law of Oxford or Cambridge. He must have got a fiat from the Archbishop of Canterbury ordering the Dean of the Arches to admit him as an advocate; and it should be noted that the issue of the fiat was in the absolute discretion of the Archbishop, so that

---

[1] 13 Chas. II, St. 1, c. 12.
[2] The charter will be found in *Parl. Papers*, 1859, sess. I, xxii, 20–22.
[3] 23 Geo. III, c. xxx.

he could not be compelled by writ of mandamus to grant it.[1] The candidate, having got his fiat, must have been admitted as an advocate by the Dean of the Arches at a session of his court. After admission "a year of silence" was imposed on him, during which time he must have attended the courts. Any person thus admitted was qualified to be admitted as an advocate in the court of Admiralty. The advocates were the higher branch of the profession. The lower branch were called proctors. They were regulated partly by an ordinance of the Archbishop of Canterbury made in 1696, which prescribed as a condition for entry into the profession service under articles to a proctor for a period of seven years, and partly by the rules made by the courts before which they practised.[2]

The buildings of Doctors' Commons contained the dwellings of the advocates, a hall, a dining room, and a library. It was in the hall of the Commons that the ecclesiastical courts and the court of Admiralty were held from 1572 onwards. The best description of the appearance of the hall and of a session of the court is to be found in the following passage from *David Copperfield*:[3]

Mr Spenlow conducted me through a paved court yard formed of grave brick houses, which I inferred, from the Doctors' names upon the doors, to be the official abiding places of the learned advocates...; and into a large dull room, not unlike a chapel to my thinking, on the left hand. The upper part of the room was fenced off from the rest; and there on two sides of a raised platform of horse shoe form, sitting on easy old fashioned dining room chairs, were sundry gentlemen in red gowns and grey wigs whom I found to be the Doctors aforesaid. Blinking over a little desk like a pulpit desk, in the curve of the horse shoe, was an old gentleman, whom, if I had seen him in an aviary,

---

[1] R. v. *Archbishop of Canterbury* (1807) 8 East 213.
[2] Holdsworth, *H.E.L.* xii, 76–77.
[3] Chap. xxiii.

I should certainly have taken for an owl, but who, I learned, was the presiding judge. In the space within the horseshoe, lower than these, were sundry other gentlemen of Mr Spenlow's rank, and dressed like him in black gowns with white fur upon them, sitting at a long green table. . . . The public represented by a boy with a comforter, and a shabby genteel man secretly eating crumbs out of his coat pockets, was warming itself at a stove in the centre of the court. The languid stillness of the place was only broken by the chirping of this fire and by the voice of one of the Doctors, who was wandering slowly through a perfect library of evidence, and stopping to put up, from time to time, at little roadside inns of argument on the journey. Altogether I have never, on any occasion, made one at such a cosey, dosey, old fashioned, time forgotten, sleepy-headed little family party in all my life; and I felt that it would be quite a soothing opiate to belong to it in any character—except perhaps as a suitor.

Dickens was not a lawyer. We who are lawyers must not forget that this description, though substantially true from the point of view of a spectator, is not the whole truth. It does no doubt represent the external appearance of the court on an ordinary day, when it was dealing with a dull case. But it is well to remember that it was at these little family parties that the foundations of our modern Admiralty law were laid, that our modern prize law was created, that much international law was made, and that many of the principles of our modern probate and divorce law were worked out.

The advocates had a very varied practice which was conducted in many various courts. It is not therefore surprising to find that the majority of the small body of advocates had official positions in one or other of the courts in which they practised; and even if an advocate did not hold one of these positions, he might always be called upon to act as one of the civilian members of the High Court of Delegates,[1] or as a deputy for the judge

[1] Holdsworth, *H.E.L.* i, 605.

of the court of Admiralty.[1] These characteristics of the practice of the civilians were hit off exactly by Dickens. He said:[2]

You shall go to Doctors' Commons one day, and find them blundering through half the nautical terms in Young's Dictionary, apropos of the "Nancy" having run down the "Sarah Jane", or Mr Pegotty and the Yarmouth boatmen having put off in a gale of wind with an anchor and cable to the "Nelson" Indiaman in distress; and you shall go there another day, and find them deep in the evidence, pro and con, respecting a clergyman who has mis-behaved himself; and you shall find the judge in the nautical case, the advocate in the clergyman's case, or contrari-wise. They are like actors: now a man's a judge, and now he is not a judge; now he's one thing, now he's another! Now he's something else, change and change about; but it's always a very pleasant, profitable little affair of private theatricals, presented to an uncommonly select audience.

The two most famous of these civilians were Sir Leoline Jenkins and Lord Stowell. The work of the first was done in the latter part of the seventeenth century. The work of the second was done in the late eighteenth and early nineteenth centuries. I shall give some account of them and their work, and then I shall say something of the way in which the law made by the civilians was, like the equity created by the Chancellors, co-ordinated with other parts of English law.

SIR LEOLINE JENKINS[3]

Jenkins was born in 1623. He was educated at Jesus College, Oxford, of which college he became principal in 1660. While at Oxford he made the civil and canon

[1] Travers Twiss, *Black Book of the Admiralty* (R.S.), iv, 459, n. 1.
[2] *David Copperfield*, chap. xxiii.
[3] The principal authority for his life is W. Wynne's *Life*, prefixed to the series of letters written during Jenkins's embassies to Cologne and Nimeguen; Holdsworth, *H.E.L.* xii, 647–661; see also two papers by D. J. Llewellyn Davies, *Transactions of the Grotius Society*, xxi, 149; *British Year Book of International Law*, 1934, 21.

law his principal study, and he became a member of Doctors' Commons in 1664. In 1665, on the outbreak of the war with Holland, he was made a member of the commission to exercise prize jurisdiction; and he and other civilians compiled a body of rules for its exercise. In 1665 he became assistant judge of the court of Admiralty, and in 1668 sole judge. In the latter year he was also made judge of the Prerogative court of the Archbishop of Canterbury. In 1669 he was sent on a diplomatic mission to France, in 1673 and 1675 he conducted important diplomatic missions in Germany and Holland, and in 1679 he was appointed ambassador extraordinary at the Hague. He served in the Parliaments of 1679–80, and 1680–81 as member for the university of Oxford, and was a strong supporter of the court, and therefore an opponent of the exclusion bill. In 1680 he was made secretary of state. Though a strong royalist he was no advocate for absolute monarchy. He was opposed to "altering or transgressing those bounds the law had fixed, between the just prerogatives of the Crown and the legal rights of the subject";[1] and he was not in favour of the quo warranto proceedings against the City of London. In 1684 he resigned his office of secretary of state to the great regret of the King. He died in the following year.

At a period when the standard of personal and public morality was low, Jenkins, like Hale, set an example to his contemporaries. He was extremely conscientious, genuinely religious, and so convinced of the truth of the Anglican creed that he tried to convert the Duke of York —the future James II. As a judge he was affable, courteous, and charitable to poor suitors, and especially to poor seamen. But he kept a firm control over the business of the court, and over the conduct of the advocates. His abilities impressed his contemporaries.[2] Though he was no courtier he won the respect of Charles II; for Charles

[1] Wynne, i, p. xlviii.   [2] See Pepys, *Diary*, March 26, 1667.

was an acute judge of character, and could respect the qualities in others which he lacked himself.

Jenkins made his mark both as an expositor and as a critic of the law.

His work as an expositor of the law. Like other civilians, Jenkins stressed the importance of encouraging the study of Roman law. In his argument on behalf of a bill to establish the jurisdiction of the Admiralty, he said:

> I hope it will not be thought invidious, if I choose the words of a great and wise Prince, his Majesty's royal grandfather. I do greatly esteem (says he) the Civil Law; the profession thereof serving more for general learning, and being most necessary for matters of treaty with foreign nations. And I think that if it should be taken away, it would make an entry to barbarism, and blemish the honour of this kingdom. For it is in a manner *Lex Gentium*, and maintaineth intercourse with all foreign nations.[1]

As a diplomat and as a judge of the Prize court Jenkins was obliged to study and apply international law. Like Gentili and Zouche and Bynkershoek, he belonged to the historical or positivist school of international lawyers. In the course of an argument addressed to the King, directed to prove the proposition that one parcel of enemy goods on a ship was not a sufficient ground to condemn the ship, he said,

> the reason I conceive to be, that it is not agreeable to the law of nations—by the law of nations I do not mean the Civil Imperial Law, but the generally received customs among the European governments which are most renowned for their justice, valour, and civility.[2]

This law of nations, he held, could not be infringed except by the express provisions of a treaty or statute or

---

[1] Wynne, i, p. lxxxiv; Jenkins was quoting James I's speech to Parliament in 1609, *Works* (ed. 1616), 532; Holdsworth, *H.E.L.* iv, 233, n. 5; and both the Protector Somerset and Francis Bacon had been of the same opinion, *ibid.* iv, 233.

[2] Jenkins MSS (All Souls Library), no. 216.

an order in council. Thus, though as judge of the Prize court he disapproved of orders in council given by the Crown, which seemed to him to be contrary to the principles of international law, he held that the court was bound by them.[1] This view as to the binding force of these orders in council was held by Lord Stowell,[2] but it is contrary to the most recent decision of the Privy Council, which overrules the law as laid down in the late seventeenth, the eighteenth, and the early nineteenth centuries,[3] and holds that an order in council can no more alter an established rule of international law than it can alter an established rule of English law. He advised the King that in time of war a man cannot have two domiciles, "whereby he shall be made subject by each of them to war or reprisals at one and the same time".[4] Commercial domicile was, he said, the decisive factor in these cases. He also advised that according to the rules of international law foreign judgments, on matters within the foreign court's jurisdiction, must be respected; and therefore that the judgment of a Prize court, vesting the property in a ship in the captors, was conclusive, and effect must be given to it by an English court.[5]

[1] Holdsworth, *H.E.L.* i, 566; Jenkins was of opinion that the interpretation of treaties was a matter for the Privy Council, and that the Prize court must accept that interpretation, Wynne, ii, 732–733, though he sometimes gave advice as to their interpretation, *ibid.* ii, 733–734, *S.P. Dom.* (1668–69), 36; similarly, although the question of what goods were contraband and what not was to be decided partly by treaties and partly by the law of nations, *Law and Custom of the Sea*, ii, 57–58, 290–291, Penrice, the judge of the Admiralty, in 1745 asked the lords of the Admiralty for a ruling as to whether pitch and tar in Swedish ships were contraband, and, like Jenkins, he considered the interpretation of treaties to be a matter of state, *ibid.* ii, 318–320; on the other hand Sir James Marriott, in an opinion which he gave in 1764, stressed the independence of the Prize court, *Calendar of Home Office Papers*, 1760–65, 454, 455; see Roscoe, *History of the Prize Court*, 40–44.

[2] Holdsworth, *H.E.L.* i, 567 n. 4; below, pp. 228, 230.

[3] *The Zamora* [1916] 2 A.C. 77; see Holdsworth, *H.E.L.* i, 567–568.

[4] Wynne, ii, 785.   [5] *Ibid.* ii, 761–763.

As judge of the Prize court he laid down some very fundamental principles governing the exercise of the Prize jurisdiction. He insisted upon the duty of a neutral state to treat belligerents impartially;[1] and the necessity of doing justice to neutrals, who, he pointed out, had a right to trade with the enemy except in case of breach of blockade or contraband.[2] He told the secretary of state that the claims of neutrals must be heard; that if neutral goods were shipped on Dutch ships before the neutrals had notice of the outbreak of war, they ought to be restored; and that if this justice were refused it would be a just cause of reprisals.[3] In 1668 he explained that, by the *jus commune*, a friend's ship could not be confiscated because it carried enemy goods; but that an enemy ship made enemy goods.[4] The stress which he laid upon the ultimate destination of a ship, and the proofs which he demanded that the destination was genuinely neutral, foreshadow the doctrine of continuous voyage.[5]

The fact that the civil jurisdiction of the court of Admiralty was crippled by the common law courts prevented him from doing much for the development of maritime law. His learned and conclusive argument in favour of a bill to settle the jurisdiction of the Admiralty, and to give it a larger jurisdiction in maritime causes, failed to convince the House of Lords.[6] But it should be noted that one of the arguments which he advanced for the bill is almost prophetic, in that it explains the reason why the development of commercial law in England was slow. If, he said, the bill passed, foreigners would understand the reasons for the decisions of the court, and foreign civilians could advise them whether to acquiesce in the decision or to appeal from it; "whereas now, all

---

[1] *Transactions of the Grotius Society*, xxi, 154.
[2] *Ibid.* xxi, 155.   [3] Wynne, ii, 702.   [4] *Ibid.* ii, 719.
[5] *British Year Book of International Law*, 1934, 29–33.
[6] Wynne, i, pp. lxxvi–lxxxv; Holdsworth, *H.E.L.* i, 555, 557.

foreigners do complain extremely, that they can have no other account of their cause, but that the *foreman of the jury said*, they found against him".[1] Till Lord Mansfield's time, this was the reason why, as Buller J. said, the cases "produced no established principle".[2]

His work as a critic of the law. Jenkins helped Nottingham and North to draft the statute of Frauds.[3] He drafted the clauses which laid down the rules as to the conditions in which nuncupative wills of personalty were valid, as to their probate, as to the revocation of wills in writing, as to soldiers' and sailors' wills, and as to the testamentary jurisdiction of the ecclesiastical courts.[4] Though he did not draft the statute of Distribution,[5] he approved of its policy, and he has left a paper in which he states the reasons why it ought to be passed.[6] He attempted without success to reform the High Court of Delegates. The chief defect of that court was the fact that it was composed of a body of poorly paid persons appointed *pro hac vice*.[7] Jenkins proposed, and Doctors' Commons approved his suggestion, that a permanent commission, properly paid, should be appointed; and he prepared a draft set of rules for the procedure of the court.[8] He prepared a bill to prevent clandestine marriages[9]—thus anticipating Lord Hardwicke's proposals; and also bills to revive the authority of rural deans, and to get rid of peculiars.[10] Like Francis Bacon, he objected to the use of excommunication as part of the ordinary process of the ecclesiastical courts; and he revived a

---

[1] Wynne, i, p. lxxxiv.
[2] *Lickbarrow* v. *Mason* (1787) 2 T.R. at p. 73; above, p. 168, n. 1.
[3] Holdsworth, *H.E.L.* vi, 382, 384.
[4] 29 Chas. II, c. 3, §§ 19–24.
[5] Holdsworth, *H.E.L.* iii, 559–560.
[6] Wynne, ii, 695–697.   [7] Holdsworth, *H.E.L.* i, 605.
[8] Wynne, i, p. lii; Coote, *English Civilians*, 87.
[9] Wynne, i, p. lii.
[10] *Ibid.*; for peculiars see Holdsworth, *H.E.L.* i, 600.

suggestion made in 1584 that, for the writ *de excommuni-
cato capiendo*, a writ *de contumace capiendo* should be substituted.[1] It was not till 1813 that effect was given to
this suggestion.[2] Jenkins was easily the greatest civilian
of his day; and, till the end of the eighteenth century,
the greatest civilian that England had yet produced.

At the beginning of the eighteenth century some of
the civilians served as ambassadors and secretaries of
state;[3] and some made their mark in the House of
Commons.[4] In George II's reign there were thoughts
of making Sir George Lee, the judge of the Prerogative
court, the chancellor of the exchequer. But, as Horace
Walpole said,[5] "the business of civilian had confined him
to too narrow a sphere for the extensive knowledge of
men that is requisite to a prime minister[6]". In fact the
trade of lawyer and judge and the trade of politician were
coming to be more sharply differentiated. In the latter
half of the eighteenth century the civilians who held the
posts of judge of the Prerogative court and of the court
of Admiralty were lawyers pure and simple. They were
all competent and some were eminent.[7] But none was
as eminent as Jenkins till 1798, when Sir William Scott,
the future Lord Stowell, was appointed the judge of the
court of Admiralty. He was the most eminent civilian
that this country has ever produced, and he has exercised
a greater influence than any other upon all the branches
of law which fell within the sphere of the civilians'
practice.

[1] Wynne, i, pp. lii–liii; Holdsworth, *H.E.L.* i, 631–632.
[2] 53 Geo. III, c. 127.
[3] Trumbull, Hedges, Newton, see Holdsworth, *H.E.L.* xii, 661–663.
[4] Lee and Hay, *ibid.* xii, 663.
[5] *Memoirs of the Last Ten Years of George II's Reign*, i, 78.
[6] By that he meant a leading minister—he was not using the phrase
in its technical sense.
[7] For some account of them see Holdsworth, *H.E.L.* xii, 665–676.

LORD STOWELL[1]

William Scott, Lord Stowell, was the elder brother of John Scott, Lord Eldon;[2] and there are many similarities in their careers. Lord Sankey has pointed out[3] that "they were knighted within two months of each other: they attended their first levée together, one as Advocate-General, the other as Solicitor-General: they were made Privy Councillors the same day, and hardly had William been made a judge of the Admiralty Court when John was made Chief Justice of the Common Pleas, and subsequently Lord Chancellor." It may be added that both were fellows of University College, Oxford; that William resigned his position as judge of the court of Admiralty the year after John resigned his position as Lord Chancellor; and that just as John completed the development of the modern system of equity, William settled many of the most fundamental principles of Admiralty and ecclesiastical law, and created the system of prize law which governs both England and the United States. The one great contrast between them is the form in which their contributions to English law is expressed. There is no spark of literature in Eldon's judgments, but we shall see that many of Stowell's judgments are literature, and sometimes great literature.

William Scott was born in 1745. He was educated at Newcastle at the same school as his brother John. In 1761 he came up to Oxford as a scholar of Corpus Christi College, and in 1764 he became a fellow of University College, Oxford. He intended to enter the legal profession, and in 1762 he had become a student at the Middle Temple. But the attractions of an academic life caused a considerable delay in the fulfilment of this

[1] Roscoe, *Lord Stowell*; Townsend, *Lives of Twelve Eminent Judges*, ii, 279–365; *D.N.B.*; "Lord Stowell", by Lord Sankey, *L.Q.R.* lii, 327.
[2] Above, pp. 190–198.
[3] *L.Q.R.* lii, 343.

intention. He became a tutor of University College in 1765, and Camden Reader in ancient history in 1774. That he was a capable tutor and reader is shown by Gibbon's allusion in his autobiography to "the merit and reputation of Sir William Scott",[1] and by contemporary and later opinion as to the merits of his lectures as Camden Reader.[2] He was a famous figure in the university; and, like Blackstone,[3] did some useful work for the Bodleian library.[4] This academic prelude to Scott's legal career left a permanent impress upon his later work. Through his friend and colleague Chambers, afterwards as we have seen a judge at Calcutta,[5] it introduced him to Dr Johnson, and procured his election to Johnson's famous literary club. It made him a jurist, and, as in the case of Blackstone,[6] it gave to his judgments a literary form and style which are unique.

In 1777 he decided to resume his legal studies— though he did not finally leave Oxford till 1780, when he was called to the bar by the Middle Temple. But though he was called to the bar, he had wisely decided that his classical and academic training fitted him better for a civilian than for a common law practice. In 1779 he was admitted as an advocate to Doctors' Commons. There his success was rapid. In 1782 he was appointed advocate-general to the Admiralty; and in 1783 his brother could say that "his success is wonderful, and he has been fortunate beyond example".[7] In 1788 he was appointed judge of the consistory court of the diocese of London— a post which he held till 1821—and King's advocate-general. In 1790 he became a member of Parliament, and in 1798 the judge of the court of Admiralty. In 1821

---

[1] Gibbon, *Autobiographies*, Memoir F, 93–94.
[2] Townsend, *Lives of Twelve Eminent Judges*, ii, 285–286.
[3] Below, pp. 240–242.
[4] Townsend, *Lives of Twelve Eminent Judges*, ii, 287–288.
[5] Above, p. 191.   [6] Below, p. 244.
[7] Cited Townsend, *Lives of Twelve Eminent Judges*, ii, 293.

his great services to the state as judge of that court were fitly rewarded by a peerage, and he became Lord Stowell. Failing health caused him to resign his judgeship of the court of Admiralty in 1828. He died in 1836.

Stowell's fame as a lawyer is due partly to his intellectual qualities, partly to the stage of development which ecclesiastical maritime and prize law had reached when he became a judge, and partly to the long duration of the Napoleonic wars.

In the first place, Stowell had a remarkable combination of intellectual qualities. He had a clear logical mind which enabled him to grasp rapidly the essential issues in the case which he was trying, to come to the right conclusions upon the facts, and to state and explain the principles which must be applied in the light of these facts to determine these issues. He had a full mind— a mind well stored with classical and modern learning and literature, and with the technical rules both of the civil law and of English law. He had the synthetic mind of an historian which enabled him to appreciate the manner in which rules of law had developed in the past, and the form which their future development ought in consequence to take. He had, in addition, that measure of legal statesmanship which is the mark of the greatest of our lawyers. That quality was more especially needed by a judge of a Prize court; and it is because Stowell possessed it that he was able to create our system of prize law. Lastly, he had as I have said, a power of literary expression which gave to his judgments a form which enhanced the effect of his grasp of principle, his mastery of the authorities, and his statesmanlike solutions of difficult problems. "If ever the praise of being luminous", said Brougham,[1] "could be bestowed on human composition, it was upon his judgments."

In the second place, Stowell's influence was due to the

[1] *Statesmen of the Time of George III*, iv, 67, cited *L.Q.R.* lii, 335.

stage of development which ecclesiastical maritime and prize law had reached when he became a judge. It was not till 1798, the year Stowell became the judge of the court of Admiralty, that we begin to get a regular series of the reports of cases decided in that court. It was not till 1822, when Haggard published his reports of cases decided in the consistory court of London from 1789–1821, that regular reports of cases decided in the ecclesiastical courts began to appear. This absence of reports had for some time past aroused criticism; for in their absence the principles upon which these courts acted were mysterious both to English and to foreign lawyers. There was, in fact, some justification for their comparison of the civilians "to the Talmudists among the Jews, who only dealt in oral traditions and secret writings";[1] for, as Mr Roscoe has said,[2] the law they applied was often contained only in their notebooks and memories, and was sometimes little more than a legal tradition which could not be accurately verified. But this scarcity of authority gave Stowell's genius free play. It enabled him to harmonize and systematize ecclesiastical maritime and prize law. "For a generation", Lord Sumner has said,[3] "he was rather a law-giver than a judge in the ordinary sense of the term. Upon many maritime points

---

[1] "It has long been complained that there are no public reports of decisions in the court of Admiralty, or Ecclesiastical and Testamentary courts among civilians. Their jealousy of the common lawyers, and a concealment of what passes among the little knot of practitioners, seems to have occasioned that respectable and learned profession to be compared to the Talmudists among the Jews, who only dealt in oral traditions and secret writings. No persons were allowed to be professed practical conjurers but the Sanhedrin themselves", Preface to the reports of Hay and Marriott's decisions, i.

[2] "In the note books and in the memories of the advocates of Doctors' Commons, precedents also existed which were utilized both by the advocates and by the judge, but they were hardly more than legal traditions often liable to be misunderstood, for they could not be accurately verified", Roscoe, *Life of Lord Stowell*, 34.

[3] *D.N.B. sub voc.* W. Scott.

his judgments are still the only law; and, little popular as they were at the moment among the Americans who suffered by them, they have been accepted by the United States courts also as authoritative." At the same time it was the fact that he was well reported by Christopher Robinson, Edwards, Dodson, and Haggard that made it possible for his judgments to become the original authority for very many principles and rules. It was in fact a happy accident that the first appearance of regular reports should coincide with the judicial career of the greatest civilian whom this country has ever produced.

In the third place, the long duration of the Napoleonic war gave Stowell the chance of settling permanently the prize law of Great Britain. In prize cases prohibitions were not issued after Coke's fall in 1616,[1] so that the court of Admiralty had a free hand in the development of prize law. During the course of the eighteenth century it was recognized that the prize jurisdiction of the court was quite distinct from its instance jurisdiction,[2] and that it administered not municipal, but international law.[3] Here was Stowell's opportunity; for the ecclesiastical and maritime jurisdiction of the courts over which he presided was very small as compared with the mass of prize cases which the Napoleonic war brought to his court.

He used his opportunity so well that he created a system of prize law which was not, like the prize law of some continental states, "an unsystematic and indefinite collection of administrative decrees, decisions, and academic opinions",[4] but a definite body of principles and rules. This definite body of principles and rules, which depend on Lord Stowell's decisions, is the international law administered by the Prize court; and it is safe to say that it is more definite and better obeyed than

---

[1] Marsden, *Law and Custom of the Sea*, i, 359.
[2] *Lindo* v. *Rodney* (1781) 2 Dougl. at p. 614.
[3] *Ibid.* at p. 616.   [4] Roscoe, *Life of Lord Stowell*, 51.

any other part of international law. The reason for these characteristics of British prize law is the fact that its development by decided cases has given it the precision of a body of municipal law. The best illustration of this fact is the decision of the Privy Council in the case of *The Zamora*,[1] which, as we have seen, overrules a dictum of Lord Stowell,[2] and lays it down that an order in council can no more alter an established rule of the international law administered by the Prize court than it can alter an established rule of English law.

Lord Stowell's greatest work was done in the sphere of prize law. It is only possible here to mention by way of illustration one or two of the cases in which he built up this body of law. In the case of *The Recovery*[3] he insisted that the Prize court "is a court of the law of nations, though sitting here under the authority of the King of Great Britain. It belongs to other nations as well as to our own; and what foreigners have a right to demand from it is the administration of the *law of nations* simply, and exclusively of the introduction of principles borrowed from our own municipal jurisprudence." Consequently, several of his judgments expound important principles of international law, for instance, the rule that a blockade to be binding must be effective,[4] and the independence and equality of all states;[5] and his decisions on such topics as continuous voyage,[6] contraband,[7] blockade,[8] purchases of ships from a belligerent by a neutral,[9] the duty of a belligerent who destroys a neutral's ship to com-

---

[1] [1916] 2 A.C. 77; above, p. 219.
[2] *The Fox* (1811) Edw. at pp. 312–313.
[3] (1807) 6 C. Rob. at pp. 348–349; cp. *The Fox* (1811) Edw. at p. 312.
[4] *The Betsey* (1798) 1 C. Rob. 92.
[5] *The Le Louis* (1817) 2 Dods. at p. 243.
[6] *The Maria* (1805) 5 C. Rob. 365.
[7] *The Jonge Margaretha* (1799) 1 C. Rob. 188.
[8] Roscoe, *Life of Lord Stowell*, 54–55.
[9] *The Bernon* (1798) 1 C. Rob. 101.

pensate the neutral,[1] commercial domicil,[2] are the basis
of the modern law. And so well and truly was that law
constructed that, in spite of changes in mercantile conditions, and changes in the procedure of the court, it was
found adequate in the war of 1914–18. The principles
which he laid down were found capable of adaptation to
changed conditions, so that, as Mr Roscoe has said,[3]
they remain "fixed more firmly than ever as the corner
stone of one branch of British jurisprudence".

But Lord Stowell's work in constructing the British
system of prize law was not his only work. Many of his
judgments on various points of maritime law fixed the
law for the future. Thus his judgments on the power of
the master of a ship to hypothecate the cargo to raise
money to enable the ship to complete her voyage,[4] and
his judgments on the law as to salvage,[5] are the foundation of the modern law on these topics. So too his judgments on such points of ecclesiastical law as the marriage
law, questions of ecclesiastical conduct and discipline,
and modes of burial,[6] are the foundations upon which
the modern law rests. His decision in the case of
The Slave Grace, R. v. Allan,[7] to the effect that a slave
brought to England who returned with her master to her
original country, where slavery was a recognized status,
reverted to her condition as a slave, aroused much comment. But on principle the law laid down, after a very
elaborate argument, is sound, and won the approbation
of that great American judge and professor—Mr Justice

---

[1]   *The Felicity* (1819) 2 Dods. 381.
[2]   *The Harmony* (1800) 2 C. Rob. 322.
[3]   *Life of Lord Stowell*, 91.
[4]   *The Gratitudine* (1801) 3 C. Rob. 240.
[5]   *The Maria* (1809) Edw. 175; *The Blenden Hall* (1814) 1 Dods.
414.
[6]   Townsend, *Lives of Twelve Eminent Judges*, ii, 317–327, 343–
347, 349–350; *L.Q.R.* lii, 337–339.
[7]   (1827) 2 Hagg. Ad. 94.

Story.[1] Both this case and the case of *Dalrymple* v. *Dalrymple*[2] show that Lord Stowell had grasped some very fundamental principles of the as yet very new topic of Private International Law.

It is, I think, true to say that what Hardwicke and Eldon did for equity and what Mansfield did for the common law, Stowell did for all those branches of law which fell within the sphere of the civilians' practice. Their achievement was possible not only because they were all very great lawyers, but also because they held their offices for sufficiently long periods to make their influence felt, and because they all came at periods when English law especially needed this kind of guidance. Consequently they all succeeded in creating large parts of the law which governs us to-day.

Very few of Lord Stowell's judgments have been questioned by his successors, and, where they have been dissented from, the dissent has not met with universal approbation. Many people consider that his dicta in the case of *The Fox*[3] are preferable to the decision of the Privy Council in the case of *The Zamora*.[4] His views as to the necessary conditions of a valid marriage, which he expounded in the case of *Dalrymple* v. *Dalrymple*,[5] were dissented from by three of the lords who decided the case of *R.* v. *Millis*;[6] but three others agreed with him, and the case was only settled in accordance with the opinion of the first three lords because their opinion agreed with the opinion of the court below. But, as Pollock and Maitland say, "it is the vanquished cause that will please the historian of the Middle Ages".[7] In other words,

---

[1] See 2 S.T. (N.S.) 303 n. (*a*).   [2] (1811) 2 Hagg. Con. 54.

[3] (1811) Edw. at pp. 312–313.

[4] [1916] 2 A.C. 77; see Holdsworth, *H.E.L.* i, 566–568; above, pp. 219, 228.

[5] (1811) 2 Hagg. Con. 54.

[6] (1843–44) 10 Cl. and Fin. 534.

[7] *H.E.L.* (1st ed.), ii, 370.

Lord Stowell's opinion was better history and sounder law.

The literary quality of Lord Stowell's judgments was not attained without labour. "He is said to have had the press stopped for the correction of a single line, and to have been anxious even in the marshalling of his colons"; and Phillimore testifies to the repeated revisions and corrections of his manuscripts and proofs.[1] An anthology of striking passages could be selected from his judgments. One of the best known, and for an Indian audience the most apposite, is the passage from his judgment in *The Indian Chief*,[2] in which he explains why an American residing at Calcutta must be deemed to have a British commercial domicil, and was therefore amenable to the law against trading with the enemy. It had been argued that, being resident at Calcutta, he was a subject, not of the King of Great Britain, but of the Mogul, so that not being a British subject, he was liable to no penalty for trading with Great Britain's enemies. That argument Stowell answered as follows:[3]

Wherever even a mere factory is founded in the eastern parts of the world, European persons trading under the shelter and protection of those establishments, are conceived to take their national character from that association under which they live and carry on their commerce. It is a rule of the law of nations, applying peculiarly to those countries, and is different from what prevails ordinarily in Europe and western parts of the world, in which men take their present national character from the general character of the country in which they are resident; and this distinction arises from the nature and habit of the countries: In the western parts of the world alien merchants mix in the society of the natives; access and intermixture are permitted: and they become incorporated to almost the full extent. But in the East, from the oldest times, an immiscible character has been kept up;

[1] Townsend, *Lives of Twelve Eminent Judges*, ii, 320.
[2] (1801) 3 C. Rob. 12, 22.   [3] *Ibid.* at pp. 28–29.

foreigners are not admitted into the general body and mass of the society of the nation; they continue strangers and sojourners as all their fathers were—

Doris amara suam non intermiscuit undam.

Many of Stowell's judgments on points of ecclesiastical and maritime law show that he combined with his learning as a civilian a very adequate knowledge of English law. In fact a knowledge of all those branches of English law which bordered upon the various branches of the civilian's practice was necessary to all civilians, because without it they would have been ignorant of the limits of the jurisdiction of the courts in which they practised. The decisions of the common law courts and the court of Chancery had, throughout the eighteenth century, been defining those limits, and had been co-ordinating the branches of law administered by the civilians with the common law and equity. As we shall now see these branches of law had, like equity, been co-ordinated with other branches of English law, in a manner which paved the way to the larger measure of assimilation which came in the nineteenth century.

THE CO-ORDINATION OF THE LAW MADE BY THE CIVILIANS WITH OTHER PARTS OF ENGLISH LAW

The civilian learning was regarded by the practitioners in the courts of law and equity as a recondite and rather mysterious subject, known only to the advocates and proctors of Doctors' Commons. There was some justification for this view. In the first place, we have seen that it was not till the end of the eighteenth and the beginning of the nineteenth centuries that reports of cases in the ecclesiastical courts and the court of Admiralty began to appear;[1] so that, apart from text-books, which always assumed a knowledge of the canon and civil law which few

---

[1] Above, p. 226.

practitioners in the courts of common law and equity possessed, it was a traditional learning,[1] of somewhat the same esoteric character as that of the medieval practitioners in the courts of common law in the days of the Year Books.[2] In the second place, the procedure of the ecclesiastical courts and the court of Admiralty, and therefore the technical environment in which the civilians administered their law, were very different from the procedure of the courts of common law and the court of Chancery, and therefore from the technical environment to which those practitioners were accustomed. These procedural differences, and the technical differences which resulted from them, were greater than those which separated the courts of common law from the court of Chancery. Therefore the bodies of law which were administered and developed in this different technical environment assumed a shape which was strange to the practitioners in the courts of law and equity.

But the civilians were an organized profession and a learned profession;[3] and the matters which fell within the jurisdiction of the courts in which they practised covered no inconsiderable field. Though the jurisdiction of the ecclesiastical courts was not so extensive as it had been in the Middle Ages, it was still considerable; and though the instance jurisdiction of the court of Admiralty had been crippled by the common law courts, it still had an exclusive prize jurisdiction. There was a considerable literature in English upon the various branches of the civilians' practice; and there was a still more considerable continental literature upon many of the topics which fell within it. It is not surprising, therefore, that the civilians were able to originate and develop

[1] Roscoe, *Life of Lord Stowell*, 34, cited above, p. 226, n. 1.

[2] Holdsworth, *H.E.L.* ii, 541–542; cp. Holdsworth, *Sources and Literature of English Law*, 89.

[3] Above, pp. 213–214, 215.

bodies of doctrine upon the various topics, falling within the jurisdiction of their courts, which made a considerable and important contribution to the English legal system. It was therefore necessary that the jurisdiction of these courts and the law which they made should be co-ordinated with the jurisdiction of the courts of common law and equity, and with the principles of law and equity which those courts were developing.

The civilians, under the superintendence of the courts of common law and the court of Chancery, helped to define the relations of these bodies of doctrine both to common law and to equity. Just as, during the eighteenth century, the courts of common law and equity had learned to define their spheres of jurisdiction and to work in partnership with one another,[1] so, during this century, the ecclesiastical courts and the court of Admiralty had learned to work in partnership with the courts of law and equity. Blackstone said of the relations which existed in his day between the ecclesiastical courts and the courts of law and equity that, though the ecclesiastical courts

continue to this day to decide many questions which are properly of temporal cognizance, yet justice is in general so ably and impartially administered in these tribunals (especially of the superior kind) and the boundaries of their power are now so well known and established, that no material inconvenience at present arises from this jurisdiction still continuing in the antient channel.[2]

And the same thing can be said of the jurisdiction of the court of Admiralty—the boundaries of its jurisdiction were well established and well known.

This co-ordination of the law made by the civilians with the rules of law and equity was the work of the eighteenth century. It was effected by means of de-cisions as to when either a writ of prohibition or an

[1] Above, pp 201, 204–5, 207–8.
[2] *Commentaries*, iii, 98–99.

injunction could be obtained. For instance, it was held
that the common law courts had jurisdiction when the
question at issue was whether a person had a title to
property such as tithes, when the question was whether
debts were due to or by the estate of a deceased person,
when the question was whether a criminal offence in
breach of a statute had been committed—so that in all
these cases a writ of prohibition would issue if the
ecclesiastical courts or the court of Admiralty assumed
jurisdiction.[1] It was held that the court of Chancery had
jurisdiction over all matters relating to trusts, over fraud,
over the construction of wills, over questions involving
the maintenance of infants—so that in all these cases the
court would issue an injunction against proceedings in
any other court.[2] These cases in which the question
whether or not a writ of prohibition or an injunction
should issue was discussed, show that the boundaries of
the jurisdiction of all these courts were being settled, that
the old rivalry between them was ceasing, and that they
were beginning to work together as partners. This was
a condition precedent to the co-ordination of these
different bodies of law. That co-ordination was helped
forward by the fact that common lawyers were occasionally heard in the court of Admiralty, by the fact that
civilians were sometimes heard in the common law courts
and the court of Chancery, and by the fact that common
law judges were generally members of the High Court
of Delegates which heard appeals in ecclesiastical causes.[3]

The reforms of the nineteenth century, which swept
away the old procedure of the ecclesiastical courts and
the court of Admiralty, removed the principal cause
which had separated the branches of law administered
by the civilians in their courts at Doctors' Commons
from the branches of law administered in the courts

[1] Holdsworth, *H.E.L.* xii, 698–699.
[2] *Ibid.* xii, 699–700.   [3] *Ibid.* xii, 700–701.

of common law and the court of Chancery. With its removal, Doctors' Commons itself was appropriately dissolved;[1] and the business which was once the preserve of the civilians was thrown open to the members of the common law and Chancery bars. But there are two respects in which the system of pleading and procedure evolved by the civilians has influenced the course of English legal history. In the first place, ideas taken from this system, just as ideas taken from the old common law and Chancery systems of procedure and pleading,[2] have influenced the new procedure inaugurated by the Judicature Act. Thus, as Phillimore has pointed out,[3] "the mode of pleading now in use in the High Court of Justice was modelled on that in use in the Admiralty court, which again was derived from that used in the ecclesiastical courts, though considerably condensed";[4] and the rule of practice, prevailing in the ecclesiastical courts, which sometimes allowed the courts to give the relief to which the parties were entitled, though the suit had been instituted for a different kind of relief, helped to introduce the practice of allowing counter-claims in actions in the High Court.[5] In the second place, just as our modern common law and our modern system of equity derive many of their characteristic features from the old systems of procedure in which and through which they were developed, so much of our modern law as to probate and administration, some of our modern law as to marriage, and much of our maritime and prize law, derive many

---

[1] In 1857 its charter was surrendered under a power contained in the statute which created the new court of Probate, and its property was divided among its members, 20, 21 Vict. c. 77, §§ 116, 117.

[2] Holdsworth, *H.E.L.* ix, 328–330, 407.

[3] *Ecclesiastical Law* (2nd ed.), ii, 959 n. (*x*).

[4] The analogy between the precedent of a libel in the court of Admiralty in a cause of damage, as given in Marriott, *Formulare Instrumentorum*, 148–159, and a modern statement of claim, is striking.

[5] Phillimore, *Ecclesiastical Law* (2nd ed.), ii, 956.

of their characteristic features from the system of procedure and pleading used by the civilians. The Probate, Divorce, and Admiralty Division of the High Court administers nearly all of those branches of law which once fell within the sphere of the civilians' practice; so that it, together with the Chancery Division, are an ever-present reminder of the diversity of the origins of different parts of the English legal system.

Lecture XI

BLACKSTONE, BENTHAM, AND AUSTIN

THE eighteenth century, like the Middle Ages, was a well-defined period in the history of England and of English law because it had a very distinct intellectual character. At the end of the century the new political ideas propagated by the French Revolution, the new economic ideas propagated by the Industrial Revolution, and the consequent changes in social ideas, altered fundamentally many of those ideas which had given to the eighteenth century this distinct intellectual character. Just as in the sixteenth century the three allied movements of Renaissance, Reformation, and Reception of Roman law substituted modern for medieval ideas,[1] so in the eighteenth and early nineteenth centuries, the ideas propagated by the French Revolution and the Industrial Revolution substituted the ideas suited to a new industrial and increasingly democratic society, for the ideas suited to the rural and aristocratic society of the eighteenth century. At both these periods the reforms in the law which were consequent on these changes, were effected more gradually and more peaceably in England than in continental states; and so the law was adapted to the new order with no violent break in the continuity of its development. The fact that this gradual and peaceable adaptation was possible was due partly to the constitutional character of the government of the English state, which made it a government to which most Englishmen were sincerely attached and of which they were proud, and partly to the way in which English law was adapted by the Legislature and the judges to meet the new needs.

[1] Above, pp. 69–70.

The law as developed by the great eighteenth-century lawyers was summed up by Blackstone. Though that law had been amended in the eighteenth century and adapted to the needs of that century, very much more extensive reforms were wanted to adapt it to the needs of the following century; and because they were more extensive they could only be made by the Legislature. Lawyers of the type of Hardwicke, Eldon, Mansfield, and Blackstone, whose outlook was the eighteenth-century outlook, were not disposed to welcome extensive legislative reforms; so that it was not till the lawyers of Bentham's new analytical school gained political influence that these reforms began to be undertaken. Bentham supplied a principle—the principle of utility—upon which these reforms should be made, and a programme of reform based on this principle. His disciple Austin supplied a jurisprudential theory to fit the needs of this reformed legal system. *A priori* analytical theories were then the fashionable theories—they influenced politics as well as law, and they were all powerful in the realm of economics. But the reforms in the law inspired by these theories were made gradually and carefully. They were skilfully pieced on to the existing fabric of English law which Blackstone had expounded; for though Bentham's principle and programme and Austin's theory were based on *a priori* reasoning, they were applied in practice by learned lawyers who had been educated in the professional historic tradition of English law. And so when Bentham's programme had been carried out, and Austin's theory had been assimilated, when these *a priori* analytical theories gave place to the evolutionary theories which Darwin's hypothesis made fashionable, it was not difficult for English lawyers to subscribe to the new historical school, which has deprived the principle of Bentham and the theory of Austin of much of the authority which they once enjoyed.

In this lecture I shall illustrate the intellectual outlook of the eighteenth century upon matters legal as it appears in one of its most typical representatives—Blackstone; and then I shall describe the very different intellectual outlook of Bentham and Austin, and the effects of their principles and theories upon English law. In the following lecture I shall describe the growth of the historical school of English lawyers, and the way in which it has placed the professional historic tradition of English law on a new basis, which has enabled English law to be adapted to new conditions with greater knowledge and understanding than was intellectually possible to wholehearted supporters of Bentham's principle of utility and Austin's theory of jurisprudence.

BLACKSTONE[1]

Lytton Strachey[2] has said of the eighteenth century that

in art, in thought, in the whole conduct of life, what it aimed at was the just, the truly proportioned, the approved and absolute best. Its ideals were stationary because they were so high; and the strict conformity which they enjoined was merely the expression of a hatred and scorn of everything short of perfection. Whether such ideals were ever realized, whether their realization was even possible, may indeed be doubted: what cannot be doubted is that they formed the framework of the eighteenth century mind.

This high ideal can be seen in the ideas and achievement of such lawyers as Hardwicke and Mansfield, and such statesmen as Burke. In legal literature it finds its expression in Blackstone's *Commentaries*.

Blackstone was born July 10, 1723. He was educated

---

[1] Holdsworth, *H.E.L.* xii, 702–736; Foss, *Lives of the Judges*, viii, 243–251; Dicey, "Blackstone's *Commentaries*", *Camb. Law Journal*, iv, 286–307; *Yale Law Journal*, xxvii, 599–618; xxviii, 542–560; *D.N.B.*

[2] *Characters and Commentaries*, 13.

at Charterhouse School and Pembroke College, Oxford; and in November, 1743, was elected a fellow of All Souls College, Oxford. He was called to the bar in 1746, but he made little progress, and returned to Oxford in 1753. There he did useful work as judge of the Chancellor's court; and, as delegate of the university press, he made some salutary reforms. He fortunately failed to become regius professor of civil law, because Newcastle—the prime minister—was not sufficiently assured of the correctness of his political views. Fortunately, because Sir William Murray—the future Lord Mansfield—persuaded him to break new ground by giving lectures on English law at Oxford. He began to give these lectures in 1753. When Viner left his property to the university to found a professorship of English law, the success of these lectures made it inevitable that Blackstone should be appointed the first Vinerian professor. He gave them as Vinerian professor from 1758 to 1766, and they were the basis of his *Commentaries*, which were published between 1765 and 1769. One reason why the *Commentaries* attained that final touch of excellence which entitles them to be called classical, is the fact that they originated in courses of lectures repeated every year for thirteen years.[1] Another reason is the fact that, at the end of that time, they were composed with great care by a man who was a learned lawyer, a learned historian, and a man of letters, whose mind was at once orderly and systematic.

Blackstone's lectures made him famous. In 1759 he resumed his practice in London; in 1761 he became a member of the House of Commons; and in 1763 he was made solicitor-general to the Queen. He was not a sufficiently ready debater to be a success in the House of Commons, as is shown by the episode which occurred in the House when his own *Commentaries* were cited

[1] For the MSS of Blackstone's lectures see Holdsworth, *H.E.L.* xii, 747–750.

against him to prove that a member who had been expelled was capable of being re-elected. In 1770 he became a judge of the court of Common Pleas.[1] His reports show that he was an able judge. The two most notable of his decisions were given in the cases of *Perrin* v. *Blake*[2] and *Scott* v. *Shepherd*.[3] He died February 14, 1780.

It is his *Commentaries* which entitle him to be numbered amongst the Makers of English Law. He prefixed to his *Commentaries* his inaugural lecture on the study of the law in which he gave a short history of legal education in England, and made a powerful plea for including the study of English law among the subjects taught at the university. This lecture forms the first section of his Introduction. In the ensuing three sections of the Introduction he speaks of the nature of law in general, of the laws of England, and of the countries subject to the laws of England. The work itself is divided into four books, to each of which a volume is allotted. The first book deals in eighteen chapters with the Rights of Persons. After dealing in the first chapter with the absolute rights of free persons, he goes on to deal in the ensuing eight chapters with those persons or bodies to which the government of the state is entrusted.[4] These chapters thus deal with constitutional law. In the tenth chapter he deals with the distinctions between natives, aliens, and denizens. In chapters eleven to thirteen he deals with "the sorts and conditions of men" under the three

---

[1] He was a judge of the King's Bench from February 16 to June 22, 1770, since he took the place of Yates J. who wished to change over to the Common Pleas; on the death of Yates J. he became a judge of the Common Pleas.

[2] (1772) Hargrave, *Law Tracts*, i, 490.

[3] (1773) 2 W. Bl. at pp. 895–898.

[4] The Parliament—the King and his Title—the King's Royal Family—the Councils belonging to the King—the King's duties—the King's Prerogative—the King's Revenue—Subordinate Magistrates.

heads of the clergy, the "civil state" or the laity, and soldiers and sailors. In chapters fourteen to seventeen a transition is made to private law; and the relations of master and servant, husband and wife, parent and child, and guardian and ward are described. The last chapter deals with corporations. The second book deals with the Rights of Things. It is a treatise on the law of property. The first twenty-three chapters contain the best short account that has ever been written of the law of real property. The remaining nine chapters deal with personal property—always an heterogeneous subject in English law. The third book deals with Private Wrongs. After two chapters on the redress of wrongs by act of the parties and by the operation of law, the four ensuing chapters describe the courts in which redress can be obtained. In the seventh chapter the jurisdiction of these various courts over different kinds of wrongs is described. The next three chapters deal with injuries to persons, to personal property, and to real property. Chapters eleven to sixteen deal with particular kinds of wrongs to property real and personal;[1] and chapter seventeen deals with injuries proceeding from or affecting the Crown. A transition is then made to the procedure followed by the courts in giving redress. Chapters eighteen to twenty-one deal with common law procedure and pleading;[2] and chapters twenty-two and three deal with different kinds of trial, and with trial by jury. The next three chapters deal with judgment, proceedings in the nature of appeals, and execution. The last chapter deals with proceedings in courts of equity. The fourth book deals with Public Wrongs. It is a very able summary in thirty-two chapters of the criminal law substantive and adjective. The whole work concludes with a chapter on

---

[1] Dispossession or Ouster of Chattels Real—Trespass—Nuisance—Waste—Subtraction—Disturbance.

[2] The Original Writ—Process—Pleading—Issue and Demurrer.

the rise, progress, and gradual improvement of the laws of England. Eight editions of the *Commentaries* were published in Blackstone's lifetime; and fifteen editions were produced by various editors between 1783 and 1849. In that year the first edition of Stephen's *Commentaries*, which were based on Blackstone's *Commentaries*, appeared. Stephen's work is now in its nineteenth edition.

When the book appeared it was at once acclaimed as a classic by lawyers and men of letters. Mansfield said that it was the ideal student's text-book;[1] and Gibbon read it three times and made a careful analysis of the first volume.[2] Even Bentham praised its literary qualities and admitted that its statements of the law were generally accurate.[3] Later lawyers such as Fitz-James Stephen[4] and Lord Campbell[5] have endorsed this verdict. What are the reasons for this unanimous verdict? First, as Dicey has said, "the *Commentaries* live by their style".[6] He was, said Bentham,[7] "the first of all institutional writers who has taught Jurisprudence to speak the language of the Scholar and the Gentleman". Secondly, the *Commentaries* state the law of Blackstone's day with great accuracy. Thirdly, they were composed with great literary tact—important principles are emphasized, and the student's attention is not distracted by the statement of subordinate rules and the elaboration of technical minutiae. Fourthly, they were the most complete statement of English law that had yet appeared. This quality of completeness has been emphasized by Lord Campbell,[8]

---

[1] Holliday, *Life of Lord Mansfield*, 89–90.
[2] Holdsworth, *H.E.L.* xii, 750–754.
[3] *A Comment on the Commentaries* (Everett's ed.), 147.
[4] *History of Criminal Law*, ii, 214–215.
[5] *Lives of the Chief Justices*, ii, 62.
[6] *Camb. Law Journal*, iv, 294.
[7] *Fragment on Government* (Montague's ed.), Pref. p. 116.
[8] *Lives of the Chief Justices*, ii, 62.

by Maitland,[1] by Fitz-James Stephen,[2] and by Professor
Lévy-Ullmann.[3] As we might expect, so great a book has
had a considerable influence on the future development
of the law. In the first place, Blackstone's summary of
the main principles of English law was of great assistance
to the law reformers of the nineteenth century, because
it gave them a clear view of the law which they proposed
to reform. Similarly, his work was and is of great assistance to us modern lawyers, because it helps us to steer
our way through that labyrinth of statutes which have
changed the face of English law. Secondly, the immense
popularity of the *Commentaries* in America, both before
and after the Declaration of Independence,[4] has helped
to add to the link of a common language that other link
of common legal principles. The gift by the Americans
of Blackstone's statue in 1924 was a graceful return, not
merely for hospitality, but for the work of the man who
had played a great part in the forging of that link of
common legal principles. Thirdly, Blackstone was the
pioneer of our modern system of the university teaching
of law. His ideas on this subject were accepted first in
the United States, and later in this country; and in both
countries their acceptance has effected a great improvement in the literature of the law, and therefore in the
law itself.

Blackstone's book described the law of the eighteenth
century. It was a child of its age, not only in the perfection of its form and style, but also in its ideas. But
when he was writing it, and still more when he was
revising its later editions, the eighteenth century was
passing. New economic conditions and new political
ideas were producing a demand for extensive reforms in

---

[1] Bracton's *Note Book*, i, 7–8.
[2] *History of Criminal Law*, ii, 214–215.
[3] *La Système Juridique de l'Angleterre*, i, 269.
[4] Hammond, *Blackstone's "Commentaries"*, Pref. p. ix; cp. Holdsworth, *Some Lessons from our Legal History*, 174–176.

the law; and that demand grew more and more insistent in the years which followed. Therefore, Blackstone's book, which was not only a faithful picture of the law of his day, but a glowing appreciation of its merits, became the target of criticism which became more bitter as the need for reform became more pressing. To a consideration of this criticism we must now turn.

Bentham and his school of analytical jurists were Blackstone's principal critics. We shall see that Bentham made his name by his *Fragment on Government* in which he opened his attack on Blackstone.[1] That attack was based on two main grounds. In the first place, Bentham denounced Blackstone as the indiscriminate apologist for all things established. There is an element of truth in this criticism; but as I have elsewhere shown[2] very much less truth in it than is generally supposed. In the second place, Bentham said that, as a jurisprudential thinker, Blackstone was weak and confused. That criticism is based on a fundamental misunderstanding of the *Commentaries*. In that part of the *Commentaries* which Bentham criticized, Blackstone was attempting to sketch the evolution of the English constitution and of its salient features. To apply, as Bentham did, to an historical sketch of this kind an analysis based on the principle of utility and the doctrine of sovereignty is unreasonable and misplaced. Such a criticism afforded abundant opportunities for condemnation; but, like Hobbes's criticism of Coke,[3] it was unfair because it approached the subject from a point of view totally different from that of the work criticized.

When the age of reform began in the nineteenth century the leaders of thought were the new Whigs who had learned from Bentham, and not the old Whigs who had learned from Burke. This was the reason why the

[1] Below, p. 249.   [2] Holdsworth, *H.E.L.* xii, 728–730.
[3] Above, pp. 126–127.

legend of Blackstone's undiscriminating optimism, and his incompetence as a political and a jurisprudential thinker, was perpetuated; and it helped for nearly a century to diminish the fame of the *Commentaries*. But these controversies are now a century old. We suffer from other ills than those which oppressed the age to which Bentham spoke; and so we can take a more impartial view of the strong and the weak points of Bentham and Blackstone.

Bentham did great things for English law by helping forward many long-needed reforms. Similarly, Austin helped English lawyers to clarify their ideas upon such fundamental matters as law, sovereignty, rights, and duties. But the school of historical lawyers which arose in the middle of the nineteenth century has deprived the school of Bentham and Austin of that sovereign control over legal thought which they exercised earlier in that century. Men like Maine and Pollock and Maitland in England, like Holmes, Ames, Thayer and Wigmore in America, have taught lawyers a larger philosophy of law, which does not disdain the lessons of the past or the wisdom which can be extracted from old law. And so to us Blackstone is not, as Bentham pictures him, the enemy to all reformation, and the inaccurate thinker who used his literary gifts to bolster up established abuses. Rather, he is the literary artist, the historical scholar, and the accomplished lawyer, who has woven into a harmonious texture all the variegated strands which made up the fabric of that English law of the old regime, which, in England, in India, and in the United States, is the foundation of large parts of the law which governs us to-day.

BENTHAM[1]

Jeremy Bentham was born February 15, 1748. His father was an attorney, and he wished to make his precocious son a famous lawyer. But though Bentham was called to the bar by Lincoln's Inn in 1769,[2] he refused to practise. From the first he was interested not in practice, but in jurisprudential and political speculations. As early as 1776 he had started a work on jurisprudence, which was published in 1789 under the title of *The Principles of Morals and Legislation*. In it his jurisprudential theories and the manner in which they should be applied to the reform of existing legal systems are explained. It was in 1776 also that he published anonymously his *Fragment on Government*, which was an attack upon the Introduction to Blackstone's *Commentaries*. He said with some exaggeration that it was "the very first publication by which men at large were invited to break loose from the trammels of authority and ancestor wisdom in the field of law".[3] With some exaggeration, because in the seventeenth century Hobbes had by methods and reasoning not dissimilar attacked Coke's writings.[4] The *Fragment* was originally a part of a larger work, entitled *A Comment on the Commentaries*, which has been recently published by Mr Everett. This larger work contains many acute criticisms of English law, including a very sound piece of criticism on Mansfield's attempts to reform the law by judicial decision.[5] But it is more especially a book for lawyers. Bentham acted wisely when he detached his *Fragment* and published it separately; for it appealed to a wider audience,

[1] *D.N.B.*; Dicey, *Law and Opinion*; Halévy, *Growth of Philosophic Radicalism*; Mill, *Dissertations and Discussions*, i, 330–392.

[2] *Black Books of Lincoln's Inn*, iii, 400; he was made a bencher in 1817, *ibid.* iv, 147.

[3] Bentham, *Works*, i, 260, n.

[4] Above, pp. 126–127.   [5] Cited above, p. 173.

and Blackstone had in his Introduction laid himself open to more obvious criticism.

The *Fragment* was written in so attractive a style that it was ascribed to some of the greatest lawyers of the day —to Lord Mansfield, to Lord Camden, and to Dunning.[1] When its authorship became known it made Bentham's name. Shelburne called on him, and welcomed him to Bowood where he met some of the leading lawyers and statesmen of the day. In 1785 Bentham visited his brother Samuel who was in the service of the Russian government. While there he wrote his *Defence of Usury*, and began his studies in the criminal law. These included a plan for a model prison—the *Panopticon*—and his *Principles of Penal Law*. The Legislature was at first inclined to take up the former project, but later on abandoned it, and compensated Bentham for the expenses which he had incurred.

From 1790 onwards Bentham was engaged on many literary works and advocated many projects. He wrote a book on political tactics for the use of the French National Assembly, which made him in return a French citizen; a criticism of the poor law, in which he anticipated many of the principles carried out in 1834; and a pamphlet entitled *The Truth* v. *Ashhurst* in which he controverted the generally received constitutional principles explained by Ashhurst J. to the grand jury of Middlesex. He was constantly writing; but he rarely completed anything; and, as we shall see, his most important books were edited and completed by his friends and admirers.[2]

Bentham at the outset was no democrat—as his tract on *Anarchical Fallacies* shows. But the time was not favourable for the consideration of far-reaching projects for the reform of English law; and so his ideas and his projects for reform attracted little or no attention in

[1] Bentham, *Works*, i, 240.   [2] Below, p. 254.

England. He was better known abroad, since some of his most important works had been edited and translated into French by Dumont and published in France. It was partly because the English governing classes refused to listen to his projects, and partly because in 1809 he came under the influence of James Mill, that he threw in his lot with the radicals, and became a democrat. Mill and Bentham together effected what neither could have effected alone. "Bentham gave Mill a doctrine, and Mill gave Bentham a school."[1] From that time onwards Bentham was regarded as the friend and oracle of all persons at home or abroad who were interested in reforms in the law; and justifiably, for, to the end of his long life, he continued to devote himself to writing on law, jurisprudence, ethics, logic, and political economy. To the end he carried on a large correspondence with his friends, and with statesmen British and foreign. He died in 1832 on the day before the Reform Act received the royal assent—famous throughout Europe and America, and in England the head of a school of lawyers belonging to many political parties who, under his inspiration, were preparing to adapt English law to the needs of the new industrial age.[2] What were the reasons why Bentham had, at the time of his death, attained this great position?

In the first place, Bentham, when he first began to write, gave expression to ideas which many were beginning to entertain. Some time before Bentham made his name as Blackstone's critic, Gibbon, in some notes which he made to his abstract of the first Book of the *Commentaries*, had expressed views very similar to his. Like Bentham he was opposed to the mystery in which some legal doctrines had been shrouded by the lawyers; he preferred the enacted to the unenacted law; and he believed in testing the expediency of a law by the criterion

[1] Halévy, *Growth of Philosophic Radicalism*, 251.
[2] *Ibid.* 479.

of utility.[1] Bentham tells us that, "some time after the appearance of the *Fragment* (1776), the House of Commons was found to contain a small knot of young men, in whose minds a disposition to contribute to the improvement of the law had begun to manifest itself".[2] But on what principle were these reforms to be made? Bentham was ready with an answer—the principle of utility. That principle, applied by a sovereign Legislature, was to be the principle which was to settle both what reforms were needed and how they were to be made. The application of this principle in this way to existing institutions, and to the reasoning by which, in Blackstone's *Commentaries*, those institutions were supported, led to some surprising conclusions. Shelburne, and others who admired the *Fragment*, could not help seeing that here was a principle which could be used as a guide to suggest and to justify changes which must sooner or later be made, if the law and institutions of England were to be brought into conformity with the new conditions which were rapidly arising. Thus the ground was prepared for the reception of Bentham's theories.

In the second place, though Bentham did not invent the principle of utility, though he was not alone in thinking that it ought to be applied to test the merits of a law, he applied it in much greater detail and with much more consistency than any other jurist had ever applied it. He applied it in much greater detail, analysing the pleasures and pains of various orders which flowed from objectionable courses of conduct, the pleasures and pains involved in punishing them, and striking a balance which proved the justification for their suppression and indicated the mode in which they should be suppressed. He applied it also with much more consistency. He took nothing for granted, and tried all existing laws and institutions by this test—Do they in their present form

[1] Holdsworth, *H.E.L.* xii, 730.   [2] *Works*, i, 241.

make for the greatest happiness of the greatest number? If not they must be condemned. Therefore he was, as Mill has said, "the great questioner of things established".[1] And there were no limits to his questioning. Men like Hardwicke, Burke, Mansfield, and Blackstone, though not opposed to all reforms, would have agreed with Horace Walpole that "there is a wide difference between correcting abuses and removing land marks".[2] Bentham did not recognize this distinction. And, unlike very many of his contemporaries, the French Revolution made no difference to his determination to criticize abuses in all departments of the law. It is because there were no limits to his questioning that his teaching, as Mill has said, "expelled mysticism from the philosophy of law".[3]

In the third place, Bentham was not merely critical. As Mill says, "he made it a point of conscience, not to assail error until he thought he could plant instead the corresponding truth".[4] And his positive suggestions were all founded on elaborate demonstrations of the fact that the changes which he suggested complied with his test of utility. It was the fact that Bentham submitted all existing laws and institutions and all his suggested reforms to this test, that is the secret of his influence, because, as Maine has said, it furnished lawyers and statesmen with "a distinct object to aim at in the pursuit of improvement".[5] It is for this reason that it did for English law what the theory of Natural law did for Roman law.[6]

In the fourth place, Bentham "took up the theory of sovereignty where Hobbes left it";[7] and he made one

---

[1] *Dissertations and Discussions*, i, 332.
[2] *Letters* (ed. Toynbee), xiii, 86.
[3] *Dissertations and Discussions*, i, 373.   [4] *Ibid.* i, 338.
[5] *Ancient Law*, 78.   [6] *Ibid.* 79.
[7] Pollock, *History of the Science of Politics*, 96.

considerable addition to it. Not only did he use it to
define the state and the law, not only did he use it to
prove that law enacted by a sovereign is the only law of
which a legal system should consist, and that it attained
its most perfect shape in a code, he also maintained that
it was the duty of the sovereign to be an active legislator
in order to make the principle of utility prevail throughout the legal system. "The formula of the greatest
happiness is made a hook to put in the nostrils of
Leviathan, that he may be tamed and harnessed to the
chariot of utility."[1] Naturally, he emphasized the deficiencies of judge-made law, and both he and Austin
poured scorn on Lord Mansfield's idea that the judges
were better fitted for the work of law reform than the
Legislature.[2] Bentham, as Dicey says,[3] "forced the faith
in scientific legislation upon the attention of a generation
of Englishmen by whom its truth or importance was
denied or forgotten".

It was these ideas and principles applied in detail to
many branches of law, and to several distinct branches
of knowledge, that give Bentham his great position
amongst the Makers of English Law; for, as Brougham
said, he was the first to try all the provisions of the law
by the test of expediency, and to inquire how far they
were adapted to "the circumstances of society, to the
wants of man, and to the promotion of human happiness".[4] On such matters as the reform of the statute
book, the codification of the law, the reform of the judicial
system, the reform of the criminal code and the law of
evidence, the reform of the law of real property, liberty
of conscience, the reform of the poor law, Bentham's

[1] Pollock, *History of the Science of Politics*, 101.
[2] Bentham, *Works*, vii, 311; Austin's views on this matter are cited
by Mill, *Dissertations and Discussions*, iii, 252.
[3] *Law and Opinion* (1st ed.), 135.
[4] Brougham's *Speeches*, ii, 288, cited Dicey, *Law and Opinion* (1st
ed.), 126.

books and ideas educated those who reformed all these branches of the law. It is this achievement which makes the period of legislative reform which had begun before 1832, and continued with much greater intensity after 1832, the period of Benthamism.

Some part of Bentham's success was due to his good fortune. He lived long enough to make his influence felt, and he was rich enough to be able to devote his whole time to his speculations. But perhaps his greatest piece of good fortune was the unexpected result of two of his intellectual defects. One of these defects was his incapacity to finish and publish his writings. He was always writing and rewriting but never finally finishing anything.[1] The other defect was the terrible jargon of invented words and interminable sentences which he used in his later days in order to ensure accuracy.[2] Both these defects were cured by devoted disciples such as Dumont and J. S. Mill, who took his manuscripts, completed them, and made them intelligible.[1] They interpreted Bentham and made it possible for his ideas to influence the minds of lawyers and statesmen. And here again he was fortunate. It would have been impossible without a revolution to have carried out literally and in detail his major suggestions for the reform of the law. But these suggestions were passed through the minds of practical lawyers and statesmen, such as

[1] J. S. Mill in his *Autobiography*, 114–116, tells us how he amalgamated three masses of MSS, and translated Bentham's "involved and parenthetical sentences", when he produced the *Rationale of Judicial Evidence*.

[2] "Preoccupation with terminology never ceased to engage Bentham's attention; he attempted to solve its problems by inventing a vocabulary of his own. Thereby he incurred the reproach which he levelled at lawyers, of fashioning their notions 'as unlike as possible to those of other men'; and though in some instances, like the term 'codify' and 'international law', he definitely added to the language, too often he merely substituted one difficulty for another", C. K. Allen, "The Young Bentham", *L.Q.R.* xliv, 506.

Brougham and Mackintosh and Romilly and many others, who, sometimes to Bentham's disgust, modified them, in order to give them a practical shape.[1] Bentham's reputation owes something to all these pieces of good fortune. Both his own abilities and single-minded industry, and his good fortune, combined to give him his influence and his fame.

The defects of Bentham's philosophy of law are patent. He ignored all other schools of thought, and he ignored history. His knowledge of human nature was limited. He believed that his principles could be applied to any nation at any stage of civilization, and he was therefore ready to construct a code for any country in the world. A code he thought would solve all difficulties— ignoring the truth that the best code cannot solve those questions of fact which are often the most difficult questions that come before a court.[2] He ignored the advantages of and indeed the necessity for lawyer-made law, whether in the form of case law or in the form of authoritative books. Some of these defects, it is true, helped to give added efficacy to the crusade for reform carried on by Bentham and his followers; for they enabled them to ignore difficulties and objections. But when the reforms which Bentham advocated had been effected, these defects in his philosophy began to be realized, and a demand arose for a philosophy of law which was more in accord with the facts of history and of human nature.

The merits and defects of Bentham's legal philosophy naturally appear in the work of his disciple Austin—but in a different setting; for Bentham, as Maine said, is a writer on legislation—on law as it ought to be: Austin is

---

[1] See Dillon, "Bentham's Influence", *Essays in Anglo-American Legal History*, i, 502, n. 1.
[2] See Maine, *Early Institutions*, 49–50.

a writer on jurisprudence—on law as it is.[1] But Austin's jurisprudence is founded on a legal system formed on Bentham's model; and in their *a priori* method of approach, in their belief in the principle of utility, in their definition of sovereignty and law, and in their views as to the place which should be taken by direct legislation in a legal system, they hold identical views.

AUSTIN[2]

The lives of John Austin and Jeremy Bentham were very different. Bentham was rich, healthy, happy in his life of study, happy in the respect which, at the end of his life, was felt for him by statesmen of all parties and by the legal profession. Austin was poor, his constitution was weak, he was a failure as a teacher of law, the merits of his writings were unrecognized by all but a few, and, when he died, he was almost unknown amongst lawyers. His fame was, to a large extent, posthumous, and was due to J. S. Mill's essay, and to the publication of the new edition of his *Jurisprudence* in 1861.

John Austin was born March 3, 1790. At the age of sixteen he entered the army, but left it five years later, and was called to the bar by the Inner Temple in 1818. In 1820 he married his very gifted wife, who appended to the second edition of his *Jurisprudence* a touching sketch of her husband's character and his struggles against an adverse fate. After their marriage they lived in Queen Square next door to Bentham, so that they were in close touch with the Benthamite circle. Both were brilliant talkers, and to their house came some of the leading liberal lawyers and statesmen of the day. But ill-health and inability to work quickly prevented Austin

---

[1] *Early Institutions*, 343–344.

[2] Mrs Austin's memoir prefixed to the editions of his *Jurisprudence* which were published in 1861 and 1869; Mill, *Dissertations and Discussions*, iii, 206–274; *D.N.B.*

from succeeding at the bar. In 1826 he was appointed professor of jurisprudence at London University; and he qualified himself for the post by an intensive course of study in Germany. But though his lectures attracted able men they were not a success. Though he had enthusiasm for his subject, though he could explain very clearly, and could even be eloquent, his extreme conscientiousness made him overload his matter with so much verbiage in his attempt to attain accuracy, that it is often as unreadable as an Act of Parliament. He resigned his chair in 1832, and a course of lectures which he gave at the Inner Temple was equally unsuccessful. It is certain that these failures were not due wholly to Austin's shortcomings as a lecturer. It is only fair to Austin to remember that amongst his audience were men who became famous, and that J. S. Mill who heard his lectures says that they left "an indelible impression" on those who heard them.[1] Austin's failures were principally due to the fact that legal education had sunk to so low a level, that it was hardly to be expected that any great number of lawyers would feel any interest in an attempt to expound the theory of law. In 1833 Austin was appointed a member of the criminal code commission; but he was unable to see eye to eye with his colleagues, and resigned. His most successful work was done as the colleague of Cornewall Lewis on a commission to enquire into the government of Malta. After his return from Malta in 1837 ill-health prevented him from doing more than write an occasional pamphlet; and the diffidence which made him undervalue his achievement in the sphere of jurisprudence, prevented him from revising and republishing the book on Jurisprudence, which he had published in 1832. He died in 1859.

Only the first edition of his book on Jurisprudence was completed and published by himself; and it is clear

[1] *Dissertations and Discussions*, iii, 220.

that he regarded it only as a provisional publication. J. S. Mill has told us something of the reasons why he never produced a complete treatise on his subject.

He had so high a standard of what ought to be done, so exaggerated a sense of deficiencies in his own performances, and was so unable to content himself with the amount of elaboration sufficient for the occasion and the purpose, that he not only spoilt much of his work for ordinary use by over labouring it, but spent so much time and exertion in superfluous study and thought, that when his task ought to have been completed, he had generally worked himself into an illness, without having half finished what he undertook.[1]

In these circumstances it is surprising that he produced enough to entitle him to a place amongst the Makers of English Law in the nineteenth century.

In recent years writers on jurisprudence have neglected the qualities which have given Austin's work a permanent place amongst the select band of English lawyers who have written notable books on legal theory. They have concentrated their attention upon the defects which were the necessary results of the intellectual characteristics of the period when he wrote. Seeing that fashions change in men's outlook on legal theory with changes in the intellectual outlook of different periods, as quickly as they change in any other branch of philosophy or political theory, this phenomenon is not surprising. Austin like Bentham was a thinker of the analytical school: later in the century an historical school arose which attacked both the premises and the conclusions of the analytical school. "In the last decade of the nineteenth century," says Dean Pound, "it was for a time the fashion for every dabbler in jurisprudence to have a fling at Austin. Now it is the fashion for everyone to fling a brick at nineteenth-century historical juris-

[1] *Autobiography*, 75.

prudence." It is not therefore surprising to find that many now think that the criticism of the historical school "did him no permanent harm", with the result that Austin is "coming into his own again".[1] Let us look first at the defects of Austin's work which the historical school has emphasized, and then consider briefly why, in spite of these defects, he is one of the most important figures in the English literature of jurisprudence.

I think that the defects of Austin's work are due to the fact that he was too faithful a follower of Bentham and his school. As we have seen, his early married life was passed in the shadow of Bentham and his school; and though in one or two points he differs from Bentham, for instance in his admission of the need for judge-made law[2] and in his appreciation of Coke,[3] it is clear that the influence of Bentham on his work was overwhelming. In fact the two most characteristic features of his work are derived from Bentham. The first of these features is his treatment of the doctrine of sovereignty, and his views as to the definition of a political society. He treats these matters in more detail and analyses them more elaborately than Bentham, but in fundamentals both hold the same views. The second of these features is his insistence on the principle of utility which he identifies with the law of God. This thesis is developed in his second, third and fourth lectures. The relevance of these lectures to his subject—the philosophy of positive law—has often been questioned. Austin was conscious that their relevance was not obvious, and attempts to meet this objection by saying that the principle of utility is the principle which "not only ought to guide but has commonly in fact guided the legislator"; so that he could not "explain distinctly and precisely the scope and purport of a law"

---

[1] Pound, *Fashions in Juristic Thinking*, Lecture delivered at the Holdsworth Club at Birmingham University, May 7, 1937, 12–13.
[2] *Jurisprudence* (3rd ed.), i, 224.   [3] *Ibid.* ii, 1130.

without a reference to it.[1] In fact Austin's conception of
jurisprudence made it necessary that he should discuss
the principle of utility. That conception depended
on the idea held by the followers of Bentham that all
branches of knowledge—political economy, history, law
—could be treated as exact sciences, which were founded
on truths as certain and universal as the truths of mathematics.[2] But if jurisprudence was a science of this
character it must depend on a series of moral truths which
could be treated as axioms. It was inevitable that these
axioms should consist of deductions from that theory of
utility upon which, according to Bentham, all truth
depended. It was equally inevitable that Austin should
accept them without question and expound them as the
necessary foundation of his analysis, for unless he had
accepted them and expounded them he could not have
attained his object, which was the creation of a science
of positive law based on a set of principles permanently
and universally true.[3] In other matters also Austin was
a faithful follower of Bentham. Like Bentham he treated
history as a series of object lessons in the errors of other
schools of thought, and not as a means to explain legal
rules; and like him he would have liked to scrap existing
rules and replace them by a new code—he resigned his
membership of the criminal law commission because his
colleagues did not see eye to eye with him on this matter.

[1] *Jurisprudence*, i, 125.

[2] "The ambition of the Benthamites was to establish all the sciences
on the model of the deductive sciences. In political economy, Ricardo
and James Mill compared the certainty of the propositions they were
advancing to the certainty of the propositions of Euclid", Halévy,
Growth of Philosophic Radicalism, 493–494.

[3] "Bentham and Austin sometimes write as if they thought that,
although obscured by false theory, false logic, and false statement, there
is somewhere behind all the delusions which they expose a framework
of permanent legal conceptions which is discoverable by a trained eye,
looking through a dry light, and to which a rational Code may always be
fitted", Maine, *Early Law and Custom*, 360.

He imitated Bentham in the truculence of his criticism of those who disagreed with his views. He agreed with Bentham in his hatred of Blackstone, and he even denied any merit to Blackstone's literary style.[1] Hooker's eloquent and noble conception of law[2] was described by him as "fustian".[3]

These are Austin's defects. But I think that they are outweighed by his merits. In the first place, he has defined with accuracy and clarity fundamental legal conceptions. This, as Mill rightly says,[4] is his great contribution to juristic thought. In the second place, though he neglects history and though his idea that there can be an exact science of positive law is a delusion, he does give us a useful analysis of the legal phenomena of mature legal systems. In the third place, Mill was right when he said that the study of Austin's writings was a lesson in "the difficult art of precise thought".[5] It is for this reason that his writings have an educational value for the lawyer as great as, but different from, the writings of Bentham. The nature of this educational value is clearly explained by Mill in the following passage:[6]

Mr Austin once said of himself, that if he had any special intellectual vocation it was that of "untying knots". In this judgment he estimated his own qualifications very correctly. The untying of intellectual knots; the clearing up of the puzzles arising from complex combinations of ideas confusedly appre-hended, and not analysed into their elements; the building up of definite conceptions where only indefinite ones existed, and where the current phrases disguised and perpetuated the indefiniteness; the disentangling of the classifications and distinctions grounded on differences in the things themselves, from those arising out of

---

[1] *Jurisprudence*, i, 71.
[2] *Ecclesiastical Polity*, bk. I, § 16, cited Holdsworth, *H.E.L.* iv, 212.
[3] *Jurisprudence*, i, 217.
[4] *Dissertations and Discussions*, iii, 220.
[5] *Ibid.* iii, 207.
[6] *Ibid.* iii, 207–208.

the mere accidents of their history, and, when disentangled, applying the distinctions (often for the first time) clearly, consistently, and uniformly—these were, of the many admirable characteristics of Mr Austin's work as a jurist, those which most especially distinguished him. This untying of knots was not particularly characteristic of Bentham. He cut them rather. He preferred to draw his pen through the whole of the past, and begin anew at the beginning.

Consequently, Austin's work has had a considerable influence in educating and shaping legal thought during the latter half of the nineteenth century, and therefore in rendering more efficacious those many reforms in the law which changing political, social and economic needs have rendered necessary. "So stimulating is Austin as an author," says Jethro Brown,[1] "so rare is his power of analysis, and so far reaching has been his influence upon later thought, that no student of legal science in the Anglo-Saxon world...can afford to remain wholly unacquainted with the Austinian text."

The services which Bentham and Austin have rendered to English law in reforming its substance and in clearing the minds of English lawyers are undoubted. But both Bentham and Austin were too apt to speak contemptuously of the work of the great lawyers of the past, because their ideas and reasoning were not based on the theory of utility which they regarded as the absolute and ultimate truth; and they were too apt to treat as mere nonsense, and sometimes as dishonest nonsense, legal theories which ignored it. This habit of mind was naturally reflected by their admirers. The result is that they have sometimes exaggerated the very real services which Bentham and Austin have rendered to English law. Thus Macaulay said that Bentham "found jurisprudence a gibberish and left it a science";[2] and Mill

---

[1] *The Austinian Theory of Law*, xi.   [2] Essay on Mirabeau.

agreed.[1] But, if those verdicts are true, how was it that English lawyers were able to make their legal system one of the great legal systems of the world? How did they manage in the eighteenth century to construct and work a Constitution which was universally admired? How did they manage to think out for themselves wholly original ideas on the law of property, contract, and tort? The truth is that English lawyers have never ignored legal theories, but they have declined, as Blackstone's *Commentaries* show, to be mastered by any one of them. They have preferred to build upon the stable foundation of the concrete facts of life and the needs of human beings, rather than upon the shifting sands of the conflicting theories of ingenious philosophers. Bentham's theories were rarely applied in their entirety. They were used by practical lawyers to make much needed reforms in English law in a manner which entailed the minimum of change in the established principles of that law. Thus they fitted the law to meet the needs of a new age without sacrificing the continuity of its development. In one case, where Bentham's recommendations were accepted in their entirety, the results were soon found to be unsatisfactory. It was due to these recommendations that the usury laws were repealed in 1854; but less than fifty years afterwards the Legislature found it necessary to check the unconscionable dealings of moneylenders, which the repeal of those laws had facilitated. Moreover, those who blame English lawyers for their indifference to legal theory forget that it was not only English lawyers who refused to accept Bentham's proposals in bulk. As M. Halévy has pointed out,[2] his influence abroad was greatest in those countries like Russia which had no philosophic tradition of their own. And as it was with

---

[1] "He found the philosophy of law a chaos, he left it a science", *Dissertations and Discussions*, i, 368.

[2] *Growth of Philosophic Radicalism*, 296.

Bentham's theories, so it was with Austin's central doctrine—his theory of sovereignty. His book on Jurisprudence was published in 1832, and during the greater part of the nineteenth century its influence was great. But the leading principles of responsible government were developed in Canada between 1840 and 1850 and were applied in the other Dominions before the end of the century. English lawyers and statesmen had fully realized his theory of sovereignty; they admitted it and used it; but they refused to become its slaves.

That English lawyers were thus able to use Bentham's and Austin's theories to reform their system in a practical manner which preserved the continuity of English legal history, is due, as I said at the beginning of this lecture, to the presence of a professional tradition amongst English lawyers which, because it was essentially historical, easily allied itself to that historical school of English lawyers which arose in the latter half of the nineteenth century. Of this professional tradition, of the rise of this historical school, and of its effects upon the development of English law, I shall speak in my next lecture.

Lecture XII

MAINE, MAITLAND, AND POLLOCK[1]

THE English system of case law, and the continuity of the development of English law public and private, have established an historical tradition amongst English lawyers, because both these causes have made it necessary for them to make researches into history in order to ascertain the law applicable to the cases which come before them. In the second half of the nineteenth century this historical tradition was both strengthened and enlightened by the rise of a new school of historically minded lawyers, which has put the study of law and history on a new basis. That school, while acknowledging the benefits conferred on English law by the reforms which were inspired by Bentham and his followers, has emancipated legal thought from the almost exclusive control of their narrow philosophy. By bringing the study and practice of English law into closer touch with the political, social, and economic history of England, and with the political, social, and economic needs of the day, it has broadened and humanized its rules and principles, because it has applied to them a criticism based on an understanding of past ideas and present needs which was impossible to the jurists of the analytical school.

In this lecture I shall begin by saying something of the historical tradition of English lawyers and of the rise of the new school of historically minded lawyers. Then I shall say something of the work and achievement of three of its most eminent members—Maine, Maitland, and Pollock.

[1] In this lecture I have used the information contained in my book on *The Historians of Anglo-American Law*, and in some passages I have not attempted to vary the wording.

THE HISTORICAL TRADITION AND THE RISE
OF THE NEW HISTORICAL SCHOOL

One of the principal effects of Coke's work was the preservation of the historic continuity of the common law,[1] and therefore the establishment of an historical tradition, which has made it necessary for all lawyers to know something of the history of the law, and has made some of our more learned lawyers no mean historians.[2] During the latter part of the seventeenth century the strength of this historical tradition made it difficult for James II to get twelve judges, and impossible for him to get twelve lawyers, to see eye to eye with him on questions of constitutional law;[3] and the improvement in the character of the bench, which followed the Revolution, strengthened it. If we look at any of the important books of the eighteenth century—at such books as Hawkins's *Pleas of the Crown*, Burn's *Justices of the Peace*, Fearne's *Contingent Remainders*, or Butler's notes to Coke upon Littleton—we can see that the lawyers who wrote them were well read in the history of the legal doctrines of English law; and it was the strength of this historical tradition which defeated Lord Mansfield's attempts to reform from the bench established doctrines of the common law.[4] In the third quarter of the eighteenth century this tradition was broadened and enlightened by Blackstone's *Commentaries*. The *Commentaries* are not only the best literary statement of the law of Blackstone's day, but also the best history of English law that had yet appeared.[5] They had a great influence, both in England

---

[1] Above, pp. 128–129.

[2] For an account of this historical tradition which has been established in the legal profession see Holdsworth, *The Historians of Anglo-American Law*, 11–29.

[3] Holdsworth, *H.E.L.* vi, 509–510.   [4] Above, pp. 167, 172–173.

[5] Holdsworth, *The Historians of Anglo-American Law*, 55–60.

and America, in maintaining the historical tradition; and
they began the process of eliminating many of those
crude legends to which Coke's credulity had given
currency.[1] When, at the end of the eighteenth and the
beginning of the nineteenth centuries, law reform, inspired by Bentham's *a priori* reasonings from the principle of utility, began, this historical tradition, broadened
and enlightened by Blackstone, was of the utmost service
in preserving the continuity of English law. Though
large parts of English law were reformed by lawyers who
had learned in Bentham's school, these lawyers had, as
we have seen,[2] absorbed the historical tradition. The
reforming statutes were generally preceded by reports
which contained careful historical statements of the law,
reasons why reform was needed, and skilful suggestions
as to how the new rules could, with least disturbance, be
substituted for the old. Perhaps the best illustration of
a reform carried out in this manner is the Fines and
Recoveries Act.[3] All through the nineteenth century,
and down to the present day, the effects of this historical
tradition can be seen in the judgments of such lawyers as
Willes, Blackburn, Cockburn, Lindley, Bowen, and
Macnaghten.

No doubt, as Maitland has pointed out,[4] the maintenance of this historical tradition has had some bad
effects on the study of legal history. In the first place, the
lawyer necessarily looks at the law from the point of view
of its bearing on the case before him. Therefore if it is
necessary for him to have recourse to medieval authorities, he reads them with the object, not of finding out
what they meant for the lawyer of the Middle Ages, but
of finding out what they have come to mean in the light
of modern decisions. Maitland says:[5]

---

[1] Above, p. 120.   [2] Above, pp. 254–255, 263.
[3] 3, 4 Will. IV, c. 74.   [4] *Collected Papers*, i, 490–491.
[5] *Ibid.* i, 491.

It is possible to find in modern books comparisons between what Bracton says and what Coke says about the law as it stood before the statutes of Edward I, and the writer of course tells us that Coke's is "the better opinion". Now if we want to know the common law of our own day Coke's authority is higher than Bracton's, and Coke's own doctrines yield easily to modern decisions. But if we are really looking for the law of Henry III's reign, Bracton's lightest word is infinitely more valuable than all the tomes of Coke. A mixture of legal dogma and legal history is in general an unsatisfactory compound.

In the second place, this historical tradition has obscured the fact that it is sometimes necessary to institute a comparison between the development of law in England and its development in foreign countries, if we would understand the full significance of the English development. Take, for instance, the history of the jury. Why did it fade out in France and develop in England?[1] The answer to that question sheds a valuable light upon many aspects of the history of the English system of procedure, civil and criminal. But English lawyers educated only in their own system of law are apt to attend only to the development of that system as portrayed by the statutes and the decisions of the courts. We may I think admit the existence of these bad effects of the historical tradition upon the scientific study of legal history, and yet hold that the maintenance of the historical tradition has been beneficial to the study of English law. That tradition has driven into the minds of practising lawyers the truth that they must study the history of the law in order to attain that mastery of legal principles which comes of understanding. At the end of the seventeenth century Roger North put this very well in the sentence which I have placed on the title-page of my History—"To say truth, although it is not necessary for

[1] Holdsworth, *H.E.L.* i, 315–316; another illustration is the light which the history of continental criminal procedure throws upon the procedure used by the court of Star Chamber, *ibid.* v, 170–196.

counsel to know what the history of a point is, but to know how it now stands resolved, yet it is a wonderful accomplishment, and without it, a lawyer cannot be accounted learned in the law."[1]

The rise of the new historical school in the nineteenth century was due to two main causes. In the first place, it was a result of the great political upheaval of the French Revolution, and the many other upheavals which followed it. In the second place, it was the result of the change in the character of scientific speculation which was the consequence of the Darwinian theory of evolution.

(1) The French rationalistic philosophers, who applied to morals and law and legal institutions a criticism of the same *a priori* kind as that which Bentham applied to English law and legal institutions, helped to shape the course of the French Revolution. But, as Vinogradoff has said,[2] "the disillusionment brought about by the excesses of the French Revolution obscured for a time the historical significance of the upheaval, and brought discredit on the cult of reason as preached by the Terrorists". This reaction took many forms; but all these forms tended to revive interest in the old institutions, the old beliefs, the old customs, which the rationalistic school had condemned, and had attempted to abolish. In the realm of law the reaction first took definite shape in the rise of the historical school which is associated with the name of Savigny. Thibaut, a well-known professor of law at Göttingen, had proposed to codify the law of the German states, taking as his model Roman law and the French civil code. Savigny protested, on the ground that the law of a nation was as dependent on its history as its language or its religion; and that therefore a code ought to reflect the history of a nation's law, and embody those national characteristics which were the product of its

---

[1] *A Discourse on the Study of the Laws*, 40.
[2] *Historical Jurisprudence*, i, 124.

history.[1] This new historical school introduced a new way of regarding law. As Vinogradoff has said,

Instead of being traced to the deliberate will of the legislator, its formation was assigned to the gradual working of customs.... As regards the State, law was assumed to be an antecedent condition, and a consequence of its activity. In this way direct legislation was thrust into the background, while customary law was studied with particular interest, and regarded as the genuine manifestation of popular consciousness.[2]

(2) The progress of this historical school was enormously helped by the change in the character of scientific speculation as to all matters affecting organic life, which was the necessary result of the Darwinian theory of evolution. As I said in my last lecture, the rationalistic school, considering only those branches of science which were concerned with inanimate nature, had tried to discover laws which were as universally true of human activities as the laws which governed inanimate nature. But this was impossible. As Sir Leslie Stephen has said,[3] "The importance of taking into account the genetic point of view, of inquiring into the growth as well as the actual constitution of things, is obvious in all the sciences which are concerned with organic life." The Darwinian theory therefore gave a new scientific backing to the upholders of the historical school, because, to use Dean Pound's terminology, it substituted a biological for a mechanical interpretation of the facts of life.[4] It reinforced the central theory of that school, that the law of any nation is dependent on its history; and that, consequently, there could be no proper understanding of a nation's law without a study of its history.

[1] *Historical Jurisprudence*, i, 128; for a good account of Savigny and his school see Prof. Kantorowicz's article, *L.Q.R.* liii, 326–343.
[2] *Historical Jurisprudence*, i, 129.
[3] *The English Utilitarians*, iii, 374.
[4] *Interpretations of Legal History*, 72.

The large and beneficial effects of the rise of this new school upon English law will be obvious when we have studied the achievement of three of its most eminent exponents—Maine, Maitland, and Pollock.

MAINE[1]

Maine was born in 1822. He was educated at Pembroke College, Cambridge, and attained great distinction as a classical scholar. As Sir Frederick Pollock has said,[2] "he entered the University an unknown young man; he left it marked as among the most brilliant scholars of his time." After taking his degree, he began to study law, became law tutor of Trinity Hall in 1845, and Regius Professor of civil law in 1847. Both as a law tutor and as professor he attained a marked success. In fact he had all the qualities of a good lecturer—a powerful voice, a style like crystal, and every sentence perfectly finished. He was called to the bar in 1850; and in 1852 he became the first reader on Roman Law at the Inns of Court. From 1862 to 1869 he was legal member of the Viceroy's council in India, and Vice-Chancellor of Calcutta University. It was then that he got that knowledge of Indian law and institutions of which he made so great a use in his books. On his return to England in 1869 he was made the first Corpus Professor of Jurisprudence at Oxford. In 1877 he became Master of Trinity Hall, and in 1887 Whewell Professor of International Law at Cambridge. He died in 1888.

Maine was influenced both by the German historical school of Savigny and by the Darwinian theory. These two influences led him to apply to jurisprudence those historical and comparative methods which in other

---

[1] *Life and Speeches of Sir Henry Maine,* by Whitley Stokes, with a memoir by Grant Duff; Pollock, *Oxford Essays,* 147–186; Vinogradoff, "The Teaching of Sir Henry Maine", *L.Q.R.* xx, 119–133.

[2] *Oxford Essays,* 149.

domains, notably philology and anthropology, had already achieved remarkable results. His wide reading, his capacity for observation, his capacity to see to the heart of a problem, and his attractive literary style, enabled him to produce books which have influenced the juridical thought of Europe and America. His great achievement is this: He converted lawyers to the belief that law and legal institutions must be studied historically if they are to be understood. Pollock in his *Oxford Lectures*[1] has stressed this point. He says:

We may at least say, looking to our own science of law, that the impulse given by Maine to its intelligent study in England and America can hardly be overrated. Within living memory the Common law was treated merely as a dogmatic and technical system. Historical explanation, beyond the dates and facts which were manifestly necessary, was regarded as at best an idle ornament, and all singularities and anomalies had to be taken as they stood, without any reason or (perhaps oftener) with a bad one. It was an unheard of process to show that they were really natural products in the development of legal conceptions.... A certain amount of awakening was no doubt effected by the analytical school.... But the analysis of modern political and legal ideas in their latest form could not lead to any rational explanation of an actual historical system.... The scientific study of legal phenomena, such as we really find them, had no place among us.... Maine not only showed that it was a possible study, but showed that it was not less interesting and fruitful than any in the whole range of the moral sciences. At one master stroke he forged a new and lasting bond between law, history, and anthropology. Jurisprudence itself has become a study of the living growth of human society through all its stages.

This, then, is the great and lasting contribution of Maine to the study of our legal history. And his contribution was made the more effective, even as Blackstone's and Maitland's were made the more effective, by

[1] At pp. 158–159.

the charm of his style—a charm which he owes to the fact that, as Sir Frederick Pollock has said, "he was a humanist before he was a jurist, and he never ceased to be a humanist".[1] And so, although many of his conclusions are not now accepted, his books will always be studied, because they show the workings of the mind of a genius in the domain of legal history, because they have an artistic form which will cause them to last long after more learned books have passed into oblivion. To quote Sir Frederick Pollock once more: "Maine can no more become obsolete through the industry and ingenuity of modern scholars than Montesquieu could be made obsolete by the legislation of Napoleon."[2]

MAITLAND[3]

Maitland was born May 28, 1850, and was educated at Eton and Trinity College, Cambridge. Though he was at the top of the Moral and Mental Science Tripos in 1872, he failed to get a fellowship at Trinity; but his fellowship dissertation, now printed in his *Collected Papers*, is a fine piece of work. He was called to the bar by Lincoln's Inn in 1876, and was made an honorary bencher in 1903. In 1883 he returned to Cambridge as reader in English law, and in 1888 he became Downing Professor of the Laws of England. His health had never been strong, and from 1898 onwards he could never stand an English winter. He died December 19, 1906, at Las Palmas.

In this lecture I propose, in the first place, to describe very briefly the intellectual characteristics which enabled Maitland to make his great contribution to English law; and, in the second place, to estimate the influence of his work upon English law and history.

---

[1] *Oxford Essays*, 150. [2] *Ibid.* 154.
[3] Fisher, *F. W. Maitland, A Biographical Sketch*; A. L. Smith, *Two Lectures and a Bibliography*.

(1) *The intellectual characteristics which enabled Maitland to make his great contribution to English law.*

First and foremost Maitland was a lawyer. Mr Rogers, in whose chambers he read, said: "He had not been with me a week before I found that I had in my chambers such a lawyer as I had never met before.... His opinions, had he suddenly been made a judge, would have been an honour to the Bench."[1] And he was not content, as Pollock said,[2] to be merely "a sound lawyer with scholarly tastes". His was a mind which would take nothing for granted, which was driven to analyse the causes and effects of legal rules and institutions. Naturally he turned to history; for history alone could supply the explanations which he sought. While still at the bar he had been greatly impressed by Stubbs's constitutional history; and he so admired Savigny's *Geschichte des Römischen Rechts* that he began to translate it.

A sound lawyer equipped with philosophy and history, and willing to use his philosophical and historical learning to criticize the technical rules of law, will produce some surprising results. The paper on the law of real property which he contributed in 1879 to the *Westminster Review*[3] marks an epoch in the method of approach to the problems of law reform. Most of the law reforms of the century had, up to that date, been inspired by lawyers of the school of Bentham. Their simple faith in *a priori* principles had accomplished much in an age in which the legal system was in danger of being choked by the accumulated rubbish of centuries. But it could not accomplish all that they had hoped. It was a faith born of inexperience; and a larger knowledge of the complexity of human nature, of social problems, and of the

[1] Fisher, *F. W. Maitland, A Biographical Sketch*, 15–16.
[2] *Quarterly Review*, ccvi, 406.
[3] *Collected Papers*, i, 162–201.

technical legal rules which successive ages had invented to solve these problems, had somewhat dimmed it. Writers of the school of Maine were demonstrating that many of these principles were based upon a very superficial view of human nature; that they could not explain all existing rules even at the present day; that they did not even exist in the past. But the writings of the historical school generally stopped short at explanation. They showed how existing legal rules came to be what they are. They showed that even the most unreasonable of them once had a reasonable basis, and that some still had more reason than whole-hearted followers of Bentham's principles might allow. But that was all. Maitland's paper showed how history, in the hands of a first-rate lawyer and philosopher, could suggest practical proposals for law reform, based not only upon a knowledge of existing law, but also upon a knowledge of the ideas which had created it. It showed that a knowledge of legal antiquities could be used, not only to teach old law and to explain present law, but also to suggest the changes needed to bring the present law into harmony with its modern environment.

And this was not all. Maitland's habit of analysing existing legal rules and institutions in the light of their history enabled him to throw new light not only on some of the most technical and difficult, but also on some of the most ordinary and familiar, features of our legal landscape. His critical mind was never dulled by familiarity. It was just these familiar things, which are generally accepted without comment and without explanation, that aroused him to investigate. And thus he gave us an explanation of the relation of equity to law, and an exposition of the great part which the Trust has played in our English life, which are as obviously true as they are strikingly original.

It was due mainly to Vinogradoff's influence that, on

his return to Cambridge, he devoted himself to the study of English legal history.[1] His edition of Bracton's *Note Book* restored to English lawyers a primary authority for the English law of the first half of the thirteenth century, which had been lost since the sixteenth century, when it was used by Fitzherbert in the composition of his Grand Abridgment.[2] His work as Literary Director of the Selden Society gave the publications of that Society an immediate prestige, which made its future safe, and set a high standard to all future contributors to its volumes. His articles on Seisin and on the Register of Writs broke new ground, and showed as decisively as his contributions to the Selden Society's publications had shown, that from medieval law both interesting history, and information valuable to modern lawyers, could be extracted.

Then came the great *History of English Law*, which gathered up the results of the nineteenth-century English and Continental and American revival of historical studies, and used them to construct a history of the origins of English law which complied with the exacting standards of modern historical scholarship. After the *History* came a series of monographs on many topics cognate to those dealt with in that history: *Domesday Book and Beyond*; *Canon Law in the Church of England*; work on the Year Books. Later came works on the problem of corporate personality—the lectures on Township and Borough, the translation of and introduction to a chapter of Gierke's great work on *Political Theories of the Middle Age*, the illuminating paper on *Corporation and Trust*; and his two excursions into the sixteenth-century history —the Rede lecture on *English Law and the Renaissance*, and his contribution to the *Cambridge Modern History*. "Nullum quod tetigit non ornavit"—this sentence from the epitaph which Dr Johnson wrote for Goldsmith's

---

[1] Fisher, *F. W. Maitland, A Biographical Sketch*, 24–25.
[2] Above, p. 22.

monument in Westminster Abbey is literally true of all Maitland's work.

What were the intellectual characteristics which stamp all Maitland's work with the mark of genius? In the first place, because he was a learned lawyer he knew the end of the story. If a legal historian does not know the end of the story he is apt to waste his time on relating the history of rules which did not survive, of tendencies which were never realized, of institutions which failed. He is in danger of becoming a mere antiquarian. Because Maitland knew the end of the story he was able to emphasize the rules and tendencies and institutions which have lived, and so to write legal history which elucidates modern law. In the second place, because he was a learned historian he was able to connect old legal rules with the political, social, or economic causes in which they originated. He was therefore able so to treat legal history that it became not only a history of the evolution of technical rules, but also a history of the evolution of a nation's ideas upon all those matters which it considers to be of sufficient importance to be settled by the state. In the third place, Maitland was never satisfied with any evidence but the best. It was this characteristic which led him to turn from the task of continuing the history of English law to the task of making a critical edition of the earlier Year Books. Such an edition was, in his eyes, a necessary preliminary to the continuation of that history. It was this characteristic which led him to make, as a preliminary condition to fully understanding the Year Books, so learned a grammar of the French talked in the law courts of the fourteenth century, that M. Paul Meyer recommended it as a text-book to students of medieval French. Lastly, there are the more personal of his intellectual characteristics. He was not content with a merely abstract statement of a rule or a theory. He liked to test his rules and theories by putting concrete cases. In a letter which he wrote to me he said: "People can't understand old law unless you give a few concrete illustrations: at least I can't." He is so alive to the human aspect of history that he can extract human traits from a Plea Roll and a Year Book. Closely allied to this characteristic is his kindly sense of humour and his constant gaiety of manner, which often conceals the learning which underlies his brilliant easily flowing argument; and, last but not least, his talent for epigram which enables him to sum up in a memorable phrase the conclusion of the whole matter.

(2) *The influence of Maitland's work upon English law and history.*

There are, I think, three directions in which the influence of Maitland's work will be far-reaching and permanent.

First, he has taught us to apply the methods of historical criticism to the sources of English law. We know now something of the influences under which Bracton wrote. We know infinitely more than we did before of the real nature of the Year Books. From his various works we get many hints as to the point of view from which we should look at many other writers upon, and sources of, English law. What the school of the humanist lawyers of the sixteenth century did for the study of Roman law, Maitland began to do for the study of English law.

Secondly, he has taught English lawyers to look at their system in its relation to other systems of law. History, as he said, involves comparison. We understand the strength and the weakness of our own system the better for such a comparison. We see better where it is at fault. We are able to appreciate or criticize intelligently suggested reforms. And, at the present day, when physical science is diminishing the size of the world, and nations are losing their former isolation, such knowledge is essential.

Thirdly, he has renewed that partnership between the history of English law and the general history of England, which existed in the seventeenth and early eighteenth centuries, but had, in more recent times, been almost dissolved. Till Maitland pointed the way to reunion, law and history had remained too long in a state of unprofitable isolation. The lawyer, immersed in technical rules, forgot the human beings for whom those rules were made and the human needs which gave them birth. The historian, because he was ignorant of the meaning of those technical rules, was apt to misapprehend the meaning of statutes and the reasoning of the courts. Maitland showed how history can humanize law, and how law can correct history. He was a consummate lawyer; but he never forgot the human beings who made and worked the institutions, or the human needs which shaped the laws, which he was describing. Under his hands even the most technical rules became living things —the expression of human policy or logic, of human passions or ideals.

In an age of great historians I think that Maitland was the greatest, I think that he was the equal of the greatest lawyers of his day, and that, as a legal historian, English law from before the time of legal memory has never known his like.

POLLOCK[1]

On the left-hand side of the entrance to Lincoln's Inn Library stands the bust of Maitland, and on the right-hand side hangs the picture of Pollock, so that those who enter the library pass between two of the greatest lawyers

[1] *For my Grandson*; the Papers on Sir Frederick Pollock in *L.Q.R.* liii, 151–206. I have reprinted my article in the *L.Q.R.* with some additions from the other articles.

of this century—lawyers whose names will go down the ages linked together, not only because they were partners in their great *History of English Law*, but also because they were alike in the extent and variety of their intellectual interests, in their devotion to the study of law and legal history, in their greatness as lawyers. "I remember", says Lord Maugham,[1] "speaking to Pollock about the achievement of Maitland, and the tone of finality with which Pollock summed up his impression. He said firmly: 'Maitland was a genius', and there was nothing more to be said." Many lawyers now say as firmly "Pollock was a genius." Their personalities were very different. Pollock had none of Maitland's charm which impressed all who came into contact with him.[2] But none the less he had a personality which made those who met him conscious that the man himself was greater than his works.[3]

Pollock was born December 10, 1845. He was educated at Eton and Trinity College, Cambridge, of which college he became a fellow in 1868 and an honorary fellow in 1920. He was called to the bar by Lincoln's Inn in 1871, and was elected a bencher in 1906. He was created a Privy Councillor in 1911. He died January 18, 1937. When he died he had long held a unique position amongst lawyers not only in England and the British Empire, but also in the United States and Europe. He

[1] *L.Q.R.* liii, 172.

[2] John Chipman Gray said of Maitland: "It is impossible for me to write or think of Maitland without recalling his personal charm. How great that was! I never saw him but once. But to have broken bread at his house among the Cotswold Hills will always be one of the happiest of my memories. If I said what I felt you would understand it, but to one who had not known him it would seem extravagant", *L.Q.R.* xxiii, 138.

[3] Lord Wright says, *L.Q.R.* liii, 166–167, "there are some men whose personalities transcend any particular things they have done. Some men are greater than their works or deeds, though these may have been great. There comes from such men an afflatus of impulse and inspiration. This is what we always felt with Pollock."

held this unique position both by reason of the extent
and accuracy of his learning in many systems and many
departments of law, and by reason of his capacity to give
to the world the results of his knowledge in a supremely
literary form. All his books, essays, notes, and reviews
upon matters legal are marked by a clarity and a felicity
of expression which is the touchstone of a master of his
craft; and there are one or two passages in some of his
essays which reach a high level of eloquence and beauty.
The literary quality of his work is due to the extent and
variety of his learning in many other subjects besides
law. He was an accomplished linguist who could write
verses in Latin, Greek, French and German; he knew
something of Eastern languages; and he was a philosopher, an historian, and something of a mathematician.
He bore his great learning lightly, and, having a subtle
sense of humour, he used his literary gifts to produce the
witty parodies and other humorous verses which are
published in *Leading Cases done into English*, and in the
volume entitled *Outside the Law*. Another good example
is his parody of a Year Book of Edward IV's reign which
is printed in the *Law Quarterly Review*.[1] The *Etchingham
Letters* are a delightful family correspondence, humorous,
packed with literary information and criticism, and
revealing with such distinctness the characters of the
correspondents and their friends, that it is difficult to
believe that they are all fictitious. What Pollock said of
Maine is even more true of himself—"he was a humanist
before he was a jurist, and he never ceased to be a
humanist";[2] for, as the writer of Pollock's obituary
notice in *The Times* said, he was "perhaps the last representative of the old broad culture"—"more like a man
of the Renaissance than a modern".[3] Nor were his
interests only literary. All his life he was a keen, though

---

[1] *L.Q.R.* liii, 183–189.   [2] *Oxford Lectures*, 150.
[3] Sir Herbert Samuel, *L.Q.R.* liii, 173.

not a very skilled,[1] fencer. He was also a mountaineer, and a member of the Inns of Court Volunteer Corps. In one of his essays in *Outside the Law* there is an interesting account of a fencing meeting which shows that he was a master of the rules of the art; he contributed to the Badminton volume on mountaineering, and acted for some time as honorary librarian to the Alpine Club; and he has left us an account of his volunteering experiences in his *For my Grandson*.[2]

Since he came of a famous legal family which has included distinguished judges amongst its members, it was almost inevitable that he should choose the law as his profession. The distinction of his academic career at Cambridge foreshadowed the distinction of his legal career. His grandfather, the chief baron, spoke truly when he said in a letter to him, "neither you nor I are mere Scholars or Mathematicians. As conspicuously in *you* as in myself, academic success has been the result of general *mental power*, and you can make yourself as good a Lawyer as Hardwicke was or Willes is."[3] He found, as his grandfather had found, that the change from the broad intellectual interests of Cambridge to the study of the law in the severely practical atmosphere of a conveyancer's chambers was somewhat discouraging. He says:

> After a year of this disjointed learning I came away with a certain rule of thumb knowledge of the conveyancer's art, pretty confused notions of the laws of England and the foundations of legal science, and considerable doubt whether I had found my proper vocation. If at that moment any definite occasion had offered for returning to Cambridge and the classics, it might have been hard to resist.[4]

Fortunately for the law no occasion offered, and equally fortunately for himself his masters in the law were two

[1] *L.Q.R.* liii, 168.   [2] At pp. 179–183.
[3] Hanworth, *Lord Chief Baron Pollock*, 196.
[4] *For my Grandson*, 162.

of the greatest lawyers of the century—Lindley and James Shaw Willes. They were inspiring teachers who imparted to him their own enthusiasm for the scientific and historical study of the law. To Lindley he said in a letter prefixed to his book on the *Principles of Contract*:

In your chambers, and by your example, I learnt the root of the matter which too many things in common practice conspire to obscure, that the law is neither a trade nor a solemn jugglery but a science. By your help and encouragement I was led to acquaint myself with that other great historical system which to this day divides, broadly speaking, the civilized world with the Common Law. To regard it not as a mere collection of rules and maxims accidentally like or unlike our own, but as the living growth of similar ideas under different conditions, and to perceive that the Roman law deserves the study and reverence of English lawyers, not merely as scholars and citizens of the world, but inasmuch as both in its history and its scientific development it is capable of throwing a light beyond price on the dark places of our own doctrine. I owe it to you and to my friend Professor Bryce that, daring to be deaf to the counsels of shallow wisdom that miscalls itself practical, I turned from the formless confusion of text-books and the dry bones of students' manuals to the immortal work of Savigny....Like one in a Platonic fable, I passed out of a cave of shadows into clear day-light.

Of Willes he said in a letter to Mr Justice Holmes prefixed to his *Law of Torts*:

He was not only a man of profound learning in the law, joined with extraordinary and varied knowledge of other kinds, but one of those whose knowledge is radiant, and kindles answering fire. To set down all I owe to him is beyond my means...but to you at least I shall say much in saying that from Willes I learnt to taste the Year Books, and to pursue the history of the law in authorities which not so long ago were collectively and compendiously described as "black letter".

Under the guidance of these teachers Pollock proved himself to be as great a lawyer as any of the distinguished lawyers of his family, and a more distinguished jurist than any of them. But he was not so well fitted as they to shine in the courts.¹ What the courts and the bench lost by his limitations the science of the law gained. In his inaugural lecture as Corpus Professor of Jurisprudence at Oxford in 1883 he said of the scientific and systematic study of English law that it was "followed by few, and scorned and depreciated by many".² His work has played no small part in removing that reproach. That his work has had so large an influence, and that it will have so permanent an influence is due not only to his great logical and philosophical abilities and his literary power, but also to his method of approach to the study of the law. That method of approach was both comparative and historical. It was comparative. We have seen that Lindley had encouraged him to study Savigny and Roman law, and to use the knowledge so gained to elucidate the principles of English law. His work on Maine's *Ancient Law* and on Indian law showed how much he had profited by this study, and how well he was fitted to be a professor of jurisprudence. At the same time he was well aware of the dangers of the comparative approach. In his *Genius of the Common Law*³ he said:

Our lady the Common Law will note other people's fashions and take a hint from them in season, but she will have no thanks for judges or legislators who steal incongruous tags and patches and offer to bedizen her raiment with them. Assimilation of foreign elements may be a very good thing. Crude and hasty borrowing of foreign details is unbecoming at best, and almost always mischievous. When you are tempted to make play with foreign ideas or terms, either for imitation or for criticism, the first thing is to be sure that you understand them.

His method of approach was also historical. In his valedictory lecture as Corpus Professor he said:⁴

---

¹ As to this matter see Lord Maugham's remarks, *L.Q.R.*liii, 171–172.
² *Oxford Lectures*, 38.   ³ At p. 116.
⁴ *Essays in the Law*, 26–27.

It is a good thing that lawyers should be better instructed in legal antiquities, and that students...should be delivered from having fictions repeated to them as history. That is matter, so far as it goes, for reasonable satisfaction....Surely there is something beyond this, and not the less because additions to positive knowledge are definable, but the spirit of an intellectual movement is not definable. Historical method has given us more than knowledge, it has made our knowledge continuous where it was formerly dispersed; it has set an ideal in the place of a bare multitude of facts.

To that ideal Pollock was ever faithful.

Pollock's contributions to legal science are many and various; and it is these contributions which will be his enduring monument. But the completeness of his legal knowledge in all departments of law, and his capacity to use it and apply it to the solution of concrete problems, enabled him to make a contribution which is by no means negligible to the administration of the law, to its restatement, and to the solution of political problems. Let us look at his work from these two points of view.

(1) His contributions to legal science were made first as an author, and, secondly, as a teacher of law.

(i) His books on Contract[1] and Tort[2] were the first books in which the principles of these branches of law were treated in a manner which was both scientific and literary. Dicey, speaking of the older books on the law of contract, said:[3]

A well-known treatise on the Law of Contract, usually placed in the hands of students at least as late as 1860, did not attempt to

---

[1] Lord Wright has said of his book on Contract that it "was a remarkable achievement for a young man only six years after his call to the bar", *L.Q.R.* liii, 162.

[2] Of this book Lord Wright says, "it is a model of comprehensiveness and analytical arrangement; it has all the charm of style which is characteristic of Pollock. It is original, independent, and philosophical", *ibid.* 164.

[3] "Blackstone's *Commentaries*", *Camb. Law Journal*, iv, 304.

analyse the nature of a contract and left on the mind of an ingenuous reader the impression that somehow or other at the very centre of the whole law of contract lay the fourth and seventeenth sections of the Statute of Frauds.

Pollock's books on these two subjects showed students and practitioners that English law was no mere collection of precedents and statutes, but a system of principles and rules which were logically coherent, and yet eminently practical, because they were the product of the long experience of the race recorded in cases decided from the first of the Year Books to modern times. For the same reason his book on *Possession in the Common Law* set forth clearly for the first time what the English theory of ownership and possession was, and showed that that theory was as logical and consistent as the different theory of Roman law. This book showed that the law on this matter had, like other parts of the common law, been built up by decided cases which settled concrete problems in many of its different branches—in the land law, in the law of tort and contract, in the law of succession. And so the book not only states the English theory of possession and ownership, but also incidentally elucidates many difficulties in these branches of the law, and notably in the law of tort. His work on the law of partnership and the land law showed that he was as accomplished in the spheres of equity and real property as in the common law. In 1894 he delivered these Tagore Lectures on the law of fraud in British India; and, along with fraud, he dealt with misrepresentation and mistake. The great *History of English Law* was, as he said in its Preface, more Maitland's work than his. But there can be no doubt that it owed much to his historical knowledge and critical powers, for it was planned in common and was revised by both. Many of his essays, notably those on *Employers' Liability, The Science of Case Law, The King's Peace, Oxford Law Studies, Sir Henry Maine and his Work,*

The History of Comparative Jurisprudence, The History of the Law of Nature, Has the Common Law received the Fiction Theory of Corporations?, The Transformation of Equity, show the extent of his knowledge of English law, of legal history, and of comparative law. Some of them are excellent illustrations of the manner in which jurisprudence should be taught, and of its use in elucidating basic principles. It was only a master of these principles who could have produced a book so clear and so helpful to beginners as *A First Book of Jurisprudence.* His book on the League of Nations showed that he was as well versed in international as in municipal law. His two books of lectures—*The Expansion of the Common Law* and *The Genius of the Common Law*—are critical studies of aspects and characteristics of the common law which only an accomplished legal historian, a master of the modern law, and a professor of jurisprudence could have written. His edition of Selden's *Table Talk* for the Selden Society illustrates his careful scholarship as well as his knowledge of Selden. His *History of the Science of Politics* illustrates the wide range of his interests in matters allied to the study of law, and his book on Spinoza illustrates his competence as a philosopher. Last but not least, his articles, notes, and reviews in the *Law Quarterly Review,* which was substantially his creation, are a unique combination of learning and criticism, often seasoned with wit and humour, which have been of immense value to all lawyers on the bench, at the bar, or in their student stage. But this last-named contribution to legal learning was something more than a literary contribution. It is closely connected with the contribution which he has made to legal science as a teacher of law.

(ii) Pollock was essentially a teacher for advanced students, and for those who were interested in legal research. His lectures were never frequented by the ordinary undergraduate; nor would he ever have made a popular college tutor. His manners at first sight seemed odd and difficult. But on further acquaintance that impression vanished. As the writer of the obituary notice in *The Times* said, "a rather odd and curt manner of speaking veiled a most genial and benevolent disposition". To any serious student he was kindness itself— always willing to advise and encourage. It was in his relations to these students that he proved himself a great teacher. If he had been a continental professor he would have conducted a famous seminar. But this institution, though it flourished in Oxford under Vinogradoff, has never taken root in the Oxford law school. Pollock accomplished results as great as, perhaps greater than, those accomplished by any continental seminar by means of the *Law Quarterly Review*. He was always ready, as I know from experience, to encourage beginners, to give them wise counsel, and to direct them how best to pursue their chosen subject. He was always generous in his appreciation of their work. His account of the genesis of the *Law Quarterly Review*[1] shows that this encouragement of research was one of the objects with which it was founded. I am sure that it and its many contemporaries in America have done for their respective law schools in another way very much the same sort of work as is done by a seminar, and much else besides. More especially they have helped the bar and the bench in their administration of the law by constructive articles, by critical notes, and by well-informed reviews of current literature. Then, too, as Literary Director of the Selden Society— a post which he held till his death—he did a similar work; for he was always ready to welcome new men and to help them with his advice and criticism.

(2) Pollock's contribution to the administration of the law, to its restatement, and to the solution of political problems is also considerable. He assisted the administration of the law in several ways. He was a member of

[1] *L.Q.R.* li, 6.

the Royal Commission on Labour in 1891, and Chair-
man of the Royal Commission on Public Records in
1910. He was appointed the judge of the Admiralty
court of the Cinque Ports in 1914. From 1895 till 1936
—the last year of his life—he was the first editor-in-chief
of the Law Reports. For some ten years before 1895 the
conduct of the Law Reports had aroused criticism; and
Pollock was one of the critics. The Council of Law
Reporting decided, he tells us,[1] "first that unity of
command was necessary, and next, on the principle of
setting a poacher to be a gamekeeper, that I should be
the new commanding officer; and so I was appointed
general editor of all the series". He helped to restate the
law by drafting the Partnership Act, 1890, and he
drafted the Indian Torts Bill which, however, never
became an Act. He helped to solve political problems
by his advice to the Government in the difficulties which
arose in connection with Venezuela in 1895,[2] and, just
before his death, by his informal advice as to the form
of the Abdication Act.

This brief summary of Pollock's work shows that he
was one of the greatest lawyers of his day, and that, at
the same time, he held a position in the legal world which
is unparalleled in our legal history. Throughout our legal
history our greatest lawyers have held judicial positions,
and they have influenced the development of the law by
their decisions and sometimes by their books: Pollock was
never in a position to give decisions which made law,[3]
but his writings have had an influence on our unenacted

---

[1] *For my Grandson*, 187.

[2] See Mr Haynes's article, *L.Q.R.* liii, 196–197; in a letter cited by
Mr Haynes, in which Pollock tells the story of his connection with the
Venezuela affair, he says, "I wrote a study of the origins of the Monroe
doctrine founded on the original correspondence between the Americans
and our F.O., which the U.S.A. Senate ordered to be printed as an
official paper. I believe it is still found useful by specialists."

[3] Though he was a judge of the Admiralty court of the Cinque Ports,
he was never called on to decide a case, *L.Q.R.* liii, 201.

law which was greater than that of many of our judges.[1] The only lawyer whose achievement can be compared with his is his life-long friend, Mr Justice Holmes. Both were great juridical thinkers who had a profound knowledge of the law of their respective countries. Both were great legal historians because their knowledge of modern law enabled them to avoid what Holmes has called "the pitfall of antiquarianism". Both were men of letters who could clothe their thoughts about law in language which makes their works literature. Holmes's most important work was, it is true, done as chief justice of Massachusetts and as judge of the Supreme Court of the United States, whilst Pollock's most important work was done as the author of classical books and essays upon English law. But in Holmes's judgments and in Pollock's books and essays we see the same reverence for and mastery of the law, the same power to illuminate the dark places of the law, and the same sense of the need to keep the law in touch with the realities of life and with the changing conditions of the age in which they lived.

At the end of one of the most eloquent passages which Pollock ever wrote he said:[2] "So venerable, so majestic, is this living temple of justice, this immemorial and yet freshly growing fabric of the Common Law, that the least of us is happy who hereafter may point to so much as one stone thereof, and say, The work of my hands is there." There are many branches of the law in which his handiwork has, and will continue to have, a permanent place; for he is one of the greatest of that select band of professors whose work places them amongst the Makers of English Law.

[1] As Lord Wright has said, "the writings of a lawyer like Pollock, constantly cited in the Courts and quoted by the judges, are entitled to claim a place under his category of unwritten law, even in a system like ours which does not normally seek its law from institutional writers", *L.Q.R.* liii, 152.

[2] *Oxford Lectures*, 111.

CONCLUSION

ALL these Makers of English Law, by their decisions or books or opinions, have helped to construct a system of law, the rules of which can be studied as a science, because they are dependent on leading principles logically developed. They have done for English law what the great Roman jurists, whose writings are preserved in the Digest, did for Roman law. For that reason the study of their works, whether in books or opinions or decided cases, is by far the most important part of the training of a lawyer. The present Master of the Rolls, Sir Wilfrid Greene, in a valuable paper which he read to the Society of Public Teachers of Law in 1936,[1] has stressed the importance to the practising lawyer of a knowledge of the leading principles which these Makers of English Law have created and developed. He says:[2]

If the advocate has a well grounded knowledge of the science of law and its principles, he is able to deal with what is one of the most difficult situations which arise in practice, namely, that in which, as the result of the way in which the facts emerge, or of the construction which the Court may be disposed to place upon a document, the principles applicable to the case turn out to be quite different from those which he had supposed. It is here that a real instinct for principle is of the greatest value. As the case proceeds, the advocate, in some department of his mind, which often has to operate unconsciously, appreciates the turn that the case is taking, realizes that he must rearrange his ideas at short notice, and is able to deal with the case in its new shape and to relate it to the new principles under which it appears to be falling.

[1] "Jurisprudence and the Practising Lawyer", *Journal of the Society of Public Teachers of Law*, 1936, 10–18.
[2] At p. 11.

It is clear that the same considerations apply equally to the judge who must weigh the evidence, the legal consequences which follow from the facts as found by himself or by a jury, and the opposing submissions of counsel on the points of law raised by the facts so found.

But it may be asked whether this study of principle is as important in an age like the present, in which the Legislature takes the largest share in the development of the law, as it was in past ages, when the law was mainly developed by the lawyers. In the opinion of the Master of the Rolls it is quite as necessary;[1] and he gives as an example its use in the application of taxing Acts which, from the fiscal point of view, deal with very many social and economic relations. "The questions", he says,[2] "which fall to be decided in the Revenue Court demand a very deep knowledge of legal principle and a sound instinct for the science of law. Without these advantages the cases will be inadequately argued and, it may be, wrongly decided." This is true of taxing Acts and other fiscal laws at all periods of our legal history. At all periods the demands of the state, and the devices used by the subject to evade these demands, have given rise to difficult legal problems. Much of the early history of the land law depends on an understanding of the nature of those fiscal resources of the King which are known as the incidents of tenure, and the devices used by the landowners to evade them;[3] the statute of Uses, which shaped the modern development of the land law, was the product of the fiscal needs of Henry VIII;[4] the first real attempt in a reported case to analyse the nature of an agreement was made in 1550 in a revenue case;[5] and as

[1] *Journal of the Society of Public Teachers of Law*, 1936, 14–15.
[2] *Ibid.* 15.
[3] Holdsworth, *Historical Introduction to the Land Law*, 35–36.
[4] *Ibid.* 153.
[5] R. M. Jackson, "The Scope of the Term Contract", *L.Q.R.* liii, 526, citing *Reniger v. Fogossa* (1550) Plowden at pp. 5, 8b–9a, 17a.

late as 1916 the construction of a revenue Act involved a consideration of the difference between legal and equitable assets and the doctrine of reconversion.[1] The same thing is true also of other Acts; and it is because our lawyers have realized its truth that they have been able to assimilate these Acts into the legal system which they have created. If they had not thus been assimilated English law would not be a system: it would be a chaos.

One of the greatest of the Makers of English Law— Sir Matthew Hale—has explained very clearly why it is important to the state and to the individual to maintain a logical system of law, and why therefore it is necessary that lawyers should so interpret statutes that they are assimilated into it. He says:[2]

Itt is one of the thinges of greatest moment in the profession of the Comon Law to keepe as neare as may be to the Certainty of the Law and the Consonance of it to it Selfe, that one age and one Tribunall may Speake the Same thinges and Carry on the Same thred of the Law in one Uniforme Rule as neare as is possible; for otherwise that wch all places and ages have Contended for in Laws namely—Certainty and to avoid Arbitrariness and that Extravagance that would fall out, if the reasons of Judges and advocates were not kept in their traces, wold in halfe an age be lost....

As to Exposition of Acts of Parlem^t and written Laws certainly Hee that hath been Educated in the Study of the Law hath a greate advantage over those that have been otherwise Exercised, lett them p'tend to or be Masters of never soe much Reason. For first they have not only the Preamble and body and provisoes of the Acts of Parlem^t before them, but they have a Cleerer Evidence of what the Practise or mischief was before which possibly is not soe obvious without readeing especially if it be an Ancient Act.

They have the oppertunitie of the Knowledge of the Exposi-

[1] O'Grady v. Wilmot [1916] 2 A.C. 231.
[2] Reflections by Hale on Hobbes's "Dialogue of the Law", Holdsworth, H.E.L. v, 506.

tions made by Judges of former times wch cannot be Soe well knowne to others.

They have within their view and Knowledge the Expositions of other Acts of Parlem^t that either have the like Clauses, or Analogye of Reasons, wch are great guides and helpes in Exposition of Laws, wch they that have the naked use of their own faculties without the help of Studye and Education are destitute of.

In these last days there has been some disposition to criticize the methods used by the lawyers to assimilate the statute law into the framework of the legal system. As the Master of the Rolls has pointed out, modern dictators are actively hostile to any principles, legal or otherwise, which impede the pursuit of the policies which they wish to pursue; and modern bureaucrats, who wish to get things done quickly, are impatient of principles which seem to impede immediate action.[1] Though we have so far escaped a dictator, our plague of bureaucrats shows no sign of abating. For the lawyer, one serious consequence is the manner in which bureaucratic methods, by ousting the control of the law over matters which ought to come within its province, tend to make it increasingly difficult to regard English law as a science of interdependent principles. Another serious consequence is the advocacy by some lawyers, whose sympathies are too much with the bureaucrats and too little with the law, of a mode of interpreting statutes which would effectually prevent their assimilation into the body of English law. These lawyers think that statutes should be interpreted, not in accordance with the old and tried canons of interpretation which are designed to secure impartial justice, but in accordance with the political or social or economic ideals which their framers had in view. Those who take this view criticize the rule that the courts must refuse to accept evidence as to debates in

[1] *Journal of the Society of Public Teachers of Law*, 1936, 17–18.

Parliament and other similar guides as to what Parliament meant, and must confine their attention to the consideration of the mischief which it appears from the words of the statute was intended to be remedied, and to the words used in the statute. Thus Professor Plucknett in his valuable *History of the Common Law* says, first, that this rule is "at variance with the practice of other systems which regard *travaux préparatoires* as particularly valuable aids to interpretation";[1] and, secondly, that the effect of this rule is that "the courts are excluded from using evidence which any historian or scientific investigator would regard as highly valuable, especially in the modern age when statutes introduce changes of social policy, and not merely of technical procedure".[2]

As to the first point, it may be conceded that difficulties have been created by the rule of exclusion, which applies to the interpretation of statutes much the same rules as are applied to the interpretation of other written documents. But it is certain that other and greater difficulties would arise if all sorts of external evidence were admitted as to what the Legislature meant when it used a particular set of words. As to the second point, it must be remembered that the task set to the historian or the scientific investigator is very different from the task set to a judge who is trying a case. The former aims at giving a true picture of the law at a particular period: the latter at doing impartial justice according to law to the parties to a litigation. If all the evidence open to the historian or scientific investigator were admissible in litigation, two disastrous results would follow. In the first place English law would not long remain a logical system of interdependent principles. The difficult task of assimilating the statutes, and making them part of a logical and reasonable system, would be made impossible if it were obligatory upon lawyers to interpret statutes in accor-

[1] At p. 299.　　　　　　　　　[2] At p. 304.

dance, not with what they said, but with what it was conjectured from external evidence they intended to say. In the second place, if this method of interpretation were allowed, there would be very little security for the maintenance of that impartial administration of justice as between the state and the individual, the attainment of which is the greatest of all the achievements of English law. And if the matter is regarded from this point of view, the fact that modern statutes deal with questions of social policy, upon which sharp differences of opinion may exist, make it not less, but more, necessary that the rules of interpretation, which do secure this impartiality, should be maintained.

The views of lawyers who advocate this new method of interpreting statutes have their jurisprudential counterpart in a modern school of writers upon jurisprudence who call themselves "fundamentalists".[1] This school advocates a return to the pure Benthamite canon of criticism—the utility of a law measured by its consequences on human action and conduct. This canon of criticism, enlightened and broadened by the new material now available for the scientific study of these consequences, should, it thinks, alone determine the effect in action and therefore the real meaning of a law.[2] Like Bentham, this new school wishes to start *ab ovo*, untrammelled by the technical principles and rules which a mature legal system has evolved, and upon which its existence as a system depends. Like Bentham, it refuses to admit that the technical reasoning, upon which the enactments of the Legislature and the decisions of the courts depend, is of much value in estimating the real consequences of a legal principle or rule, and therefore its value in practice. It maintains that when the law

[1] For an account of this school see Felix S. Cohen, "The Problems of a Functional Jurisprudence", *Mod. Law Rev.* i, 5–26.
[2] *Ibid.* i, 25–26.

reformers in England and elsewhere refused to apply literally the Benthamite canon, and used it eclectically to make reforms in a manner which preserved the technical principles and rules and therefore the historic continuity of their legal system,[1] they were perpetuating error. That this theory finds favour with some American writers may be due partly to the fact that the rigidity of the American constitution prevents the rapid changes in the law which enthusiastic social reformers desire, just as Bentham's views were coloured by the difficulties of effecting any law reforms in England in his day. However that may be, I think that the history of the way in which English law has, during the nineteenth and the present centuries, been adapted to the needs of the new industrial age, without sacrificing the continuity of its development and its character as a logical system, is a sufficient answer to this thesis. If this thesis were adopted and literally applied to a legal system, much of the political and legal experience of the nation, which is gathered up and contained in its technical principles and rules, and in the reasoning with which they are supported, would be scrapped.[2] For that experience there would be substituted the conflicting views of individual theorists as to the effect in action and therefore as to the meaning and value of any given law. A body of law founded on these shifting sands would soon cease to possess any stable principles worth mentioning.

The history of Roman law conveys a warning against

---

[1] Above, pp. 254–255, 263–264.

[2] "It is a reason for me to preferre a Law by which a Kingdome hath been happily governed four or five hundred yeares than to adventure the happiness and Peace of a Kingdome upon Some new Theory of my owne tho' I am better acquainted with the reasonableness of my owne theory than with that Law", *Reflections by Hale on Hobbes's "Dialogue of the Law"*, Holdsworth, *H.E.L.* v, 504; as Dean Pound has truly said, "the life of the law is reason tested by long experience, and experience developed by reason", *Fashions in Juristic Thinking*, 20.

the acceptance of views which tend to diminish the power of the lawyers to develop their system of law scientifically. The series of great Roman jurists ended with Modestinus because, after him, the only source of law was the direct legislation of a despotic emperor. The lawyers ceased to develop their system logically by their writings, and were employed in drafting the legislative decrees of the emperor, which gave effect to his wishes without regard to the principles of the system evolved by the lawyers.[1] The result was that when later emperors like Theodosius and Valentinian in the fifth century, and Justinian in the sixth century, wished to give new life to the study and practice of Roman law, they were obliged to have recourse to the writings of jurists who, having retained some measure of independence, had been able systematically and logically to develop legal principles. They were obliged to have recourse to the writings of jurists who lived and worked before the period when the law was developed almost entirely by imperial constitutions which the jurists were unable to assimilate into the system of Roman law, because, having lost their independence, they were obliged to interpret them in strict accordance with the shifting policy of the Legislature. We may be sure that if either the old and tried canons for the interpretation of the statutes are so altered that this process of assimilation is no longer possible to English lawyers, or if the views of the "fundamentalists" win acceptance, and if some centuries hence a ruler arises who wishes to revive and remake the scientific system of English law, it will be to the writings and decisions of some of these Makers of English Law that he will turn.

[1] Professor Jolowicz, *Historical Introduction to Roman Law*, 368, speaking of this period, says: "the completely autocratic nature of the constitution does not permit of any law making which does not come directly from the emperor"—the lawyers helped to draft the imperial constitutions, but both the constitutions and their interpretation were controlled by the emperor; cp. Muirhead, *Historical Introduction to Roman Law* (2nd ed.), 307–308.

INDEX

CAMBRIDGE: PRINTED BY W. LEWIS, M.A., AT THE UNIVERSITY PRESS